PRAISE FOR DISHONEST BROKER

Naseer H. Aruri's *Dishonest Broker: The U.S. Role in Israel and Palestine* should come packaged with the advisory: Urgent! This is a work that should be read immediately by anyone trying to understand why the so-called "peace process" has undermined the possibility of peace; why, after volumes of praise for Oslo, the struggle between Israel and the Palestinians is more bitter and protracted than ever. Aruri's book aims to clarify these and other related questions in a brief survey that is based on U.S., Palestinian, and Israeli sources that provides evidence and insights into the continuing causes of conflict as well as the nature of the Israeli occupation of the West Bank and Gaza—evidence seldom published in the U.S. media and for that reason, little known to its readers. It is U.S. policy that is Aruri's main theme in a work that exposes the false claims of U.S. impartiality and its consistent undermining of an agreement that would have led to "an end to the Israeli occupation and the establishment of a Palestinian state existing side by side with Israel."

—Professor Irene Gendzier, Boston University

DISHONEST BROKER

THE U.S. ROLE IN ISRAEL AND PALESTINE

NASEER H. ARURI

South End Press
Cambridge, MA

Library of Congress Cataloging-in-Publication Data

Aruri, Naseer Hasan, 1934-
    Dishonest broker : the US role in Israel & Palestine / Naseer Aruri.
        p. cm.
    ISBN 0-89608-688-7 (alk. paper) — ISBN 0-89608-687-9 (pbk. : alk. paper)
    1. Arab-Israeli conflict—1993—Peace. 2. United States—Foreign rela-
tions—Israel. 3. Israel—Foreign relations—United States. 4. United
States—Politics and government—1993-2001. 5. Israel—Politics and government—1993- 6. Palestinian Arabs—Politics and government—1993- 7. Diplomatic negotiations in international disputes. I. Title.

DS119.76.A773 2003
327.73054'09'045—dc21

                                                                2002042886

South End Press, 7 Brookline Street, #1
Cambridge, MA 02139-4146
www.southendpress.org

07 06 05 04 03   1 2 3 4 5

Printed in Canada

For Joyce, my wife and best friend

CONTENTS

ACKNOWLEDGMENTS

My sincere thanks go to colleagues, family members, and friends, from whom I derived inspiration and encouragement to write this book. I am greatly indebted to them for their consistent support and contributions, without which this project would not have come to fruition. My wife, Joyce, was the leading and constant advocate of the need for a new book that would attempt to present a concise history of the U.S. involvement in the Palestine-Israel conflict, particularly at the present juncture in which the current U.S. president has given Israel carte blanche in the Occupied Territories, unprecedented both in its substance and lack of ambiguity. She also read a number of chapters and offered useful criticism. My son, Jamal, has also made substantive comments and suggestions. My colleague and long-time friend, Professor Samih Farsoun of the American University in Washington, D.C. made invaluable contributions and allowed me to rely on some of the work we had written together.

My good friend, Professor Cheryl Rubenberg, was a constant source of encouragement and a penetrating critic who read some of the chapters and made valuable suggestions. I would like to acknowledge the enormous insight I gained from the numerous telephone conversations I had with my cousin, Professor Tayseer Arouri of Bir Zeit University in the occupied West Bank. He was always generous with his ideas and forthright in his scholarly analysis while under prolonged curfews, together with more than two million Palestinians in the Occupied Territories. My good friend Elaine Hagopian of Simmons College has rendered invaluable contributions, having read much of what I have written not only for this book, but for other publications that had an impact on this book. Her comments were always poignant and original. My daughter-in-law, Danielle, was extremely generous with her time and typing skills, even when she had to care for two of my granddaughters at home.

I would like to extend my gratitude to Anthony Arnove of South End Press, who was a solid source of support and enlightenment, particularly as he proposed a thoughtful scheme for updating and replacing my earlier book, *The Obstruction of Peace*. I am grateful for his help and for his shepherding of this book from the inception. I wish to gratefully acknowledge the gracious permission kindly granted by Dr. Mahdi Abdul Hadi, chairman of the Palestinian Academic Society for the Study of International Affairs (PASSIA) in Jerusalem to reproduce ten of their remarkable maps, which constitute an exceptional asset to this book. Mahmoud Abu Rmeileh, PASSIA's very able webmaster, offered vital assistance in the reproduction of these maps. I would like to express sincere thanks to two young scholars who rendered crucial assistance with footnotes: Rosemary Carroll of the University of Wisconsin, Madison, and Bader Albanna of Yale University. To all those and other unnamed persons, I offer sincere gratitude as well as exemption from any blame for errors of analysis, omission, commission, or facts. These will remain as entirely mine.

A FLAWED PEACE PROCESS

This is a book about a failed "peace process" which has been taking place since 1967 under the tutelage of the United States. It is based on an earlier work, *The Obstruction of Peace: The United States, Israel, and the Palestinians.*[1] Much of the content of that book has been deleted, while other portions have been reformulated and updated. The relationship between the United States and the two protagonists—the Palestinians and Israel—consitutes the bulk of the work. It is a relationship that has undergone some serious transformations, trials, and tribulations during the past thirty-five years. It has evolved from an outright rejectionist policy toward Palestinian participation and Palestinian rights to a policy that came to focus much on process and little on peace. The irksome, long life of the process is perhaps its most compelling indictment.

After the post–1967 war period, the special relationship between the United States and Israel turned into a strategic alliance. This ruled out the role of honest brokering for the United States, yet all other would-be peacemakers and facilitators were held at bay. The U.S. diplomatic monopoly continued to serve as the singlemost effective means to accomplish Israel's goals. It sustained Israel, protected it from international scrutiny, and engineered the gridlock that allowed it to keep negotiating indefinitely while building numerous "facts on the ground." The alliance remained intact even after the end of the Cold War, when many pundits predicted a lesser role for Israel in America's strategic calculations. Bush I saw imperial consolidation through "resolving" the Palestinian problem through a settlement based on the Begin Autonomy Plan, which was inscribed in the Camp David I Accords. His proposed "solution" was eclipsed with his own political demise in 1992. Bush I's successor, Bill Clinton, had the distinction of being the first U.S. president to bring Yasir Arafat and Yitzhak Rabin together to begin the process of solving the Palestine question. Paradoxically, Clinton was also the first president to effectively nullify the idea of trading land for peace and to explicitly alter the meaning of U.N. Resolution 242. The Oslo process created its own conflicts, which multiplied between 1993 and 2000.

By July 2000, President Clinton convened a second Camp David summit in an attempt to bypass Israel's redeployment obligations under the several codicils of the Oslo agreement and to move directly to the final status issues. For the Palestinians, they were told they could either take it or leave it, and their lack of accommodation to this diktat earned them the wrath of Washington and Tel Aviv. For Prime Minister Ehud Barak, Camp David was his exit strategy, and when it failed to provide the required exit, he blamed Arafat, with Clinton's support. That led to the further demonization of Arafat—and the entire Palestinian cause. However, what Barak failed to achieve at Camp David—the total dismantling of all previous agreements—was achieved by his successor, Ariel Sharon (with help from the conditions created by the attacks of September 11, 2001). In fact, September 11 may prove to have dealt the final blow to whatever diminished possibility had remained for a two-state settlement in Palestine/Israel. During seven visits to Washington, between March 2001 and October 2002, Sharon succeeded in getting the younger Bush to effectively cancel his father's plan, as well as that of Clinton. U.S. policy at present, notwithstanding Bush's "vision" of a two-state solution, is Israel's: fix the blame on the Palestinian partner, declare Arafat unfit to rule, and demand his removal. American diplomacy came to a grinding halt, thus providing a cover for Sharon's Israel to crush the Palestinians.

It has been widely assumed in the United States that the "peace process" can be taken at face value, with the U.S. government playing the role of disinterested party valiantly searching for resolution of the conflict. But the image of Washington as the impartial chief conciliator is contradicted by its enduring alliance with Israel. Further complicating efforts for peace is the hard political reality that thirty-five years of de facto annexation of the occupied West Bank by Israel has rendered peace, based on Israeli withdrawal from the Occupied Territories, virtually impossible. Nonetheless, the historic handshake between Rabin and Arafat at the White House in September 1993 led the public to believe (mistakenly) that the Oslo Accords were the first real step toward genuine peace. At last, an unyielding conflict had been miraculously unraveled. Nine years later, a real standoff leading to a reign of terror in a reoccupied West

Bank has dealt a crushing blow to the "peace process." Prior to the accords, Arafat was the quintessential terrorist, the devil incarnate, who was rehabilitated through Oslo, only to be demonized again, leaving his seven-year association with the "peace process" a forgotten memory.

Settlements and Fragments

The drastically increased scale of settlement activity since the signing of the Declaration of Principles (DOP) in September of 1993 makes a mockery of the peace process. Not only did official Washington look the other way as the settlements threatened to foreclose peace, but it continued to ease restrictions on U.S. tax dollars going to building settlements, and it took no position on the flow of private funds enjoying tax exemptions. Since Sharon assumed power in February 2001, more than forty new settlements have been built.[2] George W. Bush has given Sharon a freer hand in the Occupied Territories than any previous U.S. president. Lest anyone think that the utilization of suicide bombings as a strategy began with Sharon, there is evidence showing that the Beit Leid incident of January 22, 1995, was used to serve the same purpose. It provided Israel with the justification not only to halt any serious negotiations with the Palestinian Authority (PA), but also to build more settlements in the Occupied Territories at a time when the negotiations were assumed to be leading to their rollback. Back in 1995, Israeli journalist Motti Basuk provided a more honest assessment in the daily *Davar*: "[T]he Israeli army will not withdraw from even one West Bank city or village in the near future.... Palestinian terrorism and violence will enable the government to carry out its settling program with relative calm in world public opinion, certainly in U.S. public opinion."[3]

The green light to build and expand settlements openly, given shortly after the DOP was signed, was verified by numerous Israeli journalists. Hanna Kim, for example, wrote a detailed article about the Israeli government's "Comprehensive Plan" for 1995:

> Despite the government decision from November 1992 to freeze all construction in the territories, the Housing Ministry has allowed Jews to construct private buildings there, and did not include "Greater Jerusalem" in the area in which construction was frozen. Any Jew wishing to do so can hire an entrepreneur to build a home in the territories, and the Housing Ministry is obliged to supply the infrastructure.[4]

According to a 1994 report by the Israeli Peace Now movement, while Rabin's government was negotiating peace with the Palestinians, it was in fact "implementing a policy of cutting up the West Bank into Jewish and Arab areas with the intention of creating Palestinian cantons encircled by territories held by Israel." In 2002, the Israeli human rights organization B'Tselem reported that settlers and settlements enjoy virtual sovereignty over 41 percent of the West Bank, making bantustanization a *fait accompli*.[5] Bantustanization is indeed the plan being implemented by Sharon. Palestinian nationals who wish to travel between one occupied city and another have been required to obtain a special permit from the Israeli authorities since the reoccupation of seven West Bank cities in May 2002.[6] Otherwise, they are confined to their cities, most of the time at home under curfews, some of which have lasted for 130 days as of the end of October 2002. The more than 400 villages, meanwhile, remain isolated from the cities around them.

An Islamic Threat?

The U.S. public, confused about the contrast between the situation in the Middle East today and the Oslo euphoria of 1993, is told that Islamic activists and regimes in Iran, Iraq, the Sudan, and Syria, as well as militias in Southern Lebanon and Gaza, are part of a worldwide Islamic menace emerging as the central threat to the West. The utilization of the Islamic "threat" to manipulate the so-called peace process began neither with Barak and Sharon, nor with September 11. Indeed, it goes back to the end of the Cold War, when Islam replaced Communism as the principal opponent of Western liberal democracy and the values it enshrines. By the same token, it was also targeted as the principal challenger to the state of Israel.

Israeli analyst Nahum Bernea wrote rather candidly about an Israeli campaign against political Islam back in 1994. Emphasizing the benefits to Israel, he wrote that "the most important advantage" of an anti-Islamic campaign is that it:

> lets Israel please the American public. Even in the U.S. Congress some dare to say that Israel lost its former value as a major American strategic asset. To that, the anti-Islamic campaign provides an answer … Israel will become the Western vanguard in the war against Islamic enemy. The second benefit Israel derives from its anti-Islamic campaign is that it justifies the peace process.[7]

The prevailing view since the "historic handshake" in 1993, both in government and in the society at large, is that the "peace process" and the anti-Islamic campaign provide an effective cover for Israel's plan to retain control over the West Bank, irrespective of the final status talks. This was plainly admitted by Jacques Neriah, a former adviser to Prime Minister Yitzhak Rabin, in 1995. "The intention all along," he said, "was for the interim agreement to be very near the final settlement."[8] The same sentiment was echoed by Moshe Shahal, a former Israeli police minister in Rabin's cabinet: "You are not going to invest a lot of money in redeploying the army for a period of two years.... Any arrangement for the interim phase will be in contact with the final status of the settlements and borders [sic]."[9]

Rabin's foreign minister, Shimon Peres, and his deputy, Yossi Beilin, are also on record concurring with this view. Peres told a Labor Party meeting in December 1994: "There will be no evacuation from Judea/Samaria ... the Oslo agreement began and ends in Gaza."[10]

A Permanent Occupation?

The distinction between interim and final phase has been superfluous since the beginning of this Oslo process. Israel never intended to relinquish control of the West Bank, either in 1993 or during the final status talks. Today, with the far right so entrenched in power in Israel, a permanent occupation has become the norm. In Washington, where the far right is also entrenched, the Bush II administration is much too committed to Israel and much too obsessed with "terrorism" to remind Israel that agreements held under its own auspices must be honored. The Europeans have no leverage with Israel and could only answer Arafat's successive appeals for pressure on Israel with money donations to keep his faltering regime afloat. Even funding the Palestinians under occupation is coming under serious criticism in the dominant conservative circles in Israel and the United States. The lead editorial in the *Wall Street Journal Europe* on July 16, 2002, for example, accused the European Union of unwittingly contributing to terrorism:

> Now nobody considers the European Union to be a conscious sponsor of terrorism. But in the lavish aid policies toward the Palestinian Authority, the EU has indirectly contributed to the Palestinian suicide bombings it rightly denounces and has thwarted hopes for the truly legitimate Palestinian institutions the [U.N.] Commission says it wants to see.[11]

George Bush's dichotomy of good and evil, of those who are "with us" and those who are "against us," is so absolute that there is little room for any distinctions between terrorism and resistance or cause and effect. But while the U.S. media focus on the suicide bombings that kill Israeli civilians and soldiers, little or no attention is paid to Israel's state terrorism, which involves constant bureaucratic harassment, assassinations by death squads, destruction of infrastructure, confinement of civilians to towns, villages, or districts, long curfews, administrative detention, torture, and systematic confiscation of land for building settlements and roads for the exclusive use of settlers. The wanton destruction of the infrastructure of Palestinian society was never covered by the U.S. media to the extent it was detailed by even the Israeli media. For example, Amira Hass of *Ha'aretz* provided the following details about the destruction of the Palestinian Ministry of Culture in Ramallah during the month of March 2002:

> It was especially difficult to enter two floors of the building because of the pungent stench of feces and urine. Soiled toilet paper was also scattered everywhere. In some of the rooms, not far from the heaps of feces and the toilet paper, remains of rotting food were scattered. In one corner, in the room in which someone had defecated into a drawer, full cartons of fruits and vegetables had been left behind. The toilets were left overflowing with bottles filled with urine, feces, and toilet paper. Relative to other places, the soldiers did not leave behind them many sayings scrawled on the walls. Here and there were the candelabrum symbols of Israel, stars of David, praises for the Jerusalem Betar soccer team.[12]

Kathleen Christison, a former CIA analyst who has written a great deal on the Palestine question, commented on Hass's article in a way most of the mainstream media would consider not fit to print:

> This is not a tale we are ever likely to see in the American press, so the vast majority of Americans who think with Menachem Begin that nobody can preach to Israel about ethics, that Israel's army is the only moral army in the world and always employs the doctrine of "purity of arms," will go on thinking that way.
>
> But I cannot.
>
> I am forced to ask some questions that the American majority will no doubt never hear: Can it, for instance, be called terrorism if an entire unit of the Israeli army forsakes purity of arms and spends a month crapping on floors, on piles of children's artwork, in desk drawers, on photocopiers?

Is this self-defense, or "rooting out the terrorist infrastructure"?
Is it anti-Semitic to wonder what happened to the moral compass of a
society that spawns a group of young men who will intermingle their
own religious and national symbols with feces and urine, as if the draw-
ings and the excrement both constitute valued autographs?[13]

Moreover, not a single mainstream newspaper in the U.S. has ever
dared, during thirty-five years of occupation, to refer to the separate legal
standards and physical facilities applied to and available for settlers and
indigenous people in the West Bank and Gaza as a form of apartheid. In
the absence of public debate about the Middle East in the U.S. political
arena (including Congress, the media, the theater, the universities, and the
business community), and given the lack of an objective analysis of the
DOP, the realities of the conflict remain misunderstood. The reason for
the double standard is that Israel is the publicly identified ally of the U.S.
government or that it serves the "national interest" of mainstream U.S. society. In the United States, Israel is perceived as a victim, and thereby en-
joys a certain immunity against criticism. At the same time, its Palestinian
victims in the diaspora, in what is left of their land now in Israel, and under military occupation do not qualify as victims worthy of our sympathy.
The daily victims of Israel's siege policy rarely make the television news,
which covers suicide bombing incidents as "breaking news," with reports
and footage from the scene. The spectacular acts of suicide bombings
make the headlines, cover stories, and television briefs; sound bites and
dramatic reports have become a substitute for real news or insightful analysis in the prevailing culture in the United States.

Now that Sharon's military attacks of the spring and summer of 2002
have failed to insure Israeli security and force the Palestinians into total
submission, the Bush administration, the "catalyst for peace," is expected
to act, if only to rescue its sagging prestige and reassert its hegemonic influence in the Middle East. A possible course of action for Washington
was outlined by Jim Hoagland in the *Washington Post*:

> The administration must now pursue other methods of preventing the
> region from becoming a chaotic platform for greater global terrorism....
> American forces would stay for years to help develop and shield new
> and democratic leaderships in Iraq and in a Palestinian state.... This is
> no time to think small. American troops can be effective and secure on
> the West Bank only as part of a much larger force committed to the re-
> gion on a twofold mission: to fight the sources and supporters of global

terrorism, and to advance the interlocking causes of democracy in the Arab world and the survival of Israel.[14]

Hoagland's call for a military occupation of Iraq and Palestine (on the model of the U.S. war in Afghanistan) represents a challenge to Bush II by the Washington super-hawks. The Bush administration seems to believe that reordering the Middle East and Central Asia requires the crushing of Palestine, with the full might of Israel embraced as part of a common imperial effort in the area. Such inclinations coincide with the other major solution for the Occupied Territories embraced by the Likud party and its far right allies: "engineered emigration." In either case, Palestine and Palestinians will be sacrificed.

The strengthening of Turkish and Indian ties—in addition to the imposition of new puppets in Afghanistan and (the Bush administration hopes) in Iraq—is meant to allow Israel to assert its role as the local hegemon under the American global umbrella. This, in turn, is a key part of the encirclement of the strategic Middle East and Central Asia regions for the control of oil and gas. Hoagland seems to corroborate this ominous analysis:

> Straws in the wind suggest a growing acceptance at the White House of the need for an overwhelming U.S. invasion force that will remain on the ground in Iraq for several years. The U.S. presence will serve as the linchpin for democratic transformation of a major Arab country that can be a model for the region. A new Iraq would also help provide greater energy security for Americans.[15]

The kind of democracy now represented by the regime of Hamid Karzai in Afganistan is likely to provide a model for the kind of "democracy" Bush II would like to see in Iraq and Palestine. Saddam Hussein and Yasir Arafat are already targets in Bush's open-ended antiterrorist campaign. The president's infamous speech of June 24, 2002, made it plain that while the U.S. expects elections and reforms by the Palestinian Authority, the reelection of Arafat is unacceptable.[16]

Will Bush II and Sharon succeed in their grandiose scheme? Can the United States and Israel succeed in forcing "normalization" on the Arabs without Palestine? Ben-Gurion and Jabotinsky always felt that massive force would compel the Arabs to accept Israel in the area. Can this inhumane vision succeed?

Notes

1   *Obstruction of Peace: The United States, Israel and the Palestinians* (Monroe, Maine: Common Courage Press, 1995).

2   *Washington Post*, July 28, 2002.

3   *Davar*, January 27, 1995.

4   *Ha'aretz*, January 13, 1995.

5   *New York Times*, May 21, 2002.

6   *The Independent* (London), May 26, 2002.

7   *Yedioth Ahronoth*, December 16, 1994.

8   *Boston Globe*, January 30, 1995.

9   *Boston Globe*, January 30, 1995.

10 *Ha'aretz*, January 6, 1995.

11 *The Wall Street Journal Europe*, July 16, 2002.

12 *Ha'aretz,* May 6, 2002.

13 Kathleen Christison, "Israel, a Light unto Nations?" *CounterPunch*, May 11, 2002, http://www.counterpunch.org/kchristison0511.html.

14 *Washington Post*, June 30, 2002.

15 *Washington Post*, June 30, 2002.

16 *Boston Globe*, June 25, 2002; see also Chapter 11.

CHAPTER 1

PALESTINE, THE ARABS, AND U.S. POLICY

The question of Palestine consists of manifold elements—a country, Palestine, a nation, a state-in-formation, the Palestinian people, a culture, poetry, proverbs, anecdotes, embroidery, cuisine, a national ethos, and an endless struggle against foreign occupations. During the sixteenth century, the Palestinians and other Arabs fell victim to the Ottoman Turkish conquest, which lasted until World War I. Liberation did not come, however, with the end of the Ottoman era, as the victorious Western powers, the new imperialists, divided the Arab domains of Ottoman Turkey into spheres of influence, with Palestine assigned as a League of Nations mandate to be administered by Britain.

The Palestine mandate was designated as Class A, meaning that the indigenous Palestinians would require a shorter period of preparation for self-governance. That, however, did not prevent the mandatory power, Britain, from designating the country—the overwhelming majority of whose indigenous population was Palestinian—as a Jewish homeland for European settlers. Within three decades, the settler-colonial community, which had grown from 11 percent of the population to 33 percent, was able to gain control of 78 percent of the land after expelling two-thirds of the indigenous Palestinians. The Jewish military onslaught that brought the state of Israel into existence on May 15, 1948, is conventionally labeled by Israel and the West as "Israel's war of independence."

Until today, Zionists have not made it convincingly clear from whom that "independence" was wrested, and how their ethnic cleansing of the indigenous Palestinians—occurring largely during the first half of 1948, while Britain was still responsible for law and order—produced independence. The indigenous population was neither self-governing nor ruling over the Jews in Palestine. Independence from Britain, on the other hand, is oxymoronic, given that Britain's Balfour Declaration of 1917, made as part of the Mandate for Palestine, had provided the first justification for a colonial settlement (Jewish national home) in Palestine. Indeed, it was the British Mandate authorities who provided the privileges, empowerment, and protection for the Jewish settler-colonial minority.

The remaining 22 percent of Palestine, comprising the West Bank and the Gaza Strip, respectively administered by Jordan and Egypt since 1948, was conquered by Israel in June 1967. Contrary to widely held misconceptions, the Palestine problem did not begin in 1967 when Israel conquered and occupied the Gaza Strip and east-central Palestine (known as the West Bank). The invasion and occupation of the remaining Palestinian territories in 1967 were but the completion of the 1948 conquest, and, therefore, any settlement—any restitution, reparations, atonement, or compensation—would have to start with 1948.

Since 1948, the Palestine question has come to be embodied by numerous U.N. resolutions that uphold the right of the Palestinians to return to their land and property, to establish their own independent state alongside Israel, to receive compensation, and to gain restitution. These rights are collective and individual, as they are also inalienable in accordance with international law and practice. Redress to the Palestinian people, however, has been pre-empted by Israeli obstinacy and diplomatic maneuvering, cleverly bolstered by what has been misnamed as a "peace process" after the 1967 war. Restitution and compensation, let alone withdrawal from the 1967 Occupied Territories, have been assiduously removed from the active diplomatic agenda.

More U.N. resolutions were adopted after 1967, calling for an end to the occupation, dismantling of settlements, and peaceful coexistence based on two states (Palestine and Israel) existing side by side. The entire compendium of these resolutions, which span the past half century, constitutes a sort of jurisprudence for the Palestine question, a framework anchored in international law. Indeed, a global consensus had prevailed throughout the 1970s and 1980s in support of a diplomatic settlement based on that framework, but all efforts on behalf of an equitable settlement were sabotaged, ironically by none other than the manager of the "peace process" itself. U.S. and Israeli opposition to international engagement remained firmly entrenched throughout the period, ostensibly in order not to pre-empt the "peace process," or to prejudice its final outcome.

Conciliation or Collaboration?

A striking feature of U.S. policy toward the Arab-Israeli conflict since the 1967 occupation was the insistence of the U.S. government that it play the role of chief arbiter, if not sole peacemaker, when in fact it has been co-belligerent. The steady growth of the U.S.-Israeli special relationship, transformed into a full-fledged strategic alliance, during and after the Cold War, has been paralleled by a corresponding ascendancy of the U.S. diplomatic role. That role has now eclipsed all the conventional methods of conflict resolution, including mediation, multilateral initiatives, regional endeavors, and U.N.-sponsored peacemaking.

Since 1969, when Secretary of State William Rogers enunciated his "peace plan," based on the exchange of territory for peace, Arabs and Palestinians have had to repeatedly confront a dangerous illusion: that the United States was capable of delivering a fair, just, and durable peace in the region. But the duality of the U.S. diplomatic posture was a constant barrier to peace, which cannot be built on the bones of the vanquished and under the banners of the victor. Assuming the role of "honest broker," however, while being Israel's chief diplomatic backer, financial donor, and military supplier, the United States placed itself at odds with a global consensus in support of a political settlement within an international framework. As ally and protector of Israel, the U.S. government has been simply unable to credibly discharge its self-assigned mission as the catalyst for peace. This pattern is rooted in the thirty-five-year history of U.S.-Israeli relations, which constitutes the scope of this book.

The diplomatic history of the Middle East during the past thirty-five years reveals that a half dozen U.S. administrations have stood consistently in opposition to a settlement that would provide for an end to the Israeli occupation and the establishment of a Palestinian state existing side by side with Israel. Such opposition existed despite the fact that the Palestine Liberation Organization (PLO) began to align its position with that of the Arab states in the early 1970s.[1] At that time, the PLO gave up the revolutionary option and began to move toward a two-state solution. The PLO was declared the "sole legitimate representative" of the Palestinian people by the Rabat Arab Summit Conference of 1974, in return for its renunciation of the armed struggle in pursuit of the goal of a democratic secular state in all of Palestine, providing equal protection for Muslims, Christians, Jews, and others. Palestinian adherence to the much-scaled-back objective of a mini-state in the West Bank and Gaza, alongside Israel, however, failed to impress Washington. The outcome for the Palestinians was continued deprivation and denial of basic human rights, including self-determination.

At the same time, Israel managed to reject every single U.S. initiative involving a territorial settlement, even when such initiatives excluded Palestinian sovereignty. The Palestinians have thus been confronted with two powerful states intent on denying them a national existence. The two interests coincided to the extent that succeeding U.S. administrations viewed the disaffected Palestinians as a volatile antiestablishment group whose irredentist goals threatened the existing regional order. Hence the convergence of U.S. strategic designs and Israeli territorial ambitions.

Harvest Time?

The U.S. endeavor to impose its hegemony on the Middle East, which predates the Arab-Israeli war of 1967, has been relentless. The new additions to the Middle East diplomatic vocabulary—Madrid, Washington, Oslo, Taba, Camp David, Sharm al-Shaykh, and Cairo—symbolize diplomatic achievements, yet have done nothing to bring stability or peace to the region. The signing ceremonies at the White House (September 13, 1993) and at Wadi Araba (October 27, 1994), both sponsored and witnessed by President Clinton, reflected the power of the U.S.-Israeli alliance. Advocates of a variety of concepts or programs—including Arab unity, self-sufficiency, independent foreign policy, democratic governance, Palestinian self-determination, and Arab-Israeli parity and mutuality—were pushed to the sidelines. Indeed, Palestine appears to have been effectively recolonized in the age of decolonization. Its post–World War II status is being touted as a victory for Pax Americana and Pax Israel.[2]

The objectives of U.S. policy have been pursued relentlessly by U.S. politicians representing the right, "left," and center. It did not matter that the policies of liberals such as Truman, Kennedy, and Johnson were remarkably similar to those of conservatives such as John Foster Dulles and Richard Nixon. Nor was it strange that Jimmy Carter, the supposed human rights advocate and Nobel Laureate, and Ronald Reagan, the born-again cold warrior, adhered to the same line of Middle East policy, which delivered the "payoff" to Bill Clinton, the neoliberal proponent of globalization. The U.S. government position on Israel over the last several decades is a remarkable testimony to the ability of the U.S. establishment to maintain a stable foreign policy consensus, free of any real debate.

While American policy objectives remained fixed, however, the means to achieve these objectives underwent periodic adjustments. Although the tools of U.S. policy remained in place, Arabs and Palestinians in top level positions often mistakenly took such minor aberrations for substantive policy changes. Short-term fluctuations and seductive signals—which invariably included brief threats of reassessments of U.S.-Israeli relations by irritated presidents—were mistakenly read as departures, at last, in the direction of fairness. For examples, Gerald Ford's call for a "reassessment," Carter's confrontation with Menachem Begin in 1977, Baker's ordeals with Yitzhak Shamir, and Bush I's conflict over loan guarantees in 1990 were not seen by Palestinian and other Arab leaders as manifestations of normal disagreements among close allies over tactical differences, but as signs of a fundamental change in U.S. relations with Israel (and hence the Palestinians or the broader Arab world). This naivete, which overlooked the durability of strategic considerations, seems to derive from a political culture in which policy changes are often attributed to pronouncements of autocratic rulers driven by short-term imperatives or the leaders' own preferences.

Arafat's appearance at the White House Rose Garden on September 13, 1993, was seen by Arafat and his entourage as the crowning achievement of his career and the sure sign of a new American policy, when in fact Clinton, Rabin, and the informed public regarded it as the signing of his own surrender and a historic abandonment of the Palestinian people's struggle for liberation. His frivolous declaration that the Palestinians had a new friend in the White House was pathetic. Clinton clearly despised Arafat, together with the Palestinian cause. It would have made more sense had President Clinton been the one to thank Arafat three times on September 13, 1993, rather than the other way around. Arafat had, after all, enabled Clinton to proclaim the realization of objectives which U.S. policy makers had been struggling to achieve before Clinton reached voting age. The Oslo process had, in effect, reduced the Palestine question to manageable proportions. On that historic day, the United States was effectively celebrating its own victory and the eclipse of Palestine.

The Arab States as Instruments of U.S. Policy

Arab regimes are among the principal tools of U.S. foreign policy in the Middle East. The Jordanian military onslaught against the Palestinian movement in September 1970 inflicted structural damage, the effect of which continued to set back the Palestinian struggle for decades to come. Not only had the late King Hussein terminated the Palestinian-enforced de facto dual authority in Jordan, he also enabled the United States and Israel to maintain their strategic advantage in the east Mediterranean vìs-a-vìs the Soviet Union. Likewise, when Palestinian fighters regrouped in Lebanon after the "Black September" debacle of 1970 and began to threaten the delicate balance inside Lebanon and in the region, Syria was tacitly accepted by the United States and Israel as the logical candidate for the role of policeman in 1976. The Palestinian national movement once again had to be reduced to manageable proportions, this time, however, not by a conservative pro-Western monarchy, but by a self-professed "revolutionary" Arab nationalist regime. The agreement, in which Israel and Syria came to share suzerainty over Lebanon, with U.S. blessings, was the product of that mission.

Egypt was drafted subsequently to deliver the *coup de grace*, peacefully this time, against the Palestinians. Camp David had inflicted more damage on Palestinian nationalism by nonmilitary means in 1978 than the two previous armed onslaughts combined. Thus, the first Arab state to assume responsibility for strategic balance vìs-a-vìs Israel, from the mid-1950s until 1970, was transformed in the late 1970s to an enforcer of U.S. policy and a facilitator for Israel. Not only had Camp David I secured the removal of Egypt from the Arab strategic arena, it also allowed Israel to dodge its legal responsibilities to the Palestinian people and to shrug off its obligation to withdraw from Palestinian, Syrian, and Lebanese territories, in violation of U.N. Security Council resolutions and international law.

Even Iraq, the third contender for strategic balance vìs-a-vìs Israel, had allowed itself to become an instrument of U.S. foreign policy during the Iran-Iraq war in the 1980s. U.S. policy makers were gratified to see Iraq inflict damage on the Islamic republic in Iran without cost to the United States, and to weaken itself in the process, thus undermining its desire to play the role of pacesetter in the Gulf. Moreover, Iraq's war against the mullahs turned Arab attention away from the Israeli threat and toward a presumed "Shiite Iranian threat." The Palestinian cause, already battered by Camp David, was further bruised by the redefined priorities of Saddam Hussein. And when Hussein began to exaggerate his own importance for U.S. interests in the Gulf, he was reduced to size, not only with the acquiescence of Arab regimes, but also with the active participation of the Gulf states, Egypt, and Syria.

A "Window of Opportunity" for the United States

With the destruction of Iraq and the dissolution of the Soviet Union in 1991, a Palestinian-Israeli settlement based on U.S. designs suddenly became possible and desirable. The Madrid Accords would prove to be the venue for this. Although James Baker III was the architect of Madrid in 1991, much of the construction work had already begun under Baker's predecessors. The Madrid framework represented a synthesis of previous U.S. diplomatic initiatives. The two-track approach (separating Palestinian and Arab issues), the self-government concept, and transitional arrangements were derived from the Camp David Accords negotiated under Carter's auspices in 1978. The Jordanian dimension of a Palestinian-Israeli settlement is grounded in the Reagan plan of 1982.[3] The linguistic bait designed to attract the Palestinians was largely inherited from the Shultz plan of 1988, which itself incorporated the salient features of Camp David and the Reagan plan.[4]

Two characteristics are shared in common by all these initiatives. First, they were all occasioned by structural changes in either the regional or the global environment. The de-Nasserization of Egypt and the subsequent collapse of Soviet influence there in 1972 created a strategic imperative for U.S. diplomatic action. The outcome was Camp David in 1978. Moreover, the Israeli invasion of Lebanon in 1982 had so weakened the Palestinian national movement that President Reagan declared the outcome an "opportunity" for peace, which effectively removed Palestinian national rights from the active global agenda.

Having just embarked on a new Cold War with the Soviet Union and with independent nationalism, Reagan welcomed the opportunity to rearrange the strategic landscape of the Middle East. His September 1982 plan, however, was thwarted by a junior ally with strategic designs of its own. The prompt and categorical rejection of the Reagan plan by the Israeli cabinet, only a few hours after it was enunciated on prime time television, had simply sealed its fate. The plan's denial of sovereignty in the

West Bank and Gaza to both Israel and the Palestinians, in favor of Jordan, guaranteed Israel's quick rejection. The stillborn plan was thus shelved, but aspects of it were resurrected six years later in the Shultz plan, which deferred the issue of sovereignty to so-called final status negotiations. The Shultz plan also failed to impress Israel. Prime Minister Yitzhak Shamir declared it "unwelcome" in 1988, causing it to be shelved until the following year when Baker began to revive it. Baker's "opportunity" in 1991, however, proved to be more auspicious than Reagan's in 1982. The U.S. defeat of Iraq in 1991 was more decisive than the Israeli storming of Lebanon in 1982, and more damaging to the Palestinians. Hence Baker's "opportunity," which produced Madrid.

Although the Madrid formula was based on the principle of the exchange of territory for peace, in accordance with a speech by President Bush to the U.S. Congress on March 6, 1991, it was not made clear whether that exchange included the West Bank and Gaza or only the Golan Heights of Syria. In fact, the Madrid formula, through the separate negotiating tracks for Israel and the Arab states, as well as the interim arrangements for the West Bank and Gaza, effectively enabled Israel to defer West Bank and Gaza sovereignty while it derived Arab state recognition and obtained normalization within the Arab world.

The second important common denominator of the four plans by the United States is that in all of these plans the roles of the protagonists in the "peace process" were overshadowed by the strategic dimension of that process. The parties to the conflict did not always share Washington's diagnosis that the circumstances were propitious for peaceful relations. And while Israel said no to the Reagan and the Shultz plans (and later renounced its own elections plan in 1989 in order to avoid a territorial settlement), most of the Arab parties opted for negotiations, despite the adverse conditions, hoping not to displease Washington.

Given these circumstances, it is not a coincidence that all of the U.S. proposals for peace ended in failure. Camp David may have terminated the belligerency on the Israeli-Egyptian front, but it has fallen short of establishing genuine peaceful relations between the two countries, let alone the comprehensive regional peace it promised.

The U.S. government pursued its objectives relentlessly, despite its rather isolated position in the world community. Help was extended by the unintended acts of two tragic figures: Mikhail Gorbachev and Saddam

Hussein. The fateful decision of Saddam Hussein to invade Kuwait on August 2, 1990, gave George Bush the green light to reshape the strategic landscape of the Middle East, terminate the existing Arab political order, and resolve the impasse in favor of Washington's Palestinian and Arab agenda.[5] It was a windfall for a superpower facing relative economic decline and sagging credibility yet seeking to remain "number one."

The same decision spelled disaster for the Palestinian people, whose leadership decided in 1993 to acquiesce to the U.S. and Israeli agendas, even though they involved nothing more than the reformulation of old plans that excluded Palestinian self-determination and circumvented the numerous Palestinian rights that have been upheld by the international community. Even the "full autonomy" that was promised to Palestinians in Camp David I was effectively excluded.

The Palestinian people are now at a crossroads with limited options. Either they insist on total Israeli withdrawal as the only path to an independent and contiguous state in the West Bank and Gaza—with an arrangement for sharing sovereignty in Jerusalem (not merely in Abu Dis, the area Israel once considered calling the Palestinian "Jerusalem") and a just solution for the refugees in accordance with international law—or they will be forced to live under the neoapartheid system now being institutionalized by Sharon.

Oslo and Extinguishing Multilateralism

The theory and practice of the "peace process," which was based on the assumption that peace in the Middle East can only emanate from Washington, has undermined all serious efforts to bring peace to the region. The common denominator of all the U.S. plans was nonrecognition of the original injustice done to the Palestinians in 1948. None of these plans has acknowledged the unqualified right of the Palestinian people to self-determination, to real liberation from the 1967 Israeli occupation, or to restitution. While the United States had voted annually since 1948 in favor of U.N. Resolution 194, which recognizes the right of the Palestinian refugees to return to their homes and property and to receive compensation and restitution, it effectively blocked all international efforts to give any practical application to that resolution. By 1993, even that *pro forma* vote was withdrawn. The Oslo process allowed the United States and Israel to formally nullify not only U.N. Resolution 194, but the entire international framework of law related to Palestinian rights.

The United States used its U.N. Security Council veto on numerous occasions to shelter Israel from international reproach for violating the human and national rights of the Palestinian people or to deny the Palestinians international protection. The U.S.-led campaign against multilateralism was pursued so successfully that Israel and the United States now portray any mention of international law, the right of return for refugees, or even U.N. resolutions as intransigence and obstructionism. When the Oslo process began to unfold in 1993, even the pretense of international participation was sidelined. Israel, in fact, furnished the framework for a settlement, while the Palestinian leadership was asleep at the wheel, banking naively on the goodwill and trust of their Israeli counterparts, who were busily crafting a Bantustan-like arrangement. The lawyers of the Israeli foreign office insured that the agreements would exclude Palestinian sovereignty on any portion of the land extending between the River Jordan and the Mediterranean Sea. Meanwhile, the core Palestinian negotiators consisted mainly of entrepreneurs and loyalists who were eager to cash in on the many investment opportunities that Oslo was expected to bring. In hundreds of pages of the Oslo documents, one can find no mention whatsoever of such terms as occupation, withdrawal, the Geneva Convention of 1949, or Palestinian sovereignty, let alone Palestinian emancipation and independent statehood.

Not only did the Oslo process shun U.N. Security Council resolutions other than 242 and 338—albeit in a very perfunctory manner—but it was also completely open-ended. Oslo was an agreement to reach agreement, containing much about process and little about the substance of peace based on justice. Accordingly, Israel was not constrained by any international legal requirements governing its military occupation. The Oslo process has, effectively, released Israel from the occupier's obligations and rendered international law inoperable. In fact, Israel has used the Oslo process as a diplomatic cover to extend and consolidate its illegal occupation and to double the settler population, thus rendering a two-state solution a geographic impossibility. The Oslo process has been the singlemost effective instrument of the realization of strategic Israeli and Zionist goals. It has proven to be cost-effective, with Israel's policing function relegated to the Palestinian Authority. It has been sufficiently deceptive, as much of the world came to think that peace was around the corner. And it has served the interests of the right, center, and left in Israel.

Historically, settler-colonial movements relied mainly on military conquests, population expulsions, land alienation, and genocide to accomplish their goals. While Israel has been no exception, having utilized most of these techniques, the Oslo process was an unprecedented diplomatic achievement. Oslo facilitated tangible colonial achievements affecting land and population structures, yet involved minimal reliance on Israel's armed forces. When the Palestinians finally rebelled in September 2000, beginning the Al-Aqsa Intifada, Israel's armed forces were unleashed again to suppress the resistance and pre-empt a Palestinian state-in-formation.

The marginalization of international law and the corresponding ascendancy of the Israeli role, promoted and protected by the U.S.'s virtual diplomatic monopoly, have combined to create a situation in which culpability for the Palestinian catastrophe has been squarely assigned to the victim. Unlike other indigenous peoples and racial groups, the Palestinians received neither apologies nor acknowledgments of responsibility for displacement, dispossession, massacres, legalized torture, wanton destruction, home demolition, ethnic cleansing, and other atrocities committed during the past fifty-five years.

For Sharon and his allies across the Israeli spectrum, the fight with the Palestinians is existential. As such, the vanquished must pay the price. This zero-sum formulation has driven Sharon's army with impunity against virtually defenseless civilians in the cities, towns, and refugee camps of the Occupied Territories in March and April 2002. As prime minister, Sharon has been vigorously trying to force the Palestinians into submission, ending their uprising against the occupation once and for all, forcing them to accept a fragmented Bantustan solution or to leave the country. Expulsion, which is euphemistically known as "transfer" in Zionist parlance, is now supported by 46 percent of Israel's population.[6]

The Denial of Restitution

The fact that Israel was born in the sin of dispossession of another people has never been seriously acknowledged in public discussion, despite an abundance of irrefutable facts from Israel's own "revisionist historians." But how can restitution and/or atonement to the Palestinian people even be raised as issues if the genesis of the problem must remain outside the parameters of discussion? Additionally, the anti-Semitic label is frequently invoked whenever a non-Zionist narrative of Palestinian dispossession is voiced.

The excision of moral responsibility for the Palestinian catastrophe, called *al-Nakba* in Arabic, remains essential for the success of the Zionist colonial project. Nineteen forty-eight was the year of Palestinian catastrophe and, at the same time, was the year of Israel's "independence," the making of Israel. Neither event would have happened without the other. Yet no Israeli official has ever ventured to call for atonement. Such a gesture would give credibility to Palestinian grievances and appeals for basic rights, and would thus reflect unfavorably on Israel's own "credibility." Trying to find legal and moral justification for Israel's existence would be seen as a clear sign of weakness, self-doubt, and lack of moral resolve. Israel's leadership perceives an offensive strategy as the best form of defense, and thus turns history on its head. The indigenous Palestinians have been declared nonexistent. The victims have become victimizers. Colonization is development. Resistance to occupation is terrorism. And the right of return for refugees is a threat to Israel's demographic security and Jewish character. It is the victim who now has to atone and pay compensation. Only the powerful can decide whether the victim and the disempowered have been sufficiently compliant.

Israel's strategic alliance with the United States—exemplified most recently in its use of the bellicose rhetoric and methods of Bush's "war on terrorism"—is designed not only to shelter Israel from any and all Palestinian and Arab grievances, but to position it among the few privileged participants in the ongoing redefinition of the rules of international conduct and international law. Expecting Israel to acknowledge its wrongdoing in 1948, in the aftermath of the Cold War and September 11, is not a likely prospect. Yet the prospects for a genuine reconciliation and a historic compromise are not likely to succeed without this.

Notes

1   For a discussion of Palestinian relations with the Arab states after the 1967 war, see Naseer H. Aruri, "Palestinian Impasse: Constraints and Opportunities," in *The Next Arab Decade*, ed. Hisham Sharabi (Boulder: Westview Press, 1988).

2   See Naseer H. Aruri, "The Recolonization of the Arab World," *Arab Studies Quarterly* 11: 2–3 (Spring/Summer 1989): 273–86.

3   For an analysis of the Reagan plan, see Naseer H. Aruri and Fouad Moughrabi, "The Reagan Middle East Initiative," *Journal of Palestine Studies* 12: 2 (Winter 1983): 10–30.

4   "U.S. Policy in the Middle East" U.S. Department of State, Bureau of Public Affairs, *Current Policy* 27 (June 1988).

5   See the following articles on the regional and global significance of the Gulf War: Tom Naylor, "American Aims in the Persian Gulf," *Canadian Dimensions* (March 1991): 34–37; James Petras, "The Meaning of the New World Order: A Critique," *America* (May 11, 1991): 512–14; Noam Chomsky, "U.S. Gulf Policy," *Open Magazine* (January 18, 1991): 1–17; Noam Chomsky, "What We Say Goes: The Middle East in the New World Order," in *Collateral Damage,* ed. Cynthia Peters (Boston: South End Press, 1991), pp. 49–92.

6   Associated Press, April 7, 2002.

CHAPTER 2

THE EVOLUTION OF U.S. GLOBAL STRATEGY

A STRIKING CONTINUITY

Regardless of the means employed to accomplish America's policy objectives, these objectives have remained constant since the enunciation
of the Containment Policy, in accordance with the thinking of George F.
Kennan: to insure, through the threat of force, either directly or via certain regional powers, that the Middle East remains securely and irrevo-
cably in the U.S. sphere of control. The status quo the U.S. government
attempted to uphold during the second half of the twentieth century was
a region free of Soviet influence and of nationalist dominance. Arab and
Palestinian nationalism remained the single major impediment to the
maintenance of that status quo, particularly in the period following the
1967 Arab-Israeli war.[1]

Containment and the Truman Doctrine

During the 1950s, the defense of the vast economic and strategic interests
of the United States was predicated on a network of alliances pulling together conservative pro-Western regimes in the region and on the readiness of the U.S. to intervene directly. Gradually, the United States began
to replace Britain and France as the new imperial power in this strategic
region. That perception was expressed in a speech by President Truman
on Army Day in 1946: "The Near and Middle East … contains vast natural resources … lies across the most convenient route of land, air and water communication … [and] might become an arena of intense rivalry
among outside powers."[2]

The Truman Doctrine ushered in an era of U.S. intervention to contain a presumed Soviet threat. The president urged the establishment of a

mutual security program to achieve that goal, and continued, together with Britain, to search for a formula to fulfill the objectives of Western policy in the Middle East.[3] That logic led to the ill-fated Baghdad Pact, when royalist Iraq broke ranks with the Arab League and announced its decision to conclude an alliance with Turkey, a country that already had a treaty with Pakistan. Iran became the fourth regional member of the Baghdad Pact in 1955. Britain was a full-fledged member of the pact, but the United States, while it participated in some of its military committees and provided military aid, refrained from formal membership. The pact corresponded to the concept of the Northern Tier put forth by Secretary of State John Foster Dulles in 1953. At that time, he had correctly concluded that the Arab states were "more fearful of Zionism than of the communists."[4] And yet the Baghdad Pact did not bypass the Palestine problem. In fact, it polarized the Arab world along the lines of neutralism versus pro-Western orientation. That polarization was exacerbated by the Israeli raid on Gaza on February 28, 1955, which killed thirty-eight persons and exposed Egypt's military weakness. The arms that President Nasser of Egypt required to bolster his defenses were not to be found in the West, where the price was adherence to Western-sponsored military alliances. He found them, instead, in the Communist bloc after his attendance at the conference of nonaligned states at Bandung in April 1955. Chinese Premier Chou En-Lai had suggested to Nasser that the Soviets might be responsive to a request for arms, and the Egyptian-Czech arms deal was announced on September 27, 1955.[5]

The Suez Invasion of 1956

France was already unhappy with Egypt's material and diplomatic support for the Algerian struggle for independence and held Nasser responsible for the escalation of the resistance in the mid-1950s. Nasser was also objectionable to Israel, which viewed him as a new phenomenon in the region who could undermine Israeli supremacy. Israeli Prime Minister David Ben-Gurion explained, "I always feared that a personality might rise such as arose among the Arab rulers in the seventh century, or like him [Kemal Ataturk] who arose in Turkey after its defeat in the First World War. He raised their spirits, changed their character, and turned them into a fighting nation. There was and still is a danger that Nasser is this man."[6]

As the combined interests of Britain, France, and Israel led to a shared desire to deal Nasser a crushing blow, the United States appeared eager to avoid conflict. Given the imminent decline of Anglo-French influence in the region, the United States was ready to fill a power "vacuum." It did not seem to matter that the Eisenhower administration was in the midst of an election campaign. U.S. corporate interests, defined as "the national interest," required a firm stand against aggression. Less than two weeks before the Suez invasion, Secretary of State John Foster Dulles articulated these interests at a high-level policy meeting in candid terms:

> We are in the present jam because the past administration had always dealt with the Middle East from a [domestic] political standpoint and had tried to meet the wishes of the Zionists in this country. That had created a basic antagonism with the Arabs. That was what the Russians were capitalizing on. It is of the utmost importance for the welfare of the United States that we get away from a [domestic] political basis and try to develop a national nonpartisan policy. Otherwise, we may be apt to lose the whole area and possibly Africa. This would be a major disaster for Western Europe as well as the United States.[7]

President Eisenhower dispatched two letters, on October 27 and 29, 1956, to Ben-Gurion, warning that a hostile initiative by Israel could endanger the emerging close relationship between the two countries.[8] When the invasion took place on October 29, the U.S. government issued an unequivocal condemnation and worked through the United Nations to secure withdrawal of all foreign forces. President Eisenhower made a statement that would be unthinkable today:

> The actions taken can scarcely be reconciled with the principles and purposes of the United Nations to which we have all subscribed ... there can be no peace without law. And there can be no law if we were to invoke one code of international conduct for those who oppose us and another for our friends.[9]

Such pursuit of balance had also been seen earlier when the United States temporarily suspended aid to Israel on September 18, 1953, for refusing to comply with a U.N. request to suspend work on its hydroelectric project in the demilitarized zone near the Syrian border.[10] Washington also condemned the Israeli raid on the village of Qibya in the West Bank the following month and decreased aid in 1954.[11]

The Suez war would have been a catalyst for the improvement of Arab relations with the United States, which in turn was conscious of Egypt's importance for the realization of its policy objectives. Egypt was pivotal for U.S. efforts to cultivate close relationships with Saudi Arabia in order to insure steady oil supplies to Europe and to facilitate U.S. economic penetration in the Middle East—hence the U.S. reluctance to accept Israeli overtures for a formal alliance and a guarantee of security, particularly as Israel deliberately refrained from defining its boundaries. Dulles told Israel's ambassador Abba Eban rather bluntly that America could not "guarantee temporary armistice lines."[12] But later developments in U.S. policy, such as the withdrawal of U.S. funds that had been promised for the Aswan Dam project, as well as the enunciation of the Eisenhower Doctrine, derailed the attempted rapprochement.

The Eisenhower Doctrine and the Arab World

The Eisenhower Doctrine was proclaimed in a speech to a joint session of Congress on January 5, 1957, in which Eisenhower appealed for discretionary power to spend up to $200 million in aid money for the Middle East. He sought and obtained authorization to employ U.S. military forces against "overt armed aggression from any nation controlled by international communism."[13] It was made rather clear that revolutionary Egypt was the principal target of the doctrine, but the policy also paved the way for the first civil war in Lebanon and a military coup in Iraq in 1958, as well as the first U.S. military intervention in the area.

The Eisenhower Doctrine was also applied in Jordan during the spring of 1957, when the country's first government to emerge from a free parliamentary election was abruptly dismissed by King Hussein, causing massive demonstrations. Dulles extended aid of $10 million to Hussein under the Eisenhower Doctrine.[14] In Lebanon, President Camille Chamoun, seeking an unprecedented second term and facing internal opposition, was able to bring about U.S. intervention in accordance with the doctrine in 1958.

The Eisenhower Doctrine, which became law on March 9, 1957, was described as having marked "a watershed in U.S. policy toward the Middle East because it specified the area as a vital national interest."[15] From that point on, threats to the "vital American national interest" would be used to describe a wide variety of actions by nationalist forces challenging conservative regimes, resisting Israeli transgression, or questioning U.S.

hegemony. This formed a critical moment in the evolution of the U.S.-Israeli special relationship, which reached a level of maturity in the aftermath of the June 1967 war, particularly under Nixon, and became a strategic alliance during Reagan's presidency.

President Eisenhower, however, was interested in a strong Egypt, and to that end he put forward a proposal for respecting Arab neutrality in a major address to the U.N. General Assembly on August 13, 1958.[16] But the domestic American environment proved unreceptive to a major reorientation and thus a major opportunity for an international settlement of the Middle East crisis was missed. The Israeli invasion of Arab land in 1956 was to be repeated by new generations in 1967, 1978, 1982, and 2000–2002. But, unlike 1956, most of the other invasions were supported by the United States.

By the end of Eisenhower's presidency, the region was polarized between conservative pro-Western monarchies and "radical" nonaligned military republics. American policy makers postulated that the defeat of the United Arab Republic (Egypt and Syria) would remove the potential threat to the stability of the conservative regimes, preserve U.S. strategic interests, and thus assure the continued exploitation of the region's resources by American business. Prominent officials in Congress and the military reached this conclusion during Johnson's presidency.

Israel and the Nixon Doctrine

A tendency to identify United States security interests with a militarily strong Israel began to take hold in Pentagon circles in the 1960s. A Congressional subcommittee on Middle East peace concluded in April 1967 that the United Arab Republic constituted the principal obstacle to peace, thus legitimizing the future offensive which came to be known as the Six Day War. Israel had indeed anticipated a proxy role for itself prior to the 1967 war and prior to the Nixon Doctrine. A spokesman for the Israeli foreign office expressed that readiness on June 11, 1966:

> The United States has come to the conclusion that it can no longer respond to every incident around the world, that it must rely on a local power, the deterrent of a friendly power as a first line to stave off America's direct involvement. Israel feels that it fits this definition.[17]

Indeed, Israel had emerged as the principal U.S. surrogate, entrusted with blunting the nationalist tide in the West's favor. The defeat of Egypt and Syria in June 1967 and the subsequent rise to prominence in inter-Arab affairs of such conservative Arab states as Saudi Arabia were cited as a vindication of this assumption. Although the offensive against Egypt and its ideology of "Arab socialism" was not to involve the deployment of American troops, the 1967 war brought about consequences desirable not only for Israel, but for the United States as well, namely the defeat of Nasserism as a potent force in Middle Eastern politics. This fact was emphasized by the former prime minister of Israel, Levi Eshkol, in 1968:

> The value of Israel to the West in this part of the world will, I predict, be out of all proportion to its size. We will be a real bridge between the three continents, and the free world will be very thankful not only if we survive, but if we continue to thrive in secure and guaranteed frontiers.[18]

The June war, in which the American "hose and water" were placed in the hands of Israeli "firemen," anticipated the Nixon-Kissinger Doctrine, which was premised on the ability and willingness of certain countries in key regions of the world to play the role of local policemen under the direction of the United States.

The Nixon-Kissinger doctrine was articulated in several presidential speeches and policy statements, beginning with the Guam speech of November 3, 1969, and Nixon's State of the Union Address of 1970.[19] The new guiding principle postulated that unilateral intervention was expensive at home and unpopular abroad. Thus Israel, guaranteed by the U.S. a "margin of technical superiority" over all of its Arab neighbors combined, was deemed especially well suited to serve the interests of the United States.[20] The *New York Times* reported that the Nixon administration remained "firmly committed to Israel's security and to her military superiority in the Middle East, for only Israel's strength can deter attack and prevent a call for direct American intervention."[21]

The first test of this partnership concept came in 1970, during the confrontation between the Palestinian nationalist movement and the Jordanian army, when the United States alerted airborne units from its Sixth Fleet, which began to steam toward the East Mediterranean, and Israel expressed readiness to intervene in the event of a Palestinian triumph over King Hussein. After the battle of al-Karameh (March 1968), which galvanized Palestinian and Arab masses into action, the Palestinian guerilla movement began to be viewed as a serious challenge not only to Israel but to America's ambitions in the area, as well as to the conservative Arab states. The Rogers Plan of December 1969, which was based on U.N. Resolution 242, was in fact intended to effect a Jordanian settlement that would bypass the Palestinian resistance. It was followed by a determined Jordanian attempt to suppress the Palestinians, who had already begun to rival King Hussein for sovereignty in Jordan.

The unfolding of events in Jordan in the autumn of 1970 suggested a close coordination of policies between Jordan, the United States, and Israel, whose interests converged on the need to contain the Palestinian national movement. For the next quarter of a century, succeeding U.S. governments attempted to reduce the Palestinian movement to manageable proportions and render it peripheral to any Middle East settlement.

The October 1973 War and Its Diplomatic Consequences

The October 1973 Arab-Israeli war and the ensuing oil embargo enabled Secretary of State Henry Kissinger to embark on a post–Vietnam War strategy in the Middle East. Gradually, the Big Four talks on the Middle East, which began shortly after the 1967 war, had dwindled to talks between the two superpowers. By the end of the October 1973 war, the United States was beginning to act on the assumption that it was the one superpower in the Middle East. Kissinger's shuttle diplomacy, as well as the American decision to engineer the failure of the Geneva Conference at the end of 1973, marked the start of a new era in Middle East diplomacy. Afterward, the oft-mentioned "peace process" became shorthand for U.S. diplomacy, despite its consistent opposition to the internationalization—or just resolution—of the Palestine question.

Kissinger's post–October 1973 mediation revealed three objectives. The first was to bring about a general eclipse of Soviet influence in the region. The departure of some 20,000 Soviet personnel from Egypt, a standing U.S. objective, as well as Sadat's de-Nasserization program, began the process of reorienting Egypt away from nonalignment toward closer relations with the United States. The second objective was to obtain a political settlement capable of creating a transformation of the very nature of the Arab-Israeli conflict, a settlement that would remove the conflict from its ideological context and transform it into a simple conflict over territory. Such an approach was inherently detrimental to the Palestinians and

Arab nationalists, who viewed the struggle as one against settler colonialism and imperialist penetration. The third objective was to provide Egypt with such a vested interest in stability (through economic aid and territorial adjustments) that it would insure its effective removal from the Arab front against Israel.

The overall aim of Kissinger's diplomacy was to give the United States the necessary leverage not only to neutralize Egypt but also to pressure Syria and the PLO to make significant concessions to Israel. The Sinai accord, negotiated by Egypt and Israel in 1975, under U.S. auspices, was calculated to achieve that end. It granted Israel time to consolidate the occupation and build up its offensive capability vis-a-vis the Arab states on the eastern front. Moreover, it granted Israel, for the first time, what amounted to an American security guarantee. According to the September 1975 U.S.-Israel Memorandum of Agreement, the United States was to hold "consultations" with Israel in case a third party (meaning the Soviet Union) intervened militarily. Furthermore, the United States agreed to be "fully responsive ... on an ongoing and long-term basis" to Israel's military requirements. Translated into figures, the *New York Times* (October 31, 1975) put that commitment at $2.24 billion annually. The bulk of this money was used to acquire the latest equipment in the American arsenal, including the 450-mile Lance Pershing missile, F-15 and F-16A fighters, and the laser-guided "smart bombs."

Furthermore, in the U.S.-Israel Memorandum of Agreement, the United States said it would not recognize or negotiate with the PLO until it recognized Israel's right to exist and agreed to abide by U.N. Security Council Resolution 242. No reciprocal demands recognizing Palestinian national rights were made on Israel. The practical implication of Kissinger's 1975 memorandum, which decreed a diplomatic blockade against the PLO, was twofold. First, it meant that the final settlement of the Palestine question would not be based on any form of Palestinian sovereignty in the West Bank and Gaza. Second, Israel, as the principal surrogate and cornerstone of U.S. policy in the region, would be guaranteed access to military technology and the latest equipment in the U.S. arsenal. The implied marginalization of Palestinian national rights inherent in the Sinai accord was confirmed and developed further in later American plans.

The Carter Doctrine and the Regional Influentials

Israel's strategic value for the United States continued after the departure of Nixon and Kissinger from the diplomatic stage. By the end of the Ford administration, the list of regional influentials was headed by Israel, Iran, and Saudi Arabia. Israel, however, was the only one to acquire a global mission, which included arming and training U.S. clients in Central and South America and maintaining a special relationship with South Africa.[22] The Shah's regime in Iran, which was making a serious bid for the role of policeman of the Gulf, suppressed a leftist insurgency in Dhofar against pro-Western Oman. Saudi Arabia emerged as the banker and "moderating" influence in the Arab region, while Israel kept Syria, the Palestinians, and their Lebanese allies in line.

Carter's contribution to the unfolding strategy was the incorporation of Egypt into the constellation of regional powers that would relieve the burden of U.S. intervention. The Camp David formula, which created a separate peace with Israel, would free Egypt to join the ranks of the regional influentials and make its contribution to regional stability.

That strategy, however, was dealt a severe blow when the new recruits were upset by internal unrest. The Shah's regime was overthrown by the Islamic revolution in 1979. Two years later, Egypt's Sadat was assassinated by Islamist militants. Not only was Iran a principal anchor and linchpin of American interests in the Gulf, it was also a virtual test case for the Nixon Doctrine. Iran was to determine whether U.S.-trained forces would be effective in arresting social revolution in a crucial region of the third-world. The Islamic revolution created an irreparable breech in the informal security arrangements of Henry Kissinger. Undersecretary of State George Ball underscored the failure of the Nixon Doctrine in an article entitled "The Lessons from Iran":

> With Iran eliminated as the "protector" of the Gulf area, a mindless reflex is leading many to search for another surrogate country, such as Egypt or Saudi Arabia, to assume the Shah's role as "policeman." This is, it seems to me, a temptation we should sturdily avoid. If the debacle of Iran proves anything, it is that we cannot assure—as the Nixon Doctrine assumed—the security of a strategic region by stuffing a backward state with massive quantities of arms.[23]

Ball's prescription for remedy was a U.S. military buildup in the region coupled with improving the ability of the U.S. to deliver force quickly from American bases: "We should substantially beef up our presence in the Indian Ocean, assist the Saudis with surveillance and give constant reminders of our improving ability to deliver quickly, even from American bases."[24] The military buildup, which began at that time and which was promoted by the presumed "dovish" members of the Democratic establishment, such as George Ball and Cyrus Vance, developed into the military machine that the hawks in the Republican administration of George Bush I utilized in the destruction of Iraq in 1991. That buildup was originally justified on the pretext of defending the area from Soviet expansionism. But the centrality of U.S. economic interests was spelled out by key figures in the foreign policy establishment. Secretary of State Vance said in a speech before the Los Angeles World Affairs Council: "We must maintain a defense establishment modern and strong enough to protect ourselves and our allies. We must protect American investments overseas and insure continuing access to vital raw materials."

In the Iranian revolution aftermath, a strategic adaptation by the U.S. signaled a return to the principle of direct intervention without excluding reliance on partners and regional influentials. A Rapid Deployment Force, conceived by presidential adviser Zbigniew Brzezinski in 1977, would enable the United States to become the principal guarantor of its enormous economic and strategic interests in the region.

Carter's "security framework" for Southwest Asia (as U.S. policy makers began to refer to the region) was given concrete meaning by the enunciation of the Carter Doctrine on January 23, 1980: "Let our position be absolutely clear: Any attempt by any outside force to gain control of the Persian Gulf region will be regarded as an assault on the vital interests of the United States of America, and such an assault will be repelled by any means necessary, *including military force*."[25] This new commitment received added impetus with Reagan's pledge to defend Saudi Arabia against internal threats, as well: "We will not permit Saudi Arabia to be an Iran.... [There is] no way we will stand by and see it taken over."[26] That became known as the Reagan Codicil, which together with the Carter Doctrine was to mark yet another approach to the Middle East and the Arab-Israeli conflict.

The Reagan Period and the Rise of "Anti-Terrorism"

After fewer than four months in office, Ronald Reagan appeared as the most ardently anti-Communist president since Harry Truman. His policies marked a significant departure from the Carter approach, which was embellished with human rights slogans and calls for disarmament, and from Kissinger's attempts at accommodations with the U.S.S.R. With Reagan in the White House and General Alexander Haig in the State Department, Americans were told that the United States was about to "return to a geomilitary or strategic concept for its Middle East policy,"[27] that "the wheel may be turning full circle, that we are about to resume the 'containment' policies of an earlier era."[28] Reagan's proposed budget for military credits and economic support for the Middle East represented an increase of a half billion dollars over Carter's proposals. Israel was expected to receive $2.2 billion plus $600 million to "compensate" for the Saudi F-15 and Airborne Warning and Control System (AWACS) deals. Egypt's share was $1.69 billion plus $106.4 million to beef up the military base at Ras Banas. Israel and Egypt alone accounted for $4.3 billion out of $6.9 billion for military assistance in the 1982 budget—more than 80 percent.

America's huge presence in the region enabled it to shape all aspects of its clients' policies. Their weakness, which resulted from the fragmentation of the Arab world, prevented them from effectively exercising any pressure on the U.S. to dislodge the Israeli occupation. In fact, Washington was in a better position to discourage local conflicts in which local interests took precedence over global U.S. concerns. It was also in a better position to discourage political initiatives on the Palestine question from the Europeans, whose economic advantage was being offset by the U.S. military presence. While Washington was "protecting" the supply line for Europe and Japan, it was hardly possible for the latter to pursue an independent policy on the Palestine question. The buildup of the U.S. military presence acted as compensation for its lack of economic competitiveness.

The new colonial presence emerging in the Middle East was discussed openly by officials in the Reagan administration. In testimony before the Senate Foreign Relations Committee on March 19, 1981, General Haig described this framework as a "consensus of strategic concerns" that would stretch from Turkey to Pakistan.[29] He told the House Foreign Affairs Committee on the day before: "It is fundamentally important to begin to develop a consensus of strategic concerns throughout the region among Arab and Jew and to be sure that the overriding danger of Soviet inroads is not overlooked." Haig considered it a sophisticated strategy which shunned formal military alliances and recruited both Arabs and Israelis to a common cause. He told the Senate Foreign Relations Committee the following on September 17, 1981:

> Although we are building up U.S. military capabilities ... the use of U.S. military force can only be considered as a last resort. And to deter major Soviet threats, for which the U.S. role is indispensable, we also need the help of our friends, both in the region and outside it ... that is the reason why we are pursuing intensified strategic cooperation with Israel, Egypt, Saudi Arabia, and many other concerned countries ... we are not seeking to construct formal alliances or a massive structure of U.S. bases. We are pursuing a sophisticated strategy, one guided as well by a sense of urgency.[30]

Meanwhile, the Reagan administration insisted that the Arab-Israeli conflict must not stand in the way of the strategic consensus. Both Reagan and Haig stressed publicly the importance of Israel in the larger global arena. According to General Haig, the security of Saudi Arabia was intertwined with that of Israel:

> We are wholeheartedly and permanently committed to the security of Israel. Without a strong Israel, our hope to improve the prospects for peace and security in the region cannot be fulfilled. A secure Saudi Arabia and a strong U.S.-Saudi relationship are central to these same tasks.[31]

Accordingly, the central assumption of the strategic consensus was the need to subordinate the Arab-Israeli conflict and its requirement of comprehensive settlement to the Soviet "threat" and the requirement of "comprehensive security." The Palestine question, which came to be regarded by the Reagan administration as secondary, would cease to enjoy its usual priority as the region's principal concern. The project was hampered, however, by the U.S. special relationship with Israel. The U.S. had simply failed to offer the Arabs and Israel a viable formula for cooperation. The issues which divided them at the time, in 1981 and 1982, included the proposed U.S. sale of AWACS to Saudi Arabia, the Israeli raid on Iraq's nuclear research facility, the Golan annexation, the proposed Jordanian strike force, the Israeli invasion of Lebanon, and, of course, the Palestine question.

The attempt to reconcile the two endeavors foundered when the Reagan administration failed to satisfy the minimalist position of the Arab component of the strategic consensus. Neither the 1981 Fahd plan nor the 1982 Fez plan evoked even a slight measure of enthusiasm from Washington, despite strong indications of Arab willingness to recognize Israel as part of a peaceful settlement.[32] Even the Reagan plan of September 1, 1982, was allowed to drift into oblivion after it was promptly and categorically rejected by Israel.[33] The administration had also failed to make a determination on whether the Israeli use of American-supplied aircraft in the bombing of the Iraqi nuclear facility had violated the amended Arms Control Act of 1976. More blatant was the Israeli invasion of Lebanon in the summer of 1982 and U.S. complicity in that invasion, as well as its association with Israel's war aims (the attempt to draw a new political map of Lebanon, to obliterate Palestinian nationalism, and to reduce Syria to manageable proportions).[34] President Reagan spoke of an "opportunity" the war of 1982 had afforded. He placed the Israeli "achievements" within the context of America's broader goal of promoting stability in the region.

The strategic consensus had also suffered from the inability of the Reagan administration to obtain Congressional approval of money and arms for Jordan. The endeavor to set up a Jordanian Logistics Force (JLF) as a rapid deployment force for the Gulf was seen by Reagan as an assured instrument for keeping the Straits of Hormuz "open." It was also intended to put into practice the Reagan Codicil to the Carter Doctrine by facilitating intervention in internal crises in the Gulf states. But despite a clear intent to deny Jordan autonomy over its use and despite the administration's "determination to see that Israel's qualitative technological edge is maintained," Congressional opposition remained unabated.[35] It was rather ironic that the Reagan administration had planned to ask Israeli defense minister Moshe Arens to intercede with Congressional opponents of the Jordanian force.[36] But Israel remained publicly opposed to one of Reagan's principal ingredients of strategic consensus: the Jordan missile deal. Israel's opposition delivered a deadly blow to that project. Reacting to all this, in a *New York Times* interview on March 16, 1984, King Hussein offered unprecedented public criticism of U.S. policy by a Jordanian official. It seemed as though Jordan had temporarily declared independence in foreign affairs. The king said that "Israel is on our land ... by virtue of American military assistance and economic aid." He continued:

It is there by virtue of American moral and political support to the point
where the United States is succumbing to Israeli dictates.... This being
the case, there is no way by which anyone should imagine it would be
possible for Arabs to sit and talk with Israel as long as things are as they
are.... You obviously have made your choice, and your choice is Israel.
Therefore there is no hope of achieving anything.[37]

The stipulation that arms shipments be linked to Jordanian acceptance
of Camp David, among other conditions, led the King to raise a concern
about the "United States and its double standard everywhere."[38]

Such were the constraints on the Reagan administration's ability to
ease Jordan's "security problem," deemed essential to the success of the
strategic consensus. As for the second requirement—helping Jordan solve
its "negotiating problem"—it fell victim to Israel's rejection of the Reagan plan and its refusal to consider putting a freeze on the building of new
settlements in the West Bank. The most that the administration was willing to try in that regard was "only a promise to urge Israel to freeze further
settlements ... and the argument that once King Hussein comes to the table, pressures will develop in Israel for compromise."[39]

While Israel and the so-called moderate Arab states shared Reagan's
concern about the Soviet "threat," they nevertheless disagreed on the order of priorities. The "strategic consensus," in fact, suffered from a lack of
consensus. The Arabs argued that regional stability (seen as a safeguard
against revolution and Soviet influence) required a durable and just solution to the Palestine problem. Israel dismissed the Palestine question as a
secondary matter, which in turn led Washington's Arab clients to refrain
from direct cooperation with Israel. Such cooperation had to wait until the
end of the Cold War, when the containment of Saddam Hussein would
resonate far louder than the containment of Communism.

The Bush I Doctrine

The massive U.S. military deployment in the Arabian peninsula, which
began in August 1990 and culminated in the Gulf War, completed a process of recolonization of the region. This recolonization was preceded by
the U.S. naval buildup of the 1980s and the reflagging of the Kuwaiti oil
tankers during the Iraq-Iran war. The declarations and actions of President Bush in the Gulf reconfirmed, complemented, and supplemented the
Carter Doctrine (1980) and the Reagan Doctrine (1981), but reversed the

Nixon Doctrine. In 1990–91, GIs had to perform the fireman's role, and the role of mercenary, while a substantial portion of the cost for the "hose and the water" was borne by local emirs and kings and by the industrial North, which relies on Gulf oil resources.

The crisis in the Gulf was the first important indication of how the United States was going to respond to the much touted "new world order." Military intervention in that region was an ominous sign that the United States perceived its international role as essentially unchanged from the Cold War period. In the "new world order," containment has lost its original rationale as a response to the Soviet challenge. Regional interventions can no longer be explained in terms of Soviet aggression or Soviet-sponsored insurrection. The anti-Communist rhetoric of containment, however, had always masked the real enemy of American hegemonic designs: third-world nationalism and social revolution.

As the U.S. was emerging from the post–Cold War period as the uncontested superpower in a militarily unipolar world, it was more determined than ever to prevent any regional forces from questioning any aspect of the state system. That included the control of petroleum reserves, levels of production, and pricing, as well as the political or military balance of power in the region. But by invading Kuwait, Iraq had challenged the rules of the Arab state system and American hegemony in the Middle East.

Following the invasion and annexation of Kuwait by Iraq, President Bush strained to provide credible rationales for U.S. intervention. At various points, he summoned up the old rhetoric, calling for a defense of the U.S. "way of life," but without the old anti-Communist theme it was not playing well at home. Bush found it hard to defend an intervention on behalf of cheap energy when the price at the pump had risen by 50 percent and the potential cost in lives was so extreme. It was not easy to convince a cautious public that cheap gasoline was the cornerstone of the "American way."

The states and dynasties of the Gulf have continued to provide the United States with an exceedingly favorable economic climate, one in which the levels of economic penetration are maintained and enhanced. Here, much more than in Vietnam and Central America, the economic stakes are very high, and the U.S. is bound to project its military power. Hence, when President Bush claimed that his goal was to protect "our jobs" and "our way of life," he really meant, first and foremost, corporate interests, defined as a matter of national security.

The period after Iraq's invasion of Kuwait saw a sudden transformation of Hussein's image in the United States. The Iraqi president went from being a shield against Iran and custodian of business and stability to being the "most dangerous man in the world."[40] Hussein had unacceptably challenged the established order in the Gulf and called into question the legitimacy of the local regimes that anchored their stability in American protection and in turn protected American corporate interests. His sin was the attempt to play the role of regional pacesetter in an environment of decreasing oil revenues caused by the oil glut, and his ensuing clash with local overproducers Kuwait and the United Arab Emirates was transformed into a global conflict. Hence, the territorial integrity of Kuwait and the restoration of its dynasty were elevated to the status of a vital U.S. interest worthy of the most massive deployment since the Vietnam War.

To be sure, Hussein acted illegally by occupying and annexing Kuwait to Iraq. But the crisis and the subsequent war were not about legal and moral principles, or about Saddam Hussein's dismal human rights record. Many of Washington's third-world clients are among the worst abusers of human rights, violating international standards with absolute impunity, and Hussein's human rights record had been shielded from criticism when he was an ally. The Gulf War was a conflict over resources, first and foremost, and it was the first major conflict between the North and South in the post–Cold War period.

The appeal to principles enunciated by Bush I was hardly credible in view of many invasions of sovereign territory which received little or no reaction from the American government. Washington's decision to go to war was dictated by what the Bush administration perceived as regional and global imperatives of the post–Cold War period.

A New World Order?

The war option was seen as the best means to substitute U.S. military muscle for its economic power, and thus compensate for real American weakness. Hundreds of thousands of American troops were joined by those of twenty-eight other nations, most of which came to reap the benefits of the unstated goals of America's policy. For example, Britain, the most important junior partner in that endeavor, underwent a transformation in its role from the sponsor of the Sabah Dynasty in southwest Asia to itself being an instrument for U.S. domination over Arab petroleum resources. Egyptian participation was rewarded with a significant debt forgiveness. Nearly $7 billion of Egyptian debt was written off the books. As for Syria, it was provided with a green light to subdue dissidents on all sides of the Lebanese conflict and to promote the fledgling central government in Beirut under its own sovereignty. Others, such as the U.S.S.R., China, Turkey, and Ethiopia, were rewarded with loans, protection from human rights scrutiny, and intercession with the European community.

The single ally, however, that received a reward for *nonparticipation* was Israel. In addition to U.S. aid at the level of $10 million per day, it was promised the following: debt cancellation, compensation for destruction due to Iraqi scud missile attacks in the amount of $650 million, emergency military aid in the amount of $700 million, ten F-15 jets worth $65 million, and the prepositioning of $300 million worth of weapons that Israel could use in the event of war. The biggest item, however, was Israel's request for a $10 billion loan to provide housing for Soviet Jews settling in Palestine, which the Bush administration had initially held up for better diplomatic terms but finally released during the heat of presidential elections.

Saddam Hussein's first problem was an inability and unwillingness to comprehend the new rules of the game. He failed to appreciate the consequences of challenging the precepts of this new world order. His second problem was his ambition to become the third Arab leader to assume responsibility for strategic parity vìs-a-vìs Israel. An independent and advanced Arab arsenal in the aftermath of the Soviet eclipse was simply taboo, particularly if it were going to involve production, adaptation, and importation of parts for the local manufacture of weapons of mass destruction. It is one thing for a country like Iraq to import weapons from the capitalist West and help repair deficits in their balance of trade; it is quite another thing for Iraq, or any other ambitious third-world power, to aspire for independence in military technology and strategic planning. Thus, as long as Hussein was engaged in battling the Shah's successors in Iran, who were bent on challenging American primacy in the Gulf, the U.S. government aided him economically and diplomatically, and certified him as worthy of purchasing Western weapons and technology. The altered reality, however, was the emergence of Iraq from its war with Iran as an ambitious power with the capacity to develop weapons of mass de-

struction, the potential to appeal to Arab masses (as had Gamal Abdel
Nasser of Egypt), and the intention to take a lead in restoring the regional
military balance with Israel. Iraq was seen by the U.S. government and the
Zionist movement as a more dangerous foe than Egypt had been in the
1960s and 1970s or Syria had been in the 1980s. Hence the decision to
pre-empt every possible diplomatic means to settle the crisis short of
all-out war.

The real threat facing George Bush in the 1990s had less to do with
Saddam Hussein's actions, and more to do with the potential of Iraq as a
state. Now, during the second Bush presidency, the Arab states seem prepared to acquiesce in another U.S. attack on Iraq in exchange for a renewed diplomatic involvement in the Palestine-Israel conflict, the
outcome of which is far from assured.

Notes

1   "The Sources of Soviet Conduct," *Foreign Affairs* (July 1947).
2   *Department of State Bulletin*, April 21, 1946, p. 622.
3   *Department of State Bulletin*, June 4, 1951, p. 887.
4   *Department of State Bulletin*, June 15, 1953, p. 831.
5   Charles Cremeans, *The Arabs and the World* (New York: Praeger, 1963),
      p. 146.
6   Quoted in Donald Neff, *Warriors at Suez: Eisenhower Takes America into the
      Middle East* (New York: Linden Press/Simon & Schuster, 1981), pp. 439–40.
7   Neff, *Warriors at Suez,* p. 107.
8   Moshe Dayan, *Diary of the Sinai Campaign* (Jerusalem: Steinatzky
      Agency Ltd., 1966), pp. 71–73.
9   *Department of State Bulletin*, November 12, 1956, pp. 745–46.
10   Cheryl Rubenberg, *Israel and the American National Interest* (Urbana:
      University of Illinois Press, 1986), p. 64.
11   "The 1953 Qibya Raid Revisited: Excerpt From Moshe Sharett's Diaries,"
      introduced by Walid Khalidi and annotated by Neil Caplan, *Journal of
      Palestine Studies* 21: 4 (Summer 2002): 77–98.
12   Neff, *Warriors at Suez,* p. 104.
13   See an analysis of the Doctrine in Fred Halliday, *Arabia Without Sultans*
      (London: Penguin Books, 1974), p. 54.

14 From a news conference on April 23, 1957, *Department of State Bulletin*, May 13, 1957, p. 768.
15 Melvin Gurtov, *The United States Against the Third World: Anti-Nationalism and Intervention* (New York: Praeger, 1974), p. 14.
16 Malcolm Kerr, "Coming to Terms with Nasser," *International Affairs* (January 1967), pp. 73–76.
17 *New York Times*, June 12, 1966.
18 *Newsweek*, February 17, 1968.
19 *New York Times*, November 4, 1969.
20 *New York Times*, December 24, 1969.
21 *New York Times*, December 24, 1969.
22 For a discussion of Israel's role as U.S. proxy, see Israel Shahak, *Israel's Global Role: Weapons for Repression* (Belmont, MA: Association of Arab-American University Graduates, 1982); see also Milton Jamail and Margo Gutierrez, *It's No Secret: Israel's Military Involvement in Central America* (Belmont, MA: Association of Arab-American University Graduates, 1986).
23 *Boston Globe*, April 2, 1979.
24 *Boston Globe*, April 2, 1979.
25 *New York Times*, January 24, 1980.
26 *New York Times*, October 2, 1981.
27 *Christian Science Monitor*, February 19, 1981.
28 *Christian Science Monitor*, February 20, 1981.
29 *New York Times*, March 20, 1981.
30 "Secretary Haig: U.S. Strategy in the Middle East," U.S. Department of State, Bureau of Public Affairs, *Current Policy* 312.
31 See Haig's testimony before the Senate Foreign Relations Committee and the House Foreign Affairs Committee on March 19 and 20, 1981 in the *New York Times,* March 20, 1981; see also "Secretary Haig: U.S. Strategy in the Middle East," U.S. Department of State, Bureau of Public Affairs, *Current Policy* 312.
32 *Jerusalem Post*, March 12, 2002.
33 *New York Times*, September 2, 1982.
34 Ze'ev Shiff, "The Green Light," *Foreign Policy* 50 (Spring 1983).
35 *Boston Globe*, February 17, 1982.
36 *Washington Post*, October 15, 1983.
37 *Christian Science Monitor*, December 27, 1983.
38 *New York Times*, March 15, 1984.
39 *New York Times*, March 8, 1984.
40 *Newsweek* ran a story on April 9,1990, with the headline "Public Enemy No. 1." On June 4, 1990, *U.S. News & World Report* featured a cover story with a drawing of Saddam Hussein looking devious and fierce and a caption

describing him as "The World's Most Dangerous Man." On April 3, 1990, the *New York Times* carried the headline "Iraq Can Deliver, U.S. Chemical Arms Experts Say." On April 23, 1990, the *Wall Street Journal* featured an article headlined "Iraq's Buying Spree on Arms Bodes Ill for Its Neighbors."

CHAPTER 3

THE SPECIAL RELATIONSHIP AND STRATEGIC ALLIANCE DURING AND AFTER THE COLD WAR

The twelve-year period of Republican rule (1980–1992)—which included two terms for Reagan and one term for Bush I—witnessed a phenomenal expansion of the special relationship between the United States and Israel. That relationship, which developed into a strategic alliance, was nurtured and upgraded by Clinton, the first president ever to involve the pro-Israel lobby in actual Middle East policy making, and was further improved under Bush II. It was consolidated during this period in such a way that no disagreements between the two countries would undermine it. Only when a conflict was related to what Washington perceived as its national interest, expressed in Cold War terms, would the United States prevail. The 1981 disagreement over the sale of AWACS to Saudi Arabia is perhaps the only such example. Otherwise the special relationship shielded Israel from scrutiny, even when egregious violations of United States law and international law were involved. Such violations occurred during the Reagan, Bush I, Clinton, and Bush II presidencies, but they failed to have any adverse effect whatsoever on the special relationship. In fact, the relationship continues to thrive in spite of the violations, and Washington almost always yields to Israel, no matter how acrimonious its disagreements become.

Between June 7 and July 22, 1981, Israel crossed the borders of four sovereign Arab states and bombed the capitals of two states, causing severe devastation and more than 1,500 casualties. The raids on the Iraqi nuclear facility in Baghdad and the residential sections of Beirut, as well as the bombardment of the Lebanese coast from Tyre to Damur, were carried out using sophisticated American weapons, including F-16s. The principal issues during the first Bush presidency were the controversy over loan guarantees to Israel and Prime Minister Shamir's renunciation of his own plan for a Palestinian-Israeli settlement. With Clinton in the White House, controversies ceased. Israel tested the special relationship/strategic alliance with the deportation of 400 Palestinians to Lebanon, the closure of Jerusalem, and the savage four-day bombardment of Lebanon in March 1993. No protests were voiced by Clinton or Warren Christopher, making Bush and Baker, in retrospect, look like the bad boys who kept Israel under check.

Four administrations have consistently promoted the special relationship. The renewed Cold War under Reagan proved to be a fertile environment for its growth, and yet the relationship was not fundamentally changed by the end of the Cold War and the demise of the Soviet Union during the Bush I period and beyond under Clinton. This chapter will trace the evolution of the special relationship since the Reagan period and will examine the major issues that affected it or were affected by it.

The Cost of the Special Relationship to the United States

One of the most visible signs of the U.S.-Israeli special relationship/strategic alliance is the enormous amount of economic and military aid that the U.S. government has been supplying to Israel since its establishment over half a century ago. U.S. foreign aid to Israel has also been the principal instrument for expressing support for Israeli policies, most of which have been at variance with the global consensus. U.S. aid to Israel since 1949 has totaled $81.38 billion, a figure which does not include $10 billion in loan guarantees or an unknown amount of "side benefits," which tend to be excluded from accounting. Nor does this figure include monies that accrue to Israel annually from various projects and sources in the United States.[1] Last year, the *Washington Report on Middle East Affairs* estimated total aid through fiscal year 2000 at $91.82 billion. According to a Congressional research report, "it is estimated that Israel receives about $1 billion annually through philanthropy [United Jewish Appeal and other tax-deductible funds], an equal amount through commercial loans, and about $500 million or more in Israel Bonds proceeds."[2] The total is even higher when one calculates what the U.S. has had to pay in interest as a result of giving aid to Israel rather than paying down its significant debt. Richard Curtiss, editor of the *Washington Report on Middle East Affairs*, estimated the cost to taxpayers at $134.8 billion, not adjusted for inflation.[3] Curtiss adds that U.S. aid to Israel—a nation of 5.8

million people—exceeds that given to "all of the countries of sub-Saharan Africa, all of the countries of Latin America, and all of the countries of the Caribbean combined—with a total population of 1,054,000,000 people."[4]

Since 1976, Israel has received the largest amount of U.S. foreign assistance on both an annual and a cumulative basis, according to a November 2001 Congressional Research Service Report, *Israel: U.S. Foreign Assistance*. A review of U.S. assistance to Israel shows a substantial increase in aid during years in which Israel presumably demonstrated its utility to the U.S. national security establishment as a strategic asset. From 1949 through 1965, U.S. aid to Israel averaged about $63 million per year.[5] It increased to an average of $102 million annually between 1966 and 1970, and then, due to its increasing utility, jumped to about $1 billion annually during the next five years. From 1976 to 1984, U.S. aid to Israel averaged about $2.5 billion per year. With the upgrading of the special relationship to a strategic alliance during the Reagan period, U.S. aid began to escalate further, reaching about $5.5 billion annually at present, over one-third of the total U.S. foreign aid.[6]

Veteran economist Thomas Stauffer estimated the total package of U.S. support for Israel was actually much higher when hidden costs, including political, administrative, and economic costs are calculated. According to a recent lecture by Stauffer, commissioned by the U.S. Army War College, the total bill in real terms, including the cost of the Palestine-Israel conflict since 1973, is $1.6 trillion—twice as much as the cost of the Vietnam War.[7] Stauffer's carefully drawn estimates take into account a number of factors, including the assumption that the Israel bonds covered by U.S. loan guarantees are not likely to be repaid, making the United States pay both the interest and the principal, perhaps ten years out. Stauffer also takes into account the "higher cost of oil and other economic damage to the U.S, after Israel-Arab wars." For example, the United States lost $420 billion (in 2001 dollars) of ouput as a result of the 1973 oil embargo, and "a boost in oil prices cost another $450 billion." Moreover, the cost of protective measures against future embargoes, such as the Strategic Petroleum Reserve, came to another $134 billion. Stauffer adds other hidden costs to the tally, such as the cost of charities, guaranteeing commercial and housing loans, support of the Lavi fighter and Arrow missile projects, trade sanctions (which reduce U.S. exports to the

Middle East), and other Israeli-"vetoed" exports to Arab countries alleg-
edly on security grounds.

All economic aid to Israel became "forgiven loans" (grant cash transfers) in 1981, while all military loans changed to grants in 1985.[8] Moreover,
U.S. aid to Israel is made available in lump sum every October in order to
allow Israel to invest the funds in interest-bearing U.S. government securi-
ties. According to the previously cited Congressional research report, "Israel also receives $700 million in defense articles to be withdrawn from
Europe ... $650 million in emergency Economic Support Fund (ESF)
grants, a $400 million loan guarantee for housing for Soviet refugees, a
grant of $7.5 million for its foreign assistance program, a $45 million grant
for refugee settlement, and shares a $7.5 million program with Egypt for
cooperative development programs to promote the Egyptian-Israeli
treaty."[9] In addition, the Clinton administration decided in October 1994 to
compensate Israel for "redeployment costs" from Gaza and Jericho in the
amount of $95 million. That amount was deducted from the $311.8 million
settlement penalty, which Rabin's government had agreed to in its accord
with Bush I on loan guarantees in August 1992. Moreover, the Clinton administration rewarded Israel with a special grant of $1.2 billion for signing
the Wye River agreement with the Palestinian Authority in 1998.

A large amount of U.S. aid to Israel, currently running at $5.5 billion
annually, goes to purchase the jets, helicopters, missiles, and other military equipment used in Israel's wars against the Arab states and its renewed onslaught on West Bank and Gaza cities and refugee camps in
2001 and 2002. U.S. aid also pays the salaries of soldiers engaged in the
siege of the Occupied Territories and covers the cost of the ongoing fragmentation of the West Bank, including the construction of settlements and
bypass roads, among other colonial projects. And yet, U.S. politicians often justify this aid as a way to induce Israel to make peace in the region.

U.S. aid to Israel enables it to purchase weapons and to subsidize its
arms industry, estimated to be the tenth largest in the world.[10] This huge
subsidy enables the Israeli weapons industry to compete against U.S. cor-
porations such as Lockheed Martin and other giants, causing some whis-
pers of complaint in the U.S. defense industry. Joel Johnson, a vice
president at the Aerospace Industries Association of America, wondered
why "we give them money to build stuff for themselves and the U.S. taxpayer gets nothing in return."[11] To the dismay of conservatives who still

view China as an enemy, Israel did the unforgivable by helping China design its J-10 jet fighter based on Israel's own Lavi, which itself is modeled on the U.S. F-16. Moreover, Israel sold its Python III missile (patterned on the U.S. Sidewinder missile) to China without permission; members of the U.S. defense establishment have speculated that Chinese pilots might have used that missile against the U.S. spy plane captured during the confrontations between the United States and China in 2000.

The U.S.-Israeli relationship is a unique one, particularly given that Israel is a technologically advanced society with an income per capita that exceeds that of some European countries. It is exceptional both in terms of the staggering amount of subsidies given and the silence maintained around them. Even the spokesperson of the State Department's Bureau of Political-Military Affairs, Jay Greer, admitted that U.S.-Israeli relations are beyond debate and public discourse: "There's not a whole lot we can comment on.... It's a sensitive matter."[12]

The Oslo process was supposed to have ushered in an era of peace under U.S. auspices, yet arms transfers to Israel since 1993 have reached record levels—all in the name of the special relationship.

Reagan and the Special Relationship

The evolving strategic alliance between the United States and Israel was particularly enhanced by President Reagan's anti-Communist inclinations, his launching of a new Cold War, and his perception of Israel as a "unique strategic asset." Both Reagan and Alexander Haig considered Israel to be an asset of considerable if not unique significance. Reagan expressed his gratitude to Israel during an interview with U.S. journalists on February 2, 1981:

> Not only do we have a moral commitment to Israel, [but] being a country sharing our same ideals, our democratic approach to things, with a combat-experienced military, [Israel] is a force in the Middle East that actually is a benefit to us. If there were not Israel with that force, we'd have to supply that with our own, so this isn't just altruism on our part.[13]

In fact, after the fall of the Shah of Iran, Reagan dismissed the Arab regimes in the Gulf as "weak and vulnerable," asserting that Israel was "perhaps the only strategic asset in the area that the United States can really rely on."[14] Despite their abundant resources, America's Arab allies were viewed as unreliable. They, unlike Israel, were dependent upon U.S.

military personnel to keep their military establishments functioning and
on U.S. intelligence to safeguard the stability of their regimes. No similar
worries seem to have existed with regard to Israel, which merely required
the margin of military and technological superiority over the Arab states
that had been pledged by Nixon. Secretary of State Haig reiterated that
guarantee on September 17, 1981: "We are determined to maintain the
qualitative edge that is vital to Israel's security."[15] In the American view
at that time, Israel's security and the security of Saudi Arabia were intertwined. Israel, however, seemed unconvinced about the efficacy of such
linkage and succeeeded—with help from U.S. neoconservatives—in undermining it by 2001–2002. During the controversy over the sale of
AWACS to Saudi Arabia, Israel reminded Reagan that Washington's expectation of an interventionary role for Israel might be impaired by the
U.S. supply of sophisticated aircraft and weapons systems to Saudi Arabia. But Reagan made sure that the AWACS' capabilities were sufficiently
limited to render this argument invalid. The list of restrictions included no
flights outside Saudi borders, U.S. approval of security plans, U.S. inspection, continued U.S. government ownership of computer software, data exchange only with the United States, and restricted access to equipment and
maintenance. He and his staff argued that, far from undermining Israel's security, the sale to Saudi Arabia would enhance it. On October 1, 1981, Secretary Haig told the Senate Foreign Relations Committee:

> President Reagan would not have authorized this sale if he believed that it
> would jeopardize Israel's security. On the contrary, we believe that the
> risks for Israel are greater if U.S.-Saudi cooperation is disrupted and
> Saudi Arabia is left insecure or forced to turn elsewhere for equipment.[16]

The same point had already been made by Deputy Assistant Secretary for Near Eastern and South Asian Affairs Joseph W. Twinam on September 25, 1981. With regard to the implications of the sales for Israeli
security, he said:

> Israel enjoys today—and will continue to enjoy after our proposed sales
> are completed—so decisive a superiority over any combination of re-
> gional forces that the practical impact of our proposals [to sell AWACS]
> on Israeli security would be small. Contrary to claims, the AWACS can-
> not collect photographic intelligence. Nor can it collect any intelligence
> at all on ground targets. The only information it collects is the most per-
> ishable kind—aircraft tracks which become useless in a matter of min-

utes ... neither do they have any offensive capacity that could jeopardize Israeli security.[17]

In fact, the the list of restrictions placed on the AWACS sale seemed to have effectively rendered not only the weapons but Saudi sovereignty all but irrelevant.[18]

Strategic Cooperation

Ronald Reagan first presented his conception of a special relationship between the United States and Israel during his first presidential campaign in an August 15, 1979, *Washington Post* article. Having dismissed the Arab regimes in the Gulf region as "weak and vulnerable" in the wake of the Shah's demise, he proceeded to outline his expectations of Israel in three fields of service:

1. Exchange of intelligence;
2. Utilization of the Israeli infrastructure and technological expertise and services; and
3. Israeli participation even outside its frontiers in the event of a crisis involving the Soviet Union.

Reagan's ideas contributed to the framework for the U.S.-Israeli agreement on strategic cooperation announced during Menachem Begin's visit to the United States in September 1981 and concluded by the two governments on November 30, 1981. The text of the agreement revealed their resolve to strengthen strategic cooperation against "threats" to the Middle East "caused by the Soviet Union or Soviet-controlled forces from outside the region." The recognition of a regionwide police role for Israel was formalized in a provision that stipulated the need for the two countries to provide each other military assistance to cope with threats to the security of the entire region.

The November 1981 agreement was followed by yet another agreement on strategic cooperation in 1983 which, together with the June 1985 free trade agreement, institutionalized the strategic relationship. Israel was given unique access to U.S. military technology and markets and was accorded the status of non-NATO ally. The institutionalization of the strategic relationship was used by Israel as a protective shield against international criticism of its violation of international law, and as a green light in the face of any misgivings by the U.S. media or public opinion. Thus, President Reagan did not condemn the June 1981 Israeli raids on Lebanon. Instead, he issued a declaration deploring "all acts of violence" and expressing the usual regret for civilian casualties, and justified the raid by saying that Israel had been under rocket attacks.

While a great deal was heard from President Reagan and Secretary of State Haig about the need to combat "international terrorism," nothing was ever said about the need to combat terrorism at the level of state policy.[19] Though the 1952 Israeli-U.S. Mutual Defense Assistance Agreement prohibited the use of U.S. arms in any "acts of aggression against any other state," the U.S. government continued to supply and finance Israeli aggression against civilians and provide Israel with political cover. By 1985, the strategic alliance had become so strong that U.S. assistance to Israel was no longer dependent on Israeli willingness to meet Washington's standards or conditions. The suspension of U.S. military supplies to Israel in December 1981, following Israel's unilateral annexation of the occupied Golan Heights, was a meaningless gesture. As the Associated Press reported, the Reagan administration secretly notified Congress of its plans at this time to "sell" Israel an additional seventy-five F-16 fighters for more than $2.5 billion, the biggest arms deal with Israel in four years.[20] The transfer was arranged just in time for the visit of Israeli defense minister Ariel Sharon to Washington on May 26, 1982, hardly a week before his troops marched on Beirut with U.S. weapons and political protection.

On the first day of the Israeli invasion of Lebanon, Secretary Haig made a slip of the tongue when he told reporters: "We not only lost an aircraft and a helicopter yesterday, there is a claim that a second aircraft has been shot down," referring to Israeli aircraft.[21] Adding insult to injury, the United States vetoed a Security Council resolution calling for Israeli withdrawal under the threat of economic sanctions. As the Israeli invasion swept through Lebanon, Reagan and his top aides designated it as "legitimate self-defense." The contrast between President Carter's attitude during the 1978 Israeli invasion of Lebanon and that of Reagan was indeed very striking. While in 1978 Carter supported a call for Israeli withdrawal and threatened to invoke the Arms Export Control Act of 1976, which prohibited the offensive use of American weaponry, Reagan's spokesmen did not see the Israeli invasion as an offensive attack. The special relationship, transformed into a strategic alliance, was further tested in the spring of 1988, when Israel rejected the Shultz plan, which called for Palestinian elections and a transitional period of self-rule in the Occupied Territories to be followed by final status talks between Israel and the Palestinians.

The Shultz plan was designed to quell the Palestinian uprising and to reassert America's role as arbiter in the region. Yet the American posture toward Israel, before and after the Shultz plan, was one of excessive generosity. At the time that the Reagan administration was expressing concern about Israeli excesses in dealing with the Intifada in the West Bank and Gaza, it granted Israel approximately $2 billion in debt relief, bidding rights on U.S. military contracts equal to those of its NATO allies, and 80 percent of the financing for a new short-range ballistic missile system as part of the Strategic Defense Initiative, better known as Star Wars.[22] The administration's request of $3.6 billion in military aid for Israel in fiscal year 1989 represented an increase of $1.8 billion.

A memorandum of agreement, which was signed into law by President Reagan on April 22, 1988, after Shamir's rejection of the Shultz plan, further institutionalized the U.S.-Israeli strategic relationship.[23] A State Department official expressed the dismay of those who disagreed with Shultz's decision by saying that this agreement "may be seen by his opponents [in Israel] as a reward for not being serious about the peace process." A senior Israeli official confirmed this by saying "it almost looks like Shultz gave him [Shamir] a reward for not cooperating."[24]

The transformation of Israel from client to surrogate and then to strategic ally not only reflected the evolving American security policy in the region, but also hastened an ongoing marginalization of Palestinian rights in U.S. policy. By 1983, the Reagan administration had accepted the Israeli view that the Palestine question was not the principal cause of instability in the region. Henceforth, that issue would not be allowed to interfere in the special relationship between a superpower and its strategic ally.

The U.S. and Israel after the Cold War

Although the strategic alliance between Israel and the United States remained intact under Reagan's successor, relations between the two governments were not ideal. The major realignments of the strategic and political landscape of the Middle East after the end of the Cold War and the Gulf War provided the U.S. government with an opportunity to shape a new structure of relationships in which a settlement of the Arab-Israeli conflict became a U.S. national interest. The views of the Bush I administration and those of Shamir's government were not always congruent. Differences over the status of Jerusalem, the Jewish settlements, and the occupation itself resulted in crises in the relationship of the two allies.

The Loan Guarantees Controversy

The Bush I administration's threat to withhold loan guarantees as a brake on the Israeli colonization of the West Bank was perhaps the major acrimonious event which temporarily divided the strategic allies. The controversy represented a qualitative change in Washington's diplomatic approach to Israel. The linkage concept, which the Bush administration labored stubbornly to keep out of the pre–Gulf War diplomacy, was used by the Bush administration in its search for an updated basis for its special relationship with Israel. At issue in that process was a possible transformation of Israel from a predominantly global issue to an increasingly domestic matter. The aborted showdowns over the loan guarantees represented a short-lived victory for President Bush in an arena in which "humanitarian" values were highlighted by American Zionist activists and their legislative representatives, while strategic considerations were pushed to the sidelines. The U.S. national security sector was more preoccupied then with the Japanese trade surplus "threat" and the new shape and scope of an integrated Europe, as well as America's role in it. These developments entailed reduced leverage for Israel in Washington, hence its tenacious adhesion to the status quo of "not a single inch," the mad rush to build colonial settlements, and the resultant discord with the United States during Shamir's rule in 1990 and 1991.

By the time of the U.S. presidential campaign in 1991, however, George Bush endeavored to repair the damage with Israel and highlight the strategic relationship. The beleaguered incumbent, who trailed his Democratic opponent by more than 20 percent in the public opinion polls, tried to convince pro-Israel voters that the special relationship was quite alive despite the damage caused by Shamir.

Regardless of electoral politics and who was to occupy the White House later on, the future of the special relationship would be determined by the strategic establishment in light of the emerging global and regional realities. The strategic shifts in the region and in the world had two seemingly contradictory effects on Israeli hegemony. Unlike the Arab states, which were left with virtually no leverage, Israeli influence was in fact enhanced. Secretary of Defense Dick Cheney reconfirmed the U.S. commitment to the security of Israel and its military advantage in May 1991, and a new package of military and economic aid was announced during his visit there. Nonetheless, Israel's strategic relationship with the U.S. in the aftermath of the Cold War seemed to require some updating. The Soviet eclipse created a new opportunity for Baker and produced an added imperative for such a reassessment. A diminished "Soviet threat" was said to be incompatible with the notion of a strategic asset. To some people, Israel had begun to look more and more like an expensive liability. The American public became less inclined to give foreign aid after the removal of the "Soviet threat" from Washington's foreign policy lexicon and as domestic needs assumed urgent and renewed concern in the midst of recession. Sigificantly, a *Wall Street Journal*–NBC public opinion poll in 1991 found that the percentage of Americans who would give aid to the Soviet Union (58 percent) exceeded that of those who would give to Israel (44 percent).[25]

The Global Versus the Regional

An Israeli-U.S. alliance adapted to post–Cold War conditions was no longer based on the obsolete "Soviet threat," but on Israel's continued willingness and ability to offer the United States a strategic base in the eastern Mediterranean to respond to regional conflicts. Israeli strategists suggested in interviews with the *Washington Post* that in the 1990s and beyond, Israel would "present itself to Washington as a figurative home port in a sea of regional crisis."[26] The Haifa port is gradually and consistently accommodating larger U.S. naval vessels. The United States has also pre-positioned enough equipment in Israel for a mechanized battalion. The concept of "strategic asset" will also be reshaped and adapted as the Pentagon identifies new battlefields in Bush II's "war on terrorism" and his confrontation with the "Axis of Evil."

As far back as March 1991, senior Pentagon officials foresaw the development of a single superpower world (as we know from a leaked draft policy statement published in the *New York Times* at the time). Anticipating the Bush II doctrine, the United States was seen as the world's only policeman. No combination of allies or enemies would be permitted to challenge that role: "We will retain the preeminent responsibility for addressing selectively those wrongs which threaten not only our interests, but also those of our allies and friends, or which could seriously unsettle international relations."[27] This context has already proved to be fertile ground for Israel's own military planners, who have long awaited an opportunity to bridge the gap between the global orientation of the United States and Israel's regional orientation. Israeli planners correctly predicted during the early 1990s that its interests in the region and those of the post–Cold War U.S. would more closely coalesce in the coming years. The absence of Soviet-related scenarios could lead both countries to focus on the relationship between global and regional problems, such as the threat posed by Al-Qaeda. With turmoil in Algeria, Somalia, and Sudan; uncertainties in Libya, Central Asia, and the Gulf; and a dormant conflict in the former Yugoslavia, the Pentagon authors of future war scenarios have already found Israel a suitable platform. Israel is, in effect, the biggest U.S. aircraft carrier in the Mediterranean.

Israel's Regional Role and the Prospects for a Settlement

From the view of the U.S. politico-military establishment, Israel's relevance for U.S. strategic ventures was enhanced by leaps and bounds in the early 1990s in the context of an Arab-Israeli diplomatic settlement. Its regional role would be confirmed and expanded to include the Mediterranean, the Gulf, and Central Asia. Israel would no longer have to be kept out of Gulf "security" matters. It would become a vanguard in the coming crusade against what is known in the West as Islamic fundamentalism. It would be in the forefront in the fight against "terrorism" and against the spread of nuclear weapons and weapons of mass destruction to countries of the Global South. Meanwhile, the United States understood that Israel might also use its own terrorist methods and nuclear blackmail to achieve U.S.-Israeli mutual objectives.

The strategic relationship is also being rebuilt in the area of shared intelligence and the servicing of U.S. naval ships and military aircraft stationed in Europe as part of the Sixth Fleet. All U.S. F-15 planes are now serviced by Israel Aircraft Industries, while the government-owned Israel Shipyards regularly services and repairs U.S. ships at Haifa. The U.S. navy allocated funds for expanding the port of Haifa, dredging the harbor, and strengthening the piers.

Such joint ventures in military and nonmilitary matters reinforce the strategic alliance, confirming Israel's role as regional enforcer for the sole superpower. Israel has successfully positioned itself to be a strategic asset beyond the Cold War and the dissolution of the Soviet Union. On the eve of Rabin's first visit to the United States as prime minister, his foreign minister, Shimon Peres, challenged the view that Israel's strategic importance had diminished:

> If previously we had to confront the Russians, now we have to confront [a new situation].... Because the best peace paintings, hung on deteriorating walls, will fall down. We need different walls, not just different paintings. And I think it is in the interest of the U.S. to see the Middle East reconstructed.[28]

Rearranging the regional order in the Middle East implies a need for a settlement of the Arab-Israeli conflict. Yet the Bush II administration has focused on strategic cooperation and blocked meaningful diplomacy. The lessons learned from the Israeli military operations of March and April 2002 against Palestinian cities and refugee camps were quickly incorporated in the manuals of the U.S. Marine Corps. According to the *New York Times*, "[O]fficials from the Israeli Embassy, the Pentagon and Marine Corps all are unapologetic about the exchange of information about tactics, saying that they are the result of a long-standing partnership."[29]

Though human rights organizations referred to the slaughter in the Jenin refugee camp in mid-April 2002 as gruesome, and condemned the fact that Israelis used Palestinian civilians as human shields, U.S. and Israeli military experts seemed to relish the lessons derived from the massacre. U.S. military planners make no secret of their desire to learn from Israel in conducting the "war on terrorism." As Colonel Dave Booth, who oversees the Marine Corps and Israeli Defense Forces exchange, emphasized, "We're interested in what they're developing, especially since September 11 ... so there's a lot of things we could learn from them."[30] According to Randy Gangle, director of the Center for Emerging Threats and Opportunities, accounts of the Jenin fighting "reflected everything that we have been saying for the last four years about the problems we're going to face in the urban battle space." [31]

48 Dishonest Broker

Notes

1   Skirl McArthur, "A Conservative Total for U.S. Aid to Israel," *Washington Report on Middle East Affairs*, January 5, 2001.
2   Clyde Mark, *Israel: U.S. Foreign Assistance Facts*, Foreign Affairs and National Defense Division, Congressional Research Service, Library of Congress (CRS Issue Brief. Order Code: IB85066), September 4, 1991, pp. 4–5.
3   See http://www.alhewar.com/Curtiss.html.
4   See http://www.alhewar.com/Curtiss.html.
5   Mark, *Israel: U.S. Foreign Assistance Facts.*
6   "U.S. Israel Agreement of FY 2004 Security Assistance Levels," U.S. Department of State, Bureau of Public Affairs, *Current Policy* (November 20, 2002).
7   *Christian Science Monitor*, December 9, 2002.
8   *Mark, Israel: US Foreign Assistance Facts.*
9   See note 2 above.
10   Associated Press, June 20, 2002.
11   Associated Press, June 20, 2002.
12   Associated Press, June 20, 2002.
13   *Christian Science Monitor*, February 2, 1981.
14   When those quotations resurfaced in the German weekly *Welt am Sonntag* on February 7, 1982, the White House quickly denied that they represented current U.S. policy.
15   "Secretary Haig: U.S. Strategy in the Middle East," U.S. Department of State, Bureau of Public Affairs, *Current Policy* 312.
16   "Secretary Haig: Saudi Security, Middle East Peace, and U.S. Interests," Department of State, Bureau of Public Affairs, *Current Policy* 323.
17   Twinam was speaking for James Buckley, under secretary for security assistance, in an address before the National Conference of Editorial Writers in Providence, RI.
18   Secretary Haig, "Dangerous Illusions and Real Choices on AWACS," Department of State, Bureau of Public Affairs, *Current Policy* 324.
19   Naseer H. Aruri and John Carroll, "The Anti-Terrorist Crusade," *Arab Studies Quarterly* 9: 2 (Spring 1987): 173–87.
20   *New York Times*, May 26, 1982.
21   *New York Times*, June 8, 1982.
22   Clyde Mark, *Israeli-United States Relations*, Foreign Affairs and National Defense Division, Congressional Research Service, Library of Congress.
23   Text of the Memorandum of Agreement in the *Journal of Palestine Studies,* 18: 1 (Autumn 1988): 300–302.

24   *New York Times*, April 22, 1998.
25   *Wall Street Journal*, October 15, 1991.
26   *Washington Post*, July 28, 1992.
27   *New York Times*, March 8, 1992.
28   *Christian Science Monitor*, August 3, 1992.
29   *New York Times*, May 31, 2002.
30   *New York Times*, May 31, 2002.
31   *New York Times*, May 31, 2002.

CHAPTER 4

THE OBSTRUCTION OF PEACE

During the past thirty-five years, two approaches emerged for settling the Palestinian-Arab-Israeli conflict: a comprehensive settlement under international auspices and a "peace process" conducted under U.S. supervision. The two approaches remained dichotomous throughout the post-1967 war, in terms of both substance and procedure. This unbridgeable gap continued to promote an impasse until the end of the Gulf War. U.S. and allied victory in that war signaled the effective demise of the idea of convening the international conference called for in U.N. Resolution 338 after the October 1973 war, and the consecration of U.S. diplomacy as the only path toward an Arab-Israeli settlement. Secretary of State James Baker not only succeeded in replacing the international conference with a "regional" parley whose sole function was to legitimize the bilateral talks between Israel and the Arab states, but also secured Soviet and Syrian acquiescence to the change. This chapter will trace the rise and fall of the international approach to peacemaking in the region, which culminated in the apparent triumph of American unilateralism as the de facto approach for solving the Palestine question.

The mere fact that numerous international conferences have been held to tackle global conflicts in the modern period testifies to the utility of this concept as a viable means of conflict resolution. The Palestine question and its derivative, commonly referred to as the Arab-Israeli conflict, is one that is particularly suited to this method of conflict resolution. First, the problem itself was created by the imperialist powers between the two world wars, and was expanded and perpetuated by the superpowers in the aftermath of World War II. Secondly, this is a conflict in a highly strategic area of the world, in which two superpowers claimed vital interests throughout the Cold War period.

Numerous U.N. resolutions have called for the association of the major powers and third-world nations with a settlement. Even Resolution

242, which pushed Palestinian national rights to the sidelines, recognized a role for the world community by requesting the secretary-general to designate a special representative and to report to the Security Council on his efforts toward promoting a settlement. Resolution 338 of October 22, 1973, called for negotiations "between the parties concerned under appropriate auspices aimed at establishing a just and durable peace in the Middle East." The result was the ill-fated, largely ceremonious Geneva conference, which met briefly in December 1973 and was never convened again. Eighteen years later, the Madrid conference was convened under the auspices of the United States and the dying U.S.S.R. Its principal mission was to provide a semblance of an international character to a meeting that would launch bilateral negotiations on separate tracks between Israel and the Arab parties (under the careful watch of the United States). It was clearly a vindication of the U.S.-Israeli approach and a victory for the obstruction of an international settlement.

The international approach to a Middle East settlement had been championed by the Soviet Union and the Arab states and supported by the great majority of third-world nations during the 1970s and 1980s. Western Europe maintained a relatively independent position, and largely dissented from its American ally and Israel by accepting the legitimacy of the Palestinian national movement and its leadership, the Palestine Liberation Organization, and by affirming the illegality of both the 1967 occupation of Arab territories and the continued Israeli colonization of those territories. This position was proclaimed in the Venice Declaration of June 1980 and reaffirmed in subsequent statements and resolutions of various Euopean Community and later European Union (EU) forums from the 1990s until today. This approach envisioned an international framework with authority to shape a settlement in accord with recognized legal principles and accepted practices. These would include the inadmissibility of territorial acquisition by force; the principles established in U.N. Security Council Resolutions 242 and 338; and equal rights for the Palestinian people in accordance with General Assembly Resolution 3236 of November 22, 1974, which established the right of the Palestinian people to self-determination, national independence, and sovereignty. That resolution also requested that the U.N. secretary-general establish contacts with the PLO on all matters concerning Palestine.

The international consensus embodied a historic compromise, based on the exchange of territory for peace. The Arab states and the Palestinians, through the PLO, would recognize the permanence of Israel within the 1967 borders, in return for recognition of the right of the Palestinians to self-determination. Together, Resolutions 242 and 338 were universally considered to be the cornerstone of a proper settlement. This position was broadly accepted in the Arab world and gained endorsement of Arab summit conferences, from Algiers and Rabat in 1973 and 1974 to Fez and Amman in 1982 and 1987. It received an implicit sanction from the 1977 Palestine National Council (PNC) session in Cairo and an explicit acknowledgment from the 1988 PNC session in Algiers. The acknowledgment was made even more specific by PLO chairman Yasir Arafat's statements to the U.N. General Assembly session in Geneva, his subsequent press conference, and the "Stockholm Document," all in December 1988.

The U.S. "peace process" approach also claimed U.N. Security Council Resolutions 242 and 338 as a foundation for a reasonable settlement, but endorsed the concept of direct bilateral negotiations between states in a step-by-step fashion, leading toward a comprehensive settlement. The status of the exchange of territory for peace under this approach remained unclear, and seemed to allow a degree of territorial acquisition through negotiated agreement, inasmuch as Israel assumed the position that the resolution called for withdrawal "from occupied Arab territories," and not from *the* Occupied Territories. The concept of direct negotiations was designed to allow Israel to avoid the restrictions of the international framework. In particular, Israel and the United States sought to negate the rights of the Palestinian refugees to return to their homes and property or receive compensation, as well as their right to establish an independent state in accordance with General Assembly Resolution 194 of November 29, 1947.

U.S. Opposition to an International Peace Conference

Recent diplomatic history of the Middle East reveals that every U.S. administration since the 1967 Israeli occupation has thwarted an international settlement. By shielding Israel from international scrutiny, successive governments succeeded only in permitting Israel to consolidate its occupation of Palestinian and other Arab territories.

Between March 1969 and October 1973 various attempts were made to strengthen the U.N. and restore its role in negotiating a settlement. Am-

bassador Gunnar Jarring, a U.N. mediator, was charged with preparing
the grounds for implementation of Resolution 242. The Big Four talks,
which were proposed by France in January 1969, were conceived as an
added pillar for the Jarring mission. Israel's reaction to the involvement of
the Big Four was swift and unambiguously hostile. It cautioned Washington about the specter of an "imposed settlement," which would deny Israel the ability, as the victor, to impose its "peace" on the vanquished.[1]
And while the United States went along with the Big Four talks in 1969, it
insured that they remained perfunctory and would not evolve into an international peace conference. In fact, the United States used the Big Four
forum to advocate the Rhodes formula, a form of direct negotiations favored by Israel.[2] That advocacy was invigorated in the aftermath of Israel's rejection of the Rogers Plan of December 1969, which called for a
settlement based on the exchange of territory for peace in accordance with
Resolution 242. Whatever ingredients of a comprehensive settlement the
Rogers plan might have contained were sacrificed at the altar of the
U.S.-Israel special relationship. And whatever potential the Big Four
talks had as a peace conference was rendered barren by a manipulative
U.S. diplomacy.

  While the late French president Charles de Gaulle envisioned the Big
Four talks as the proper forum for a political settlement that would be
guaranteed by a subsequent big power conference, President Richard
Nixon and Henry Kissinger were determined to not allow these talks to
succeed.[3] Nixon's memoirs reveal that he wanted the United States, not
the U.N., to receive credit for a Middle East settlement. Seymour Hersh's
account of Kissinger's tenure in Nixon's White House shows that Nixon
and Kissinger's opposition to an Israeli withdrawal ordered by the U.N. or
the Big Four stemmed from a real concern that such a withdrawal would
appear as a victory for the U.S.S.R. or Arab leftists.[4] Both Moshe Dayan
and Yitzhak Rabin's memoirs corroborate Hersh's conclusion that Nixon
and Kissinger encouraged Israel to escalate the war of attrition in the Suez
Canal area and to attack the Soviet antiaircraft missiles deployed there in
the aftermath of Israel's penetration bombing in 1970.[5] These efforts to
thwart a comprehensive settlement and to frustrate an international solution
were continued by Nixon and Kissinger until the October 1973 war.

  The period between the October 1973 war and Carter's assumption
of the presidency in 1977 witnessed a triumph of U.S. diplomacy in its en-

deavor to promote separate agreements outside the U.N. framework. The Geneva conference, which was held in December 1973, produced no substantive results, and none had been expected. Absent from the conference, which was convened by the U.N. secretary-general and chaired jointly by the United States and the Soviet Union, were the other three permanent members of the Security Council and the two other principal parties to the conflict: Syria and the PLO. Syria's absence was dictated by policy disagreements, while the PLO was simply not invited.

Not unlike the previous Big Four talks, Geneva was not meant to achieve any comprehensive peace. Kissinger's manipulative diplomacy subordinated that goal to Washington's own objectives in the region. Kissinger's swift attempts to put together a meeting without any form of commitment from Israel on substantive issues, and Sadat's proclivity to separate solutions, deprived the conference of its assigned mission. Geneva, in effect, served as a smokescreen for Kissinger's "shuttle diplomacy." Indeed, Kissinger used the conference as a cover for negotiating two troop disengagement accords between Egypt and Israel in January 1974 and September 1975.[6]

Tellingly, the Israeli-Egyptian agreement reached in Geneva was signed by the Egyptian prime minister rather than the chief of staff.[7] Sadat's pledge to terminate the state of belligerency while Israel occupied most of Sinai, the Golan Heights, the West Bank, and Gaza gave it the character of a separate peace, notwithstanding Kissinger's announcement that it was a step in the direction of a comprehensive solution to the Arab-Israeli conflict.

Far from being a step toward a comprehensive peace, the September 1975 Sinai Accord was particularly harmful to the cause of peace. It came as a result of the resumption of Kissinger's step-by-step diplomacy, which was temporarily interrupted by President Gerald Ford's threatened "reassessment" of U.S.-Israeli relations in April 1975.[8] When Israel and its domestic U.S. lobby countered the president by mobilizing seventy-six U.S. senators against the recommendations to pursue a comprehensive settlement in Geneva, the administration fell back in line, and a new momentum was created for exacting concessions from the White House. In return for withdrawing from a small portion of Egyptian territory, Israel obtained from the United States important concessions, three of which proved particularly detrimental to a comprehensive settlement under international aus-

pices. First, the U.S. pledge that it would not negotiate directly with the
PLO meant the Palestine question could be treated, at best, as a territorial
and security-related matter rather than as a national question related to issues of self-determination. Second, the pledge to coordinate with Israel on
any Geneva talks gave Israel a virtual veto over U.S. policy in the Middle
East. Finally, the U.S. agreement that Arab-Israeli negotiations would be
conducted on a bilateral basis represented a formal endorsement of Israel's strategy of dividing the Arab states so as to maximize its goals at the
expense of Palestinian rights.

U.S. efforts to deter the concept of an international peace conference
were interrupted somewhat during President Carter's first nine months in
office, but after this brief interlude, it was business as usual. Carter initially attempted to revive the Geneva conference in order to achieve a
comprehensive settlement. Some of the Carter administration's top policy
advisers had been involved in drafting the Brookings Report of 1975,
which called for a comprehensive solution based on Israeli withdrawal
and Palestinian self-determination. The salient features of the Brookings
Report were incorporated into Carter's approach from January until November 1977, when Anwar Sadat made his trip to Jerusalem. In a September news conference, President Carter said that there could be no Middle
East settlement unless there was "adequate Palestinian representation" at
Geneva, and he expressed the view that the PLO represented a "substantial part" of the Palestinian people.[9] President Carter's 1977 diplomatic
offensive climaxed in an October 1, 1977, joint U.S.-U.S.S.R. statement
calling for a comprehensive political settlement in Geneva:

> The United States and the Soviet Union believe that the only right and ef-
> fective way for achieving a fundamental solution to all aspects of the
> Middle East problem in its entirety is negotiations within the framework
> of the Geneva Peace Conference, specially convened for those purposes,
> with participation in its work of the representatives of all the parties in-
> volved in the conflict including those of the Palestinian people.[10]

The reference to "legitimate rights" of the Palestinian people and its
implication of a reactivated Soviet role provoked opposition from the
U.S. Israel lobby, right-wing political forces, and the governments of
Menachem Begin and Anwar Sadat.[11] It took only four days to bring about
the virtual nullification of the October 1 statement. The Dayan-Carter
working paper of October 5, 1977, significantly undermined the Geneva

conference, while the Sadat visit to Jerusalem issued its death certificate. The Carter interlude was over.

Since that moment, Camp David has remained at the center stage of Middle East diplomacy. It signified the effective abandonment of the idea of an international peace conference, replaced by the pursuit of separate deals under U.S. auspices.

Neither the Arab proposal of August 1981, known as the Fahd plan, nor the Brezhnev plan of October 1981 convinced the U.S. government to reconsider an international approach.

The Fahd plan envisaged a role for the U.N. Security Council and was supported by Britain and France. The Brezhnev plan called for an expanded international peace conference that would include Western Europe, North Africa, and South Asia. A year later (on September 1, 1982), the United States proposed the Reagan plan, again bypassing the U.N., the Soviet Union, and Syria. Both the Arab Fez Plan of September 6 and the Brezhnev Plan of September 15, 1982 referred to a peace among *all* states in the region, including the independent Palestinian state that would be guaranteed by the Security Council or the big powers. But neither of these plans was put into effect.

United States obstruction of an international settlement persisted throughout the Reagan period and continued beyond it until the world finally accepted the Madrid conference of 1991, which served as Washington's alternative to the universal notion of an international settlement. The three decades since the October 1973 war witnessed the emergence of the United States as the de facto superpower of the region, its principal custodian and sole arbiter of peace. Israel was allowed to make a mockery of the global consensus, to escape the international scrutiny and eventually to substitute its own framework of bilateral agreement for the multilateral approach. The effective suspension of real peace in the Middle East was the price of American unilateralism.

The more the United States continued to promote itself as the sole legitimate arbiter in the Middle East, and as long as a growing number of Arab interests acquiesced in that role, the more the U.S.S.R., Syria, and other indigenous forces coalesced behind an international settlement. Nevertheless, U.S. opposition to an international conference on the Middle East remained persistent, vigorous, and unambiguous after the 1967 war. Eventually the correlation of forces resulted in the triumph of American unilateralism, and the consequent marginalization of Palestinian rights.

Notes

1   Israeli foreign minister Abba Eban expressed that concern in Washington during a March 1969 visit and tried to persuade President Nixon and Secretary of State William Rogers to abandon the talks. See Leila S. Kadi, *The Arab–Israeli Conflict: The Peaceful Proposals 1948–1972* (Beirut: NEEBIL, 1973), p. 68.

2   The Israeli cabinet's statement declared: Israel entirely opposes the plan to convene the representatives of states which lie outside the Middle East in order to prepare recommendations concerning the region. Such a procedure undermines the responsibility devolving on the states of the region to attain peace among themselves. Kadi, *The Arab–Israeli Conflict,* p. 68.

3   For an analysis of French policy toward the Middle East after the 1967 war, see Naseer H. Aruri and Natalie Hevener, "France and the Middle East, 1967–1968," *The Middle East Journal* (Autumn 1969): 484–502.

4   Seymour Hersh, *The Price of Power: Kissinger in the Nixon White House* (New York: Summit Books, 1983), pp. 216–17; see also *The Memoirs of Richard Nixon* (New York: Grosset & Dunlop, 1978) and the two volumes of Kissinger's memoirs, *The White House Years* (Boston: Little Brown, 1979) and *Years of Upheaval* (Boston: Little Brown, 1982).

5   *The Rabin Memoirs* (Boston: Little Brown, 1979).

6   "U.S. Policy in the Middle East, December 1973–November 1974," U.S. Department of State, Bureau of Public Affairs, *Current Policy* (Special Report No. 12): 12.

7   The September 1975 Sinai Accord (second disengagement agreement) was signed by Mamduh Salem at Sadat's request. See Ismail Fahmy, *Negotiating for Peace in the Middle East* (Baltimore: Johns Hopkins University Press, 1983), pp. 163–66.

8   President Ford's "reassessment" was based on recommendations by Averall Harriman, Cyrus Vance, Dean Rusk, George Ball, and William Scranton. See Cyrus Vance, *Hard Choices: Critical Years in America's Foreign Policy* (New York: Simon & Schuster, 1983); Fahmy, *Negotiating For Peace,* and Mahmoud Riad, *The Struggle for Peace in the Middle East* (London: Quartet Books, 1981).

9   *Department of State Bulletin,* October 31, 1977, p. 585.

10   *Department of State Bulletin,* November 7, 1977, pp. 639–40.
11   *New York Times*, October 2, 1977.

THE MARGINALIZATION OF THE PALESTINE QUESTION

The marginalization of the Palestine question was a natural consequence of the shifting balance in favor of American unilateralism over internationalism. Camp David, which purported to bring about a comprehensive settlement, had simply provided cover for a separate peace between Egypt and Israel, while permitting the latter a free hand in the Palestinian territories it occupied in 1967. That deal required a tacit reinterpretation of U.N. Security Council Resolution 242. Given that resolution's broad acceptance as a foundation for a settlement, it was necessary to keep it at the center of the diplomatic stage. Its demotion of Palestinian rights endeared it to Israel, yet its withdrawal clause contradicted Israeli goals. To reconcile these conflicting components, Resolution 242 was interpreted to allow for a certain accommodation of the Israeli position. For example, despite the fact that the Camp David Accords promised a comprehensive settlement on the basis of Resolution 242, the accords altered the status of the West Bank and Gaza from *occupied* territory to *disputed* territory whose sovereignty became a matter for negotiations. Moreover, the Egyptian-Israeli agreement granted Israel a virtual veto over the final disposition of the Palestinian territories occupied since 1967. Thus, Israel's withdrawal from the Sinai Peninsula, which took place in April 1982 in accordance with these agreements, was considered by Israeli leaders to be its final territorial "concession" and a fulfillment of its obligations under Resolution 242. "There will never again be a redivision of Western Eretz Israel," said Menachem Begin at that time, asserting "eternal sovereignty" over the West Bank and Gaza, and consequently blocking off even the U.S. options that had been presumed for these territories at Camp David.[1]

Carter and Palestine/Israel

The Sinai Accord of 1975 and the Camp David Accords of 1979 embodied the principle that the final settlement of the Palestine question would not be premised on the "faulty assumption" that Israel violated Palestinian rights.[2] Hence, the matter of sovereignty over the West Bank and Gaza was to be negotiable. That, in reality, was the true meaning of America's diplomatic blockade against the PLO, which was decreed by Henry Kissinger in 1975 and only lifted by the Reagan administration on its way out of office. *Boston Globe* columnist David Wilson correctly observed that the purpose of the Kissinger formula was to "protect Israel and its American ally from having to deal with the 1.7 million Palestinians under occupation."[3]

The marginalization of Palestinian national rights continued to dominate President Carter's efforts to effect an Arab-Israeli settlement. During his electoral campaign, Carter spelled out a position on the Palestinians that was consistent with those of the Nixon and Ford administrations: He would not recognize the Palestinians as a political entity, preferring instead to have Jordan administer the West Bank. By contrast, Carter's expectations from Israel were very modest and rather accommodating: "Israel must withdraw from some of the territories occupied. I would not try to force the Israelis to relinquish control of the Golan Heights or Old Jerusalem."[4]

President Carter said in his first news conference following the inauguration: "If the Palestinians should be invited to the meeting [at Geneva] as agreed by the other participating nations, along with us, it would probably be as part of one of the Arab delegations."[5] President Sadat, who had already expressed a desire for a formal link between a "Palestinian state" and Jordan, reiterated this point in the presence of Secretary of State Cyrus Vance in Cairo on February 17, 1977, adding that this should be an "official and declared link," that is, a confederation to be announced *before* a Geneva conference was convened.[6] Most Arab leaders stated that the PLO should receive an invitation as a full participant in the Middle East conference, but they were willing to exercise pressure on the PLO to accept being part of a single Arab delegation or even to stay away from the conference altogether and let the other Arabs negotiate for them.

During spring 1977, President Carter felt impelled to provide the Arab leaders with a face-saving device regarding the Palestine question. Yet he had to respond to internal and party pressures with regard to Israel and its own definition of peace. His Clinton, Massachusetts, speech on

March 16, 1977, revealed this dilemma and hinted at the way out: He would accept Israel's framework of a settlement, providing Israel accepted his obligation to provide that face-saving device to Arab leaders.[7]

Carter's dilemma, however, was intensified when the Likud bloc assumed power in Israel, for the first time, in the summer of 1977. The revisionist prime minister Menachem Begin was now publicly implying that the West Bank and Gaza were not Occupied Territories. Begin called the Occupied Territories "Judea and Samaria," and described the Palestinians living there as the "Arabs of Eretz Israel." When asked if he would find some means of pressure or persuasion should the Israeli position at Geneva be different from his own, Carter replied, "I would try to marshal the support of the leader, first of all. Secondly, the opinion of his people back home, the constituencies that might exist in our own country that would have influence around the world, opinion that exists in the European community, and in the Arab nations as well."[8] President Carter's "offensive" against Menachem Begin climaxed in the Joint Statement of the U.S.-U.S.S.R. on the Middle East on October 1, 1977, in which the U.S. agreed to associate the U.S.S.R. with the settlement in Geneva and used the phrase Palestinian "legitimate rights" for the first time.[9]

The joint declaration was met with intense opposition by Israel, as well as its constituencies in Congress and the American Jewish community, and was effectively abandoned by the Carter administration. The Dayan-Carter Working Paper of October 5 rendered the joint declaration ineffectual by declaring that "Acceptance of the Joint U.S.-U.S.S.R. Statement of October 1, 1977, by the parties is not a prerequisite for the reconvening and the conduct of the Geneva conference."[10] Meanwhile, Israeli foreign minister Moshe Dayan released a draft of the secret Working Paper to the Knesset, which revealed that Carter and Vance had not only retreated from their commitment to assure a form of PLO representation at Geneva, but in fact accepted Begin's definition of a settlement regarding the West Bank and Gaza.[11] The impasse which ensued following Carter's ill-fated "offensive" was interrupted by Anwar Sadat's sudden visit to Israel on November 19, 1977. His interest and that of Begin converged on the need to keep the Soviet Union out of Middle East diplomacy. Thus the focus of attention had shifted away from Geneva to the Middle East.

The next phase of Carter's Middle East policy began with Sadat's Jerusalem visit and ended with the Camp David Accord on September 17, 1978. Zbigniew Brzezinski's famous "bye-bye PLO" statement underscored the administration's abandonment of behind-the-scenes efforts to make the PLO a "qualified" negotiating partner. Sadat's trip ushered in a new era in the diplomatic history of the modern Middle East, in which the guidelines of a settlement would be formulated mainly by Israel. Carter and Sadat dropped whatever initiatives they might have entertained in the past. The Begin Plan, unveiled in December 1977, was put forward as Israel's "contribution to peace" in response to the Sadat trip. It envisaged the formation of an administrative council in the West Bank and Gaza with jurisdiction over local education, religious affairs, commerce, agriculture, tourism, health, and policing. Israeli authorities were to remain in charge of "security," foreign affairs, and economic matters. Israeli settlements were to continue unabated. The plan itself constituted a reaffirmation of Begin's sovereign claims in the West Bank and Gaza, and, as such, was at odds with the stated policies of both the United States and Egypt. Yet both Carter and Sadat accepted Begin's concept of autonomy as a framework for Camp David, though they differed with him on the extent of self-government it implied. Whereas Begin subscribed to limited autonomy, emphasizing that it was autonomy for the people but not the land, Carter and Sadat favored "full autonomy." A deliberate ambiguity, however, saved the three leaders from controversy and facilitated the agreement which was hailed in the Carter administration as its most impressive achievement in the Middle East. But Carter's retreat before Israel and its U.S. domestic constituencies, coupled with the Palestinian people's resolve to achieve their national rights, relegated that achievement to the status of a separate and "cold peace" between Egypt and Israel.

The Reagan Period

The Reagan plan of September 1, 1982, which denied sovereignty over the whole of the West Bank and Gaza to both Israel and the Palestinians, exemplified the trend of U.S. policy that had aimed since 1967 to thwart the international consensus and substitute its own "peace process."[12] The plan was precipitated largely by the siege of Beirut, which tarnished Israel's image and at the same time provided an impetus in the world community for linking PLO withdrawal from Beirut to Palestinian statehood.

To justify its virtual sole dissent from the international consensus, the Reagan administration felt obliged to launch its own initiative based on the "Jordan option." But the territorial and confederal aspects of the plan evoked a swift rejection from the Israeli cabinet.

The two major developments of 1988 in U.S. policy toward the Palestine question—the Shultz plan and the dialogue with the PLO—came largely in response to profound changes in the international, regional, and local situation.[13] The Shultz plan was introduced simply to reaffirm U.S. custodianship over the Middle East, to marginalize other serious plans for settlement, and to protect Israel's image, which had been tarnished by its brutal methods of suppressing the first Intifada. Shultz had endorsed Israel's attempt to contain the Intifada, but his approach differed from Israel's. He had issued an invitation to the Palestinians to explore a solution based on the Reagan Plan and Camp David, whose framework consisted of "full autonomy," transitional periods, elections for a "self-governing authority," and some kind of association with Jordan, none of which was likely to incur serious Israeli opposition.[14]

Yet, while the PLO recognized Israel's "right to exist," "renounced terrorism," and called for a two-state solution in December 1988, the Reagan administration merely agreed to no more than talking to the PLO sporadically at a fairly low level and about a highly constricted agenda. Meanwhile, Israel rejected both the Shultz plan and the idea of a "substantive dialogue" between the United States and the PLO, despite Arafat's compliance with the strict U.S. conditions for such a dialogue. The United States had done no more than agree to talk to the PLO, and George Shultz emphasized that "the first item of business on our agenda in that dialogue will be the subject of terrorism."[15] Reaffirming the U.S. position on direct negotiations and the role of the PLO in these negotiations, he said:

> We hope … that dialogue may help bring about direct negotiations that will lead to peace. How those negotiations are structured, who is there to speak on behalf of the Palestinians, is a subject that's a difficult one; we've worked on it a long time, and I imagine it will continue to be difficult.[16]

The PLO paid a high price for the dialogue, having agreed not only to Kissinger's conditions but also Reagan's codicils. These included recognizing Israel's "right" to exist (rather than merely the right "to live in peace") and the "renunciation" of, rather than the "condemnation" of, ter-

rorism. Both of these additions—which allowed Shultz to boast "I didn't
change my mind, they changed their[s]"—were used by the legal minds of
the new governments in Washington and Tel Aviv to extract new concessions from the Palestinians.[17] If Israel had the moral and legal right to exist, then why did the Palestinians wage a "war" against it for forty years?
By the same logic, the Zionist movement would have to be seen not as a
colonial-settler phenomenon, which resulted in Palestinian dispersal and
dispossession, but as a national liberation movement. Israeli and U.S. officials also argued that the 1988 Intifada was a form of violence and would
have to be "renounced" along with the Palestinian National Charter, which
negated Israel's "right" to exist. In fact, according to the first disclosure in
the West of the classified protocol of the initial negotiations between the
United States and the PLO in Tunis, the United States considered the Intifada a form of terrorism, just as it would consider the next Intifada (the
Al-Aqsa Intifada of 2000) a form of terrorism.

The Bush-Baker Strategy

The Reagan-Shultz legacy to the Bush I administration was not reversed
by the dialogue with the PLO. In fact, the Bush administration's approach
to the conflict revealed an even stronger commitment to the Israeli position. The inaction by the new administration during the first five months
was reflective both of its worldview and its sensitivity to domestic realities. Baker seemed to view the world through the prism of American domestic politics. He and the president expressed apprehension about major
initiatives that might lead to doing "dumb things."

When the Bush administration finally decided that the Middle East
could not be ignored any longer, it moved through surrogates with charac-
teristic caution and passivity. Shamir and Mubarak were induced to attach
their imprimatur to the peace plan that Washington would eventually
sponsor. The diplomatic void was filled by the so-called Shamir elections
plan, a rather safe issue for the Bush administration, which elevated the
plan to the centerpiece of its Middle East diplomacy. The plan, which received approval of the Israeli cabinet on May 4, 1989, was decorated with
slogans and buzzwords that would be popular in the American political
arena. Phrases such as "free democratic elections," a sacrosanct concept
in liberal America, "lull in violence," and "interim phases" were safe
enough for the administration to extend its approval.[18] The substance of

the elections plan, however, was characteristically rejectionist. All four points under the title "Basic Premises" insured the plan would be unworkable:

1. Direct negotiations based on the Camp David Accords;
2. "No" to negotiations with the PLO;
3. "No" to a Palestinian state; and
4. "No" to "any change in the status of Judea, Samaria, and Gaza other than in accordance with the basic guidelines of the government."

The administration, however, continued to try to "play it safe," with a major address by Secretary Baker to the American-Israel Public Affairs Committee (AIPAC) on May 22, 1989.[19] It was filled with rhetoric but short on substance, carefully avoiding the label of a U.S. plan. Even so, the demands that Baker's speech made on the Palestinians and the Arabs were more specific than those made on Israel. He urged them to produce a "constructive" response to the initiatives that the "Israeli government *has* offered." He commanded the Palestinians to "renounce the 'policy of phases' in all languages.... Amend the Covenant. Translate the dialogue of violence in the Intifada into a dialogue of politics and diplomacy." He asked the Palestinians to accept a transitional period of autonomy prior to a final settlement. He warned them not to "distort international organizations" by seeking admission to membership in the U.N. specialized agencies. He wanted them to convince the Israelis of their peaceful intentions, to accept as a real opening the elections proposed by the Shamir government, and to understand that "no one is going to deliver Israel for you." [20] Baker clearly placed the onus for breaking the impasse on the Palestinians and the Arab world, which he admonished to "take concrete steps toward accommodation with Israel," insisting that such steps could not be taken outside the framework of the so-called peace process. He, therefore, ignored previous Arab efforts on behalf of accommodation—though these spanned two decades, beginning with U.N. mediator Gunnar Jarring in 1970 and including the numerous resolutions adopted by Arab summit conferences calling for mutual recognition. He challenged the Arabs to "end the economic boycott ... stop the challenges to Israel's standing in international organizations, and repudiate the odious line that Zionism is racism." [21]

The only new element in the speech was Washington's open support for Shamir's elections plan. Yet the speech was widely interpreted in the U.S. as the first major policy pronouncement of the Bush administration and was generally described as evenhanded. If sponsoring elections through Israel was the first phase of Bush-Baker diplomacy, selling the plan to the Palestinians through Eygpt was the second phase. As Washington's secondary proxy in the region, Egypt would sweeten the bait and try to camouflage its diktat character.[22] But Mubarak's ensuing Ten-Point plan was rejected by Israel, despite its capitulatory character.

Baker's response to his recalcitrant ally was to put forward five "suggested points," again carefully avoiding the impression that there was any "American plan" and keeping the U.S. away from the center of the negotiating process.[23] The intent of the "suggested points" was to hold a meeting for the foreign ministers of Egypt, Israel, and the United States in order to decide on who would be the legitimate representative of the Palestinians. After all, Shamir was opposed not only to the PLO playing that role but also to the participation of a broad range of Palestinians, including expelled activists, Jerusalem residents, and anyone involved in the uprising.

Israeli rejectionism of its patron's suggestions had become so untenable that it disturbed even its traditional supporters in the United States. "Bleak Rejectionism" was the title of a *Washington Post* editorial on October 9, 1989, that accused Shamir of making a decision "to greet the new president in his first year ... with a hard line in order to set the tone for the rest of his term." A *New York Times* editorial on October 4,1989, titled "Is Coaxing Enough?" stated that Shamir and his allies were "tough customers" who were "unlikely to budge unless Washington makes clear, at least privately, its determination to get talks under way." [24]

That the Shamir government was stalling and perpetuating the impasse was indeed very clear. But more importantly, Shamir had renounced his own proposal under pressure from new extremist allies in the Likud coalition who believed the plan would ultimately lead to a Palestinian state. Hence the renewed crisis in U.S.-Israeli relations. Yet none of the other parties would rock the boat. Baker would not push Shamir into a corner and risk a collapse of his "national unity" government. Mubarak, with a vested interest in a settlement that would vindicate Egypt and present Camp David as the way for the future, was not ready for a confrontation with Shamir. But the PLO—which had the most to lose since it would be formally disenfranchised—decided against rejecting the repackaged Camp David terms to avoid being seen as the spoiler. It obliged Baker by providing the green light for Palestinian leaders in the Occupied Territories to meet with Israeli officials and with the Bush administration's first high-ranking delegation in May 1989.

What Washington wanted from the PLO, having exhausted all means of promoting Jordan as interlocutor, was to deliver the Palestinian leadership in the Occupied Territories—that is, to acquiesce in the ongoing process of substituting local self-government for statehood. After Jordan decided to sever constitutional links with the West Bank under the impact of the Intifada in August 1988, the PLO made the hard choice of scaling down the already minimal position it had outlined in the November 1988 declaration of independence in which it recognized Israel.[25] Meanwhile, Baker's first round was dealt a severe blow when Shamir renounced his own plan, which Baker had earlier described as "the only game in town." Baker's response was rather timid; he flashed the State Department's telephone number on the television screen, saying, "If interested in peace, call us."[26]

The outcome of Baker's renewed "peace process" was rather predictable. His AIPAC speech somehow found symmetry between the Palestinian-Arab dream of an independent state on less than 25 percent of pre-1948 Palestine and the dream of a greater Israel in the whole of Palestine. In the meantime, the PLO had not only played Arafat's "last card"—recognition of Israel—but the Intifada card as well. These cards produced a meager dialogue, which Washington utilized to preach to the PLO from its bully pulpit. But the Gulf War would serve to marginalize the Palestinian cause and the PLO even further.

The Gulf War and the Palestinians

The suspension of the "peace process" in the summer of 1990 led the PLO to shift its primary diplomatic focus in the Arab world from Egypt to Iraq. Frustrated by the breakdown of the U.S.-Egyptian endeavor to prepare for direct Israeli-Palestinian talks and angered by the fact that it had to communicate with Washington through Egypt despite the dialogue (which was later suspended anyway), the PLO began to pin its hopes for a diplomatic settlement on a perceived Iraqi potential for mutual deterrence vis-a-vis Israel.

The failure of the U.S. and Egypt to effect a diplomatic settlement, coupled with the failure of Iraq to develop military and political leverage for a settlement based on mutual recognition, placed the Palestinians at the mercy of the new balance of power in the region. The conventional wisdom was that the Palestinians had done their cause irreparable damage by identifying too closely with Iraq. President George Bush stated in Martinique in March 1990 that the Palestine Liberation Organization had "backed the wrong horse," implying that it should not, therefore, expect an invitation to the post-war negotiations. Long before Bush unleashed the Allied bombers and cruise missiles against Baghdad, media analysts in the United States and abroad pronounced the Palestinian struggle for a homeland as a principal casualty of the Gulf conflict. According to the *New Statesman*, "Whoever the winner may be in the coming cataclysm, there was certain to be one big loser: the Palestinians."[27] In a column titled "Desperation and Folly," *New York Times* columnist Anthony Lewis argued, "Over many decades Palestinian nationalism has made crucial political mistakes. This may be the worst."[28] An editorial in the same issue agreed: "By embracing Saddam Hussein, the Palestine Liberation Organization has injured its cause in every imaginable direction."[29] A cartoon by Szep depicted Arafat lying on a couch with psychiatrist Saddam Hussein by his side saying: "Other than feeling universally hated, detested and unwanted, what's your problem?"

Palestinians in the occupied West Bank and Gaza and in Jordan took to the streets to demonstrate their opposition to the U.S. military deployment during the autumn of 1990. They were certainly in tune with much of Arab public opinion, which feared the unstated objective of U.S. policy was the destruction of Iraq and its elimination as a regional power. Meanwhile, Arafat's efforts to mediate reached a dead end when the very concept of an "Arab solution," which he pursued together with other members of the Arab League, was discredited and discouraged by the Bush administration, which would not accept any settlement that would have left Iraq's military and industrial capability intact.

The leaders of the Intifada inside the Occupied Territories, who were less constrained by the exigencies of diplomacy, delivered an unequivocal condemnation of the Iraqi and Israeli occupations. In a statement issued on August 15, 1990, in Jerusalem, they affirmed "the nonlegitimacy of the acquisition of land by force and the unacceptability of resorting to military options in solving conflicts among states, which may involve the occupation of Arab lands and the Iraqi invasion of Kuwait."[30]

In any case, U.S. policy in the aftermath of the Gulf conflict was not going to be determined by a perceived Palestinian stand on that conflict. It was significant that President Bush reaffirmed the three no's of his election campaign platform after the Gulf War: "no" to an international peace conference, "no" to PLO representation in any negotiations on the Palestine question, and "no" to a Palestinian state.[31] These no's paralleled the "Basic Premises" of Shamir's plan of May 4, 1989. Not only had the United States been working in tandem with Israel since the Gulf War, but after Iraq was defeated and America's Arab clients were rescued, the U.S. government became less constrained by the previous pretense of evenhandedness. In fact, U.S. rejectionism not only stiffened, it gained more support among the Arab members of the war coalition. Egypt and some of the family regimes in the Gulf began to signal a not-so-subtle retreat from the Arab consensus on Palestine. Saudi Arabia, for example, floated the idea of a Palestinian state in Jordan, an idea which approximated the Reagan plan of 1982. Egypt and Syria agreed to a nonsubstantive regional conference instead of the international conference which the Arab states had always insisted upon. Also significant was the absence of any reference to the PLO in official Arab declarations after the Gulf War, starting with the Damascus Communiqué issued by the Arab members of the war coalition in March 1991.[32] Kuwait, together with other Gulf states and Egypt, joined the United States and Israel in another campaign to demonize Yasir Arafat and delegitimize the PLO. The combined resources marshaled to produce a post-war settlement by the United States and its strategic ally, together with those of its Arab war partners, were to prove catastrophic for Palestinian national and human rights.

The Road to Madrid

Less than a year after Shamir renounced his own plan, Baker had a second "window of opportunity," now bolstered by objective and material changes occurring at the regional and global levels. The strategic imperatives for a negotiated settlement, largely on U.S. terms and under U.S. auspices, were created by the effective collapse of the Soviet Union and the destruction of Iraq. The Soviet Union was transformed from chief diplomatic backer and arms supplier of the Arab states to U.S. appendage in the "peace process." Iraq was reduced from the champion of strategic balance with Israel to a basket case nation preoccupied with the preservation of its threatened sovereignty and territorial integrity. Thus, with deterrence having suddenly vanished at the global and regional levels, the U.S. government was left without any serious opposition for the first time since Nasser. Ironically, the major source of irritation for its diplomatic efforts was its own regional ally. The dramatic transformation of the strategic and political landscape of the Middle East in the aftermath of the Cold War and the destruction of Iraq paved the way for George Bush to attempt to shape a new structure of relationships in which an Arab-Israeli settlement became a U.S. national interest.

The Eclipse of Arab Solidarity

The Gulf War had effectively demolished the official Arab consensus on Palestine, eroded Arab solidarity, and exposed regime insecurity in the Gulf region. The Arab world became more divided than at any time since the establishment of the Arab League. Arab solidarity against Israel had broken down, and an important source of pressure for Israeli concessions was thereby eliminated. Moreover, the indebtedness of the poorer Arab countries, as well as the virtual protectorate status of the richer Arab states, seemed to translate into a loss of relative sovereignty and leverage.[33] There was hardly any economic or diplomatic leverage left for these countries, and with the destruction of Iraq as a regional power, the military leverage was also eliminated for the foreseeable future.

These developments dismantled the joint Palestinian-Arab strategy developed at the Rabat summit in 1974, whose pillars consisted of Arab economic and diplomatic leverage and Palestinian "moderation" (that is, its acceptance of a two-state solution rather than the secular democratic state in all of Palestine). That enabled the Bush administration to obtain Arab and Palestinian acquiescence in its framework for negotiations, tilted heavily against the Arab side.

The Gulf War also removed the question of Palestine from the top of the Arab agenda. The conventional wisdom prevailing in the West—that the Palestinians had done their cause irreparable damage by identifying too closely with Iraq—was conveniently adopted by the Arab members of the war coalition. The Arab states seemed to have little objection to the U.S. refusal to allow the PLO a meaningful diplomatic gain in exchange for its historic concessions of 1988 and Arafat's subsequent "renunciation" of terrorism.

The Consolidation of Israeli Hegemony

The Gulf War consolidated the hardline forces in Israel, placing the Israeli peace camp on the defensive and causing its faint voice to drown in an avalanche from the rapidly rising right-wing forces. The crisis also provided the Israeli government with a natural pretext to clamp down on the Intifada with near total freedom from international scrutiny. Under cover of the Gulf crisis, Israel embarked on the destruction of everything the Intifada had achieved between 1988 and 1991 in the diplomatic, political, and economic fields and in health care and social organization. It was an "opportunity" to cripple the evolving Palestinian infrastructure, which had already been dealt a serious blow a decade earlier in Lebanon, and was to be dealt a third blow in 2000–2002.

The Gulf War also provided Israel with an opportunity to impose its diplomatic framework on any negotiations that it was expected to join. In fact, it was the only party whose demands were not scaled down for the sake of compromise, but were instead elevated. Shamir argued that only after Israel had peace with the Arab states would it feel confident enough to discuss the West Bank and Gaza.[34] That represented a change from his earlier insistence on Arab recognition of Israel as a precondition for entering peace talks between Israel and the Palestinians.[35] But the two-track approach—which provided for multilateral negotiations on environmental issues, water, refugees, economic development, and arms control, along with the bilateral talks—assured Israel a de facto recognition from the Arab states attending the "multilaterals" prior to any action by Israel to meet its obligations to the Palestinians, Syrians, and Lebanese whose territory was under occupation.

The second post–Gulf War trend was the replacement of the international peace conference with a regional conference hosted by the United States and the Soviet Union. This strange concept not only diminished the importance of U.N. Resolution 242, but also rendered a forty-five-year-old legal record, enshrined in countless U.N. resolutions, virtually irrelevant. A token U.N. presence was assured at the conference, but the observer was committed to humiliating silence. In addition, Israel set a number of other conditions that were accepted by Baker, sold to the Arabs, and incorporated into what became known as the Madrid framework. Salient among these were the following:

1. The Soviet Union would have to establish "full diplomatic relations with Israel and agree to the meeting ground rules demanded by Israel" in order to qualify as co-sponsor.[36] These ground rules included Israel's insistence that "all that would be discussed at first with the Palestinians is an interim settlement involving self-government." Final status talks would begin three years later.

2. An opening statement at such a conference by the United States must refrain from delineating any plan for settlement, a demand which Baker had complied with back in 1989 when he called his "five points" a "proposal," not a "plan."[37]

3. In view of the limited purpose of the conference, which would be a one-time event to launch direct negotiations and pave the way for discussing Israel's autonomy plan, participation would be limited to Palestinians living in the West Bank and Gaza and would exclude those living in East Jerusalem and in Israeli jails, as well as the four million refugees scattered outside Palestine.

Israel further expected the United States to persuade the Arab states to agree that the regional conference lead immediately to direct negotiations in the two tracks; that the meeting have no power to impose solutions on the parties, or to pass judgment on agreements reached in bilateral negotiations;[38] that Resolutions 242 and 338 not determine the outcome of the process; and that the U.S. promise that the PLO would have no role at any point in the process, a position which the U.S., the Arab states, and even the PLO itself had accepted.

Had the PLO insisted on representing the Palestinians, the United States and the Arab states were ready and willing to promote an alternative leadership in the Occupied Territories to negotiate a peace based on the new balance of power in the region. The deteriorating economic conditions in the Occupied Territories—created by Israel's draconian measures during the Gulf crisis—were counted upon as the catalyst that would prod the Palestinians into compliance.

An "Opportunity" for James Baker

The consequences of the Gulf War provided Baker with an opportunity to shape a new structure of relationships in which an Arab-Israeli settlement became a U.S. national interest. The PLO was extremely vulnerable. Deprived of solid and unified Arab backing in the negotiation; isolated from its constituencies in the Occupied Territories, the Gulf, Syria, and Lebanon; and faced with economic, ideological, leadership, and governance crises—the PLO was seen by the Bush administration as the weakest link in the chain of negotiations. Hence Baker's diplomacy relied on deliberate ambiguity, and substantive issues were thinly camouflaged as procedural arrangements.

Having succeeded in convening a gathering that he called an international conference, James Baker was also able to secure Soviet and Syrian acquiescence during eight trips to the region between March and September 1991. The Arab position, which was based on the necessity of an international conference, was gradually watered down with each trip. On April 19, 1991, King Hussein said that Jordan would be "very flexible" when it came to the terms of a conference.[39] Syria, on the other hand, stood by its position, insisting on U.N. participation in a conference that had a permanent structure and demanding that Israel commit itself to the exchange of land for peace.

On May 8, 1991, Baker proposed a "compromise" whereby the conference would be sponsored by the U.S. and Russia and would reconvene every six months. He also proposed that each side bring in its own interpretation of Resolution 242 with regard to Palestinian representation, which would be part of a joint Jordanian-Palestinian delegation. Even that "compromise" proved to be unacceptable to Israel and was also rejected by Syria, thus prompting Baker to return to Washington and blame both parties. He did, however, emphasize that Israel's continued settlement policy was the biggest obstacle to peace.[40] In the meantime, President Bush hinted that invitations could be issued, implying that those who failed to attend would be considered as standing in the way of peace. On July 14, President Hafez Al-Assad of Syria accepted the U.S. "compromise," stating that the plan was "an acceptable basis for achieving a comprehensive solution." This prompted Baker to return to the area to look for additional conciliatory moves by the Arabs to entice Israel to agree. But despite a firm Syrian commitment, made to Baker by Assad in Damascus, and President Mubarak's call for the Arabs to end the economic boycott of Israel in return for an Israeli suspension of settlement building, Prime Minister Shamir could only tell Baker upon his arrival in Israel on July 21 that he needed time to consider the matter. On the same day, Jordan announced its acceptance of Baker's proposal and together with Egypt and Saudi Arabia offered to suspend the economic boycott of Israel.

With Arab concessions mounting, Israel, concerned about the outcome of the public relations battle, finally decided to extend approval on
July 24, but with stipulations that Palestinian presence at the conference be
limited to non-PLO, non-Jerusalem, non-diaspora Palestinians. This exclusion amounted to about 75 percent of the Palestinian people. The Arab concessions were incorporated into a letter of invitation signed by the United
States and Russia on October 18, 1991. The letter effectively replaced all
previous U.N. resolutions as a framework for settling the Arab-Israeli conflict. It was accompanied by a "letter of assurances" to the protagonists,
which largely defined the U.S. understanding and intentions concerning the
negotiations. The main principles in the letter of invitation were:

1. Peace would be grounded in Security Council Resolutions 242 and
   338 and the principle of territory for peace, in accordance with President Bush's address to Congress on March 6, 1992. It would provide
   for Israeli security and recognition, for legitimate Palestinian political rights, and for Palestinian control over political and economic decisions that affect their lives.
2. The venue for the peace negotiations would be a "regional conference" that would lead, after four days, to direct bilateral negotiations.
   The conference would have no power to impose solutions, veto
   agreements reached by the parties, or make decisions for the parties.
   It could reconvene only with the consent of the parties.
3. The negotiations would be conducted in phases, beginning with talks on
   interim self-government arrangements. The interim self-government
   would last for five years, and during the third year, negotiations would
   begin for final status.

The letter of assurances to the Palestinians reiterated these principles
and added a few specific points to accommodate its exclusion of anything
resembling an international approach:

1. The Israeli occupation would come to an end, but that could be accomplished only through negotiations that would be comprehensive and
   would proceed along two tracks—a Palestinian and an Arab track.
2. The United Nations would be represented by an observer. Agreements would be registered with the U.N. Secretariat and reported to
   the Security Council. As long as the process went on, the United
   States would not support another process in the United Nations.
3. The Palestinians could choose their own delegation. Although the
   U.S. claimed it did not seek to determine who spoke for the Palestinians, it stipulated that the delegation members would be residents

from the Occupied Territories who agreed to the two-track concept, in phases, and who were willing to live in peace with Israel. No party could be forced to sit with anyone.

4. Jerusalem would never again be divided and its final status would be decided in negotiations. The U.S. would not recognize Israel's annexation of East Jerusalem or the extension of its municipal boundaries. Palestinians from Jerusalem would be excluded from the delegation, but a Palestinian resident in Jordan with ties to a prominent Jerusalem family would be eligible to join the Jordanian delegation. Palestinians from East Jerusalem would be able to vote in the election for an interim self-governing authority. Together with diaspora Palestinians, these people could also negotiate on final status.

The proximity of these parameters to Israel's conditions is very striking, a fact that reflects the gradual incorporation of the Israeli perspective into Baker's shuttles.

The fundamental moral and legal issue that Baker's diplomacy ignored was the wrong done to the Palestinians, in violation of the 1949 Fourth Geneva Convention Relative to the Protection of Civilians in Times of War. Security Council Resolution 681 unanimously declared in 1991 that the Geneva Convention protects the Palestinian people in the Occupied Territories from being coerced to submit to illegal agreements. It guards against the renunciation of rights guaranteed in the Geneva Convention and restricts Israeli practices in the manner of a de facto sovereign.

The shortcomings of the Madrid agreement and the deliberate ambiguity of Baker's diplomacy prevented the parties from making the kind of progress needed to meet deadlines. Self-government for the Palestinians was scheduled for implementation in October 1992, one year from the Madrid conference. Yet, after ten years and numerous other deadlines, Palestinian self-government has not happened, and it is not likely to happen in the foreseeable future. Bush II has embraced Ariel Sharon's position with hardly any qualifications.

The right-wing sector, which was in power in Israel at the time, viewed the Madrid process as an investment to buy a few more years in which Soviet immigrants and expanded settlements would help assure an effective foreclosure on a territorial peace. Shamir put it succinctly:

This mass immigration aims at forming a greater Israel ...will make Israel bigger, stronger, and better ... in the space of five years you will not be able to recognize this country. Everything will change, everything will be bigger. The strongest of the Arabs around us will be in a state of desperation and panic as they will not be able to stop the natural flow of Jewish people into their land.[41]

Not surprisingly, the Madrid process went nowhere after eleven rounds of talks in Washington, Rome, and Moscow, as Israel clung tenaciously to the policy of building settlements, thus forfeiting any kind of a territorial solution. For the Palestinians, it was an uncertain path, if not in fact a blind alley. All fundamental issues involving borders, refugees, Jerusalem, and indeed the occupation itself were deferred, as they would be in the Oslo process two years later. Self-government, as the sole concern of these negotiations in the immediate term, was seen by the Palestinians as the necessary link toward independence. Israel, on the other hand, had ruled out independence and viewed what it called self-government as a mechanism to ratify the occupation under a new and different label. Any doubt about this strategy was dispelled by the text of the Israeli plan submitted during the March 1992 round of negotiations in Washington (entitled "Ideas for Peaceful Coexistence in the Territories during the Interim Period"). The premise of that plan seemed consonant with parameters enunciated by Deputy Foreign Minister Benjamin Netanyahu in December 1991: "maximum security for Israel and minimum intervention in Palestinian life."

The text of the plan made it very clear that the concept of Israeli security disallowed the Palestinians any notion of an overall central authority, geographical space, independent economic planning, real legislative authority, or judicial review—not to mention autonomy in defense, foreign affairs, or natural resources. Minimum intervention in Palestinian life would remove direct Israeli control of fragmented municipalities. The Palestinians would have enclaves on about 5 percent of historic Palestine—exactly the same amount of land owned by Jews on the eve of the establishment of Israel.

The outcome of the Gulf crisis had so radically altered the balance of power in the region that it was nearly impossible for the Palestinians to achieve their minimal goals under U.S. diplomatic auspices. A crippling impasse rendered the Washington diplomatic rounds an exercise in futility. That situation persisted until the deadlock was temporarily interrupted at Oslo in September 1993.

Notes

1   *New York Times*, May 4, 1982.
2   Jimmy Carter's phrase, as reported in the *New York Times*, April 1, 1976.
3   *Boston Globe*, December 20, 1988.
4   *New York Times*, April 1, 1976.
5   *New York Times*, January 14, 1977.
6   *New York Times*, February 19, 1977.
7   *New York Times*, March 19, 1977.
8   *Time*, August 8, 1977.
9   *New York Times*, October 2, 1977.
10 *New York Times*, October 6, 1977.
11 *New York Times*, October 14, 1977.
12 For a discussion of the Reagan plan, see Naseer H. Aruri and Fouad Moughrabi, "The Reagan Middle East Initiative," *Journal of Palestine Studies* 12: 2 (Winter 1983): 10–30.
13 For an analysis of the Shultz plan, see Kathleen Christison, "The Arab-Israeli Policy of George Shultz," *Journal of Palestine Studies* 18: 2 (Winter 1989): 29–47.
14 "The Statement by Secretary of State George Shultz Addressed to the Palestinians in the Occupied Territories in East Jerusalem," U.S. Department of State, Bureau of Public Affairs, *Current Policy* 1055 (February 26, 1988).
15 *New York Times*, December 19, 1988.
16 *New York Times*, December 15, 1988.
17 *New York Times*, December 15, 1988.
18 *Jerusalem Post*, May 5, 1989.
19 James Baker, "Principles and Pragmatism: American Policy Towards the Arab-Israeli Conflict," U.S. Department of State, Bureau of Public Affairs, *Current Policy* 1176; see also *New York Times*, May 23, 1989.
20 *Jerusalem Post*, May 26, 1989.
21 *Jerusalem Post*, May 26, 1989.
22 Text of Mubarak's Ten-Point plan in *Boston Globe*, October 8, 1989; see also Abba Eban, "Mubarak's Offer: A Dramatic Test," *New York Times*, September 28, 1989.
23 Thomas Friedman, "Advance Reported on Middle East Talks," *New York Times*, December 7, 1989; see also Mary Curtiss, "Shamir is Seen Accepting Egypt's View of U.S. Plan," *Boston Globe*, December 8, 1989.
24 *New York Times*, October 4, 1989.
25 *New York Times*, December 15, 1989.

26   Naseer H. Aruri, "America's Passive Approach," *Middle East International* 636 (November 7, 1989).

27   Stephen Howe, "The Palestinians, Back to the Wall," *New Statesman*, August 24, 1990, p. 23.

28   *New York Times*, January 21, 1991.

29   *New York Times*, January 21, 1991.

30   *Al-Quds,* August 16, 1990.

31   Text of the 1988 Republican Party Platform in *Journal of Palestine Studies* 18: 1 (Autumn 1988): 304–306.

32   *Time,* March 18, 1991; *Boston Globe*, April 12, 1991.

33   Yahya Sadowski, "Revolution, Reform or Regression? Arab Political Options in the 1990 Gulf Crisis," *Brooking Review* (Winter 1990–1991): 17–21.

34   *Boston Globe,* March 4, 1991.

35   *Wall Street Journal,* March 6, 1991.

36   *New York Times,* April 10, 1991.

37   *New York Times,* April 10, 1991.

38   *Boston Globe,* April 12, 1991.

39   *New York Times*, April 21, 1991.

40   *Guardian* (London), May 23, 1991.

41   Avi Shlaim, *The Iron Wall: Israel and the Arab World* (New York: Norton, 2000); see also *Mariv*, June 26, 1992; *Yedioth Ahronoth*, June 22, 1992.

CHAPTER 6

THE FURTHER MARGINALIZATION OF THE PALESTINE QUESTION

AFTER OSLO

A Historic Handshake

On September 13, 1993, President Bill Clinton hosted Yasir Arafat and Yitzhak Rabin. The occasion was a White House ceremony for the signing of the "Declaration of Principles," also known as the Oslo Accords.[1] These accords must be understood in the context of American hegemony over the Middle East, which was expanded after the collapse of the Soviet Union and the U.S. military victory in the Gulf War. Though hailed as a dramatic breakthrough for peace, the accords represented the PLO's virtual surrender to the United States and its ally, Israel. Arafat and the PLO were in a weakened position, facing a new administration in Washington that had acquiesced in Israel's total closure of the Occupied Territories, massive bombardment of Lebanon, and expulsion of 413 Hamas supporters, without any semblance of due process. The act that precipitated Arafat's acceptance of the Oslo Accords, however, was the production of the "Declaration of Principles" by Secretary of State Warren Christopher on June 30, 1993. The DOP repudiated long-standing American policy. It implied that the West Bank and Gaza were "disputed" rather than "occupied" territories, and made reference to authority over people but not over territory. Arafat decided to salvage what little he could.

The Oslo Accords created a fundamental change in the political terrain on which the struggle for a diplomatic settlement had begun nearly twenty years earlier. The DOP and the "Mutual Recognition" statements, which were signed in an atmosphere of euphoria and exultation, were assumed to signal a turning point in the Arab-Israeli conflict.[2] The reluctant handshake between Arafat and Rabin was generally seen as the start of a new chapter that would usher in a new phase of peaceful coexistence.

Ardent believers said that provisions such as the ones proclaiming the West Bank and Gaza a "single territorial unit" (Article IV), held significant promise for Palestinian aspirations. They ignored, however, that such a unit was, in reality, a collection of enclaves and subenclaves severed by permanent Israeli settlements and their infrastructure. Other optimists also touted Article I, which stated that "the transitional period of interim self-government shall lead to a permanent settlement based on Security Council Resolution[s] 242 and 338," again ignoring the widely known Israeli position that Israel had already met its obligations under Resolution 242 when it made the Sinai withdrawal after Camp David.

To understand the agreement, we must place it in its proper context. This will help us answer the question of why, after more than twenty years of active but futile diplomacy, and after twenty-two months of crippling impasse in the Madrid process, was this agreement finally reached at Oslo in an atmosphere of total secrecy? A second question is how much of a departure from the existing situation it signified.

The Context

The key to the context of the PLO-Israel agreement was the new political reality created by the collapse of the Soviet Union and the destruction of Iraq, which enabled the United States to effectively emerge as the uncontested imperial power in the Middle East. It was the start of a new era and a militarily unipolar world order. With deterrence having suddenly vanished at the global and regional levels, the United States and Israel were both left without any serious opposition. This is the context in which the negotiations in Madrid, Washington, and Oslo, which eventually led to a virtual Palestinian surrender, could be seen.

During twenty-two months of negotiations (November 1991 to August 1993), the major concern in the Palestinian street was whether the negotiations would lead to genuine independence or to a fractured entity of disconnected enclaves. Having participated in the Madrid conference under conditions dictated largely by Israel (bilateral negotiations, transitional arrangements, U.N. dislodgment, and virtual U.S. diplomatic monopoly), the Palestinians were acknowledging the bitter realities of the post–Gulf War, post–Cold War period. Consequently, they expected to make major concessions, reflecting their weakness in the shifting regional and global balance of power.

The conclusions of Washington and Tel Aviv were not far apart. Bush and Baker had differed somewhat from Israel on the real meaning of U.N. Security Council Resolution 242, the exchange of land for peace, the question of colonial settlements, and the status of Jerusalem. But U.S. strategic influence, combined with the virtual absence of any Arab pressure on Washington, prevented the American "catalyst" from bridging the diplomatic gap between the Arabs and Israel with specific proposals. At issue were the following basic matters: whether the Occupied Territories were occupied or contested; whether the projected Palestinian self-governing entity had any geographic definition, a land dimension, or only a population dimension; whether its jurisdiction was derived from the popular will of the Palestinians or conferred and limited by the occupation regime, whose very existence had been deemed illegal; whether Israel could continue to exclude Jerusalem from negotiable items during the transition; and finally what future lay beyond the transition.

Madrid had signified a turning point in the Arab-Israeli conflict. Not only did the Arabs and Palestinians accept the reality of Israel, but they also recognized its legitimacy as a state, even prior to an explicit acknowledgment by Israel of its occupation of their land, a statement which Israel to this day has never made. The important legal issue involved here was that as long as Israel was unwilling to come to terms with its status as occupant within the meaning of international law, it would be able to render any agreement regarding withdrawal, security, sovereignty, and human rights completely superfluous. Without acknowledging its status as occupant, Israel would continue to shrug off its responsibility to the people while it controlled their land. It would be able to set aside, as it has been doing since 1967, the 1949 Geneva Convention.

The applicability of the Geneva Convention to the Occupied Territories was reaffirmed by Security Council Resolution 681, which was adopted unanimously in 1990. The convention protects the Palestinians from being coerced into illegal agreements—that is, agreements which violate their rights.[3] It also guards against the renunciation of their rights, and significantly, it restricts Israeli practices as a de facto sovereign. The applicability of the convention was also recognized by the United States.

The "Country Report on Human Rights Practices" for the year 1987 recognizes the applicability of both the 1907 Hague Convention and the 1949 Geneva Convention to the Israeli occupation. So did Baker's letter of assurances, though in a somewhat watered-down form.

The prospects for a negotiated settlement based on the Madrid framework began to look more grim with the ascendancy of Bill Clinton to the presidency. Meanwhile, the interests of Arafat and Rabin began to converge as Islamic resistance was threatening both of them. Arafat had become, together with his organization, increasingly irrelevant. The Intifada had given him a reprieve after his ouster from Lebanon in 1982, and now he was looking for yet another extension. The irrelevance of his organization and the erosion of his leadership were further accentuated by the growing prominence of the West Bank and Gaza negotiators who were accredited to the Washington talks by the Madrid process. While Haider Abdel Shafi led his delegation to the State Department and as Hanan Ashrawi articulated the Palestinian position to the press on a regular basis, Arafat's overseer, Nabil Sha'ath, had to take a back seat in his Washington hotel while remaining in constant touch with his boss in Tunis. The Oslo venue made a dramatic change by providing Arafat a welcome exchange of his proxy role for direct, on-the-spot involvement. His rush to Oslo was pushed along also by the mounting crisis facing his leadership: a financial and governance crisis related to Arafat's outright corruption. The United States and Israel were now more than ready to drop their reservations and objections. "Terrorism" was no longer a major stumbling block, and the road to Oslo had suddenly opened.

Having witnessed Clinton's embrace of Zionists throughout the presidential campaign and after victory, Arafat drew his own conclusions and hastened to secure his own tenure, even at the expense of Palestinian national rights. The stark choice before him was either to be involved in the "peace process" or to risk being bypassed altogether. The road to Oslo implied a role for and recognition of the PLO, but only in form and not in substance. Yet Arafat, who had presumably missed the Baker "bus," decided not to miss Clinton's train, which ultimately (and predictably) crashed.

Israel's First Test of Clinton: Mass Expulsion

The Clinton administration faced a severe test by Israel just as it was beginning its tenure in January of 1993. Three major escalations by Prime

Minister Rabin were met by open acquiescence in Washington. The expulsion of 413 Palestinians to Lebanon in December 1992 led the Clinton administration to shield Israel again from imminent U.N. Security Council sanctions. The Israeli closure of the Occupied Territories in March 1993, rendering them four isolated districts with enormous economic hardships for their Palestinian residents, failed to produce even a nudge from the self-styled arbiter supposedly concerned with "confidence-building measures." The bombardment of Lebanon in July 1993 with the declared objective of depopulating the south, which caused numerous civilian casualties and the destruction of some seventy Lebanese villages, demonstrated how confident Israel was about the passivity of the "honest broker."

Responding to criticism by right-wing members of the Knesset, and aware of public opinion polls showing that 78 percent of Israelis supported the expulsion, Prime Minister Rabin boasted on February 8, 1993, to a BBC correspondent:

> We knew we were making an unprecedented move. Which government in the past twenty years was prepared to expel or remove temporarily twenty-five, not to mention 400 people? I felt at the time a need to level an immediate, tough blow against Hamas that went beyond everything done previously. I achieved that aim, whether it involved 300 or 400.[4]

That statement hardly masked the siege mentality, which Rabin himself had asked Israelis to shed upon his assuming office only seven months earlier. "We must overcome the sense of isolation that has held us in its thrall for almost a half a century," he said in July 1992. It also reflected a grotesque sense of proportionality, whereby 400 Palestinians were summarily ejected to a makeshift mountain camp in the middle of winter in retaliation for the killing of four Israeli soldiers.

Worse yet was that during Rabin's first six months in office, the death toll among Palestinians killed by Israelis was on the increase. According to the Israeli human rights organization B'Tselem, security forces shot dead seventy-six Palestinians between August 1992 and January 1993, in contrast to sixty-three dead during the first six months of 1992. During the same period, the number of Palestinian children killed soared from six to seventeen.[5] The *Houston Chronicle* speculated about the world's reaction to a similar atrocity committed against Israelis by Palestinians:

> What would have happened if the Palestinians had held 415 Israelis hostage for over a month in a cold and barren no man's land with nothing

but tents to shelter in? What would Israel have done if the Palestinians had their hostages over holidays and said they would not be allowed to go home unless they agreed to end their occupation of Arab land? What would those in human rights circles have done from Washington to London if not one of these hostages had been given any sort of trial before being deported from their land and dumped in the cold? What would the press have said if they were submitted to intermittent showers of snow and artillery?[6]

That 1,600 Palestinian natives could quickly be rounded up, and in a few hours 413 of them blindfolded, handcuffed, and bused to the Lebanese border, without charge, trial, or any semblance of due process, is ominous enough. But the act itself represented a new dimension of Israel's expulsion policy, and was intended to set a precedent in Israel's demographic battle with the Palestinians.

Unlike the mass expulsions of 1948 and 1967, which took place under the cover of armed conflict, and unlike those of 1989 to 1990, which were executed bureaucratically on the pretext of improper residency, the December 1992 expulsion was the first mass expulsion to be carried out explicitly in the name of security. On December 16, 1992, Prime Minister Rabin, who also held the defense ministry portfolio, issued Authorization No. 97 granting military commanders in the Occupied Territories the authority to expel "inciters." Almost simultaneously, the required "legal" machinery was set up with the issuance of Military Order 1086, and the expulsion was carried out in accordance with the instant legislation. This "legislation" had amended a previous rule, which allowed those subject to expulsion orders the right of appeal to a military committee and then the Supreme Court. In fact, such appeals never succeeded; the Israeli Supreme Court had never overturned an expulsion order by the government.

Surely Yitzhak Rabin—himself a veteran of such tactics, having "removed" some 55,000 residents of Ramleh and Lydda in 1948 (a small portion of the 800,000 Palestinians who became refugees) and having served as the army chief of staff in 1967, when about 300,000 Palestinians were "removed" to Jordan—was seeking new horizons in the policy of acquiring more land and fewer people. The cumulative impact of such expulsions on the political future of the Palestinians would be devastating.

U.S. Complicity in Israel's Expulsion Policy

The expulsion of December 17, 1992, provided President Clinton with his first opportunity to embark on the road of Middle East diplomacy. Rabin wasted no time in claiming a major victory when he struck a deal with the Clinton administration on February 1, 1993. According to an agreement that Secretary of State Warren Christopher described as a "compromise," Washington said it would shield Israel from imminent sanctions in the Security Council in exchange for Israel's agreement to allow 101 of the deportees to return immediately while keeping the other 295 in exile for one year.[7] Environment Minister Yossi Sarid, who represented the supposedly dovish Meretz Party in the cabinet, confirmed U.S. support: "We are getting full backing from the United States ... [T]here is no more fear that sanctions will be imposed."[8] Sarid was simply reacting to what became common knowledge in late January 1993. According to Elaine Sciolino of the *New York Times*, "Despite the Security Council vote in favor of the immediate return of the deportees, neither Mr. Clinton, nor Mr. Christopher explicitly repeated that demand when they spoke with Mr. Rabin in separate telephone conversations last weekend, according to Israeli officials."[9]

The Clinton administration had also succeeded in blocking separate efforts by the U.N. secretary-general and by the PLO to press for some type of sanctions against Israel. After Christopher announced the agreement, saying that Israel's move should end U.N. involvement in the issue and promising that the United States "will prevent any decisions in international forums that would have operational significance against Israel," Rabin described the agreement as a "package deal" and asserted that it preserved "the principle of our ability to remove for a limited time hundreds of inciters, leaders and organizers."[10] Although the Clinton administration did not cherish being characterized as an accomplice by Rabin, no U.S. official disavowed the attribution.

Worse yet from Washington's standpoint were Rabin's leaked boasts that he was able to hoodwink the Americans. According to Agence France-Presse, Rabin boasted, "I've made a great deal with the Americans." When asked about the Palestinian's rejection of the deal, he was reported to have said: "It's no longer my problem.... Now it's Clinton's problem. He can stew in his own juices. I wanted a deal with the Americans and I've got one.... [T]he reaction of the expelled Palestinians does not interest me, it never has."[11]

Rabin's success in getting the Clinton administration to effectively acquiesce in a new dimension of Israel's expulsion policy was unprecedented. This is not to imply that the Reagan and Bush administrations have been promoters of peace and justice, but they did adhere to the principle that expulsion from Occupied Territories was illegal. The U.S. departure from this principle, which the Rabin-Christopher "compromise" of February 1 implied, explains the Israeli prime minister's glee. This first action on the Middle East by the Clinton administration reveals not only a collaborative attitude toward Israel but a deviation from international law, which was touted repeatedly in the conflict with Iraq.

During 1992, the U.S. government expressed its position on this question on at least two occasions. Voting in favor of Security Council Resolution 726 on January 6, 1992, Thomas Pickering, the U.S. ambassador to the U.N., said:

> The U.S. government believes that deportation of individuals from the Occupied Territories is a violation of Article 49 of the Geneva Convention.... Any persons charged with wrongdoing should be brought before a court of law based on the evidence and be given a fair trial, which would afford a full judicial process.[12]

As late as December 18, 1992, Secretary of State Lawrence Eagleburger reaffirmed the U.S. position, which considered expulsion a violation of the Fourth Geneva Convention of 1949. Article 49 prohibits absolutely "individual or mass forcible transfers, as well as deportations ... regardless of their motive." Human Rights Watch reminded Warren Christopher that deportations, as a form of collective punishment, are prohibited by Article 33 of the 1949 Geneva Convention (cited as a "grave breach") and are a war crime punishable under the convention in Article 147.[13] Moreover, Article 146 places specific duties on states party to the convention to suppress grave breaches by prosecuting the perpetrators. The latter requirement is significant in light of the U.S.-Israeli "compromise" of February 1, which makes the United States, a party to the convention, an accomplice in an illegal act.

Contrary to the claim made by Christopher that the Israeli offer to repatriate 101 out of 400 Palestinians was "consistent with Security Council Resolution 799," that resolution in fact made no exceptions or exemptions. The resolution did not establish new categories of permissible expulsion, partial expulsion, or temporary expulsion, as absurdly implied in that process which in Christopher's view made it "unnecessary for the matter to come before the Security Council for further action." It demanded the "immediate repatriation" of all deportees. The prohibition of deportation in international law is categorical. The departure of the Clinton administration from the requirements of international law, as well as from long-standing U.S. policy, amounted to rewarding Israel for carrying out an illegal act.

Arafat began to see that his negotiators were likely to face not only a recalcitrant Israel, but a more Israelized American policy. If the U.S. government was unwilling to enforce Resolution 799, would it ever help in the enforcement of Resolution 242? This was the crucial question he began to ponder, and which contributed to his eventual capitulation.

Paving the Way to Oslo

The real catalyst, which reinforced the ongoing secret affair in Oslo, was the crucial decision of the Clinton administration to break the impasse with so-called bridging measures—something that Bush and Baker had been reluctant to undertake. The Washington negotiations between Israel and the Palestinians, which began after the Madrid conference, failed to yield results despite eleven rounds of talks in a period of twenty-two months. Warren Christopher's proposed "Declaration of Principles" (DOP), announced June 30, 1993, contained three elements in particular that upheld the Israeli position: the implication that the West Bank and Gaza are disputed rather than occupied territory; the conspicuous absence of any reference to the exchange of land for peace or to Israeli withdrawal or even redeployment, implying that Israel has an equal right to lay claims to the land; and the U.S. requirement that the Palestinians agree, beforehand, that all matters relating to sovereignty would be outside the scope of the negotiations for the interim phase (hence discussion of Jerusalem, the still expanding settlements, and land would be deferred for several years).[14] Also, because the issues of land and the nature of authority on that land are treated separately in the U.S. paper, the focus of negotiations would be limited to authority over the people but not the territory, with the people reduced to the status of inhabitants or a minority rather than a people with national rights. This manifest departure in U.S. policy, which effectively modified the Madrid framework and the context of the

U.S. letter of assurances, was the real catalyst for the PLO-Israeli agreement of September 13, 1993.

The Oslo Accords signified a critical juncture in the Palestine-Israel conflict. For the first time in history, a Palestinian leadership endorsed a settlement that kept the Israeli occupation intact on the premise that all the outstanding issues in the conflict would be subject to negotiations during the next three to five years. The reality of the accords, however, precluded a brighter outcome in the future for several reasons:

First, there was a conspicuous shortage of principles in this "agreement to reach agreement." Contrary to the initial pronouncements of a number of U.S. journalists that "the devil is in the details," a major deficiency in fact was not the lack of details, but the desertion of principles. The text of the agreement makes no mention of the occupation, the exchange of land for peace, the inadmissibility of conquest by force, or the national rights of the Palestinian people.

Second, there was no reference whatsoever to the human rights of the Palestinians at a time when the need for guarding against abuse was more urgent than ever before. During the transitional period of "self-governance," the Palestinians would have to contend with a new Palestinian administration, in addition to the occupation regime. Dissidents who opposed the agreement would be vulnerable to abuse, especially in view of the total absence of clear and effective means of accountability, with two authorities looking over each other's shoulders.

The urgency was further accentuated by the contempt for the human rights of Palestinians already demonstrated not only by Rabin and Clinton, but also by Arafat. President Clinton had telephoned President Assad of Syria on September 15 requesting that he silence critics of the agreement.[15] The following quotation from Rabin illustrates his own disregard for human rights and preference to have Arafat do the dirty work:

> I prefer the Palestinians to cope with the problem of enforcing order in the Gaza [Strip]. The Palestinians will be better at it than we were because they will allow no appeals to the Supreme Court and will prevent the [Israeli] Association for Civil Rights from criticizing the conditions, thereby denying it access to the area. They will rule there by their own methods, freeing—and this is most important—the Israeli army soldiers from having to do what they will do.[16]

Meanwhile, the PLO chief of security, Hakam Balawi, expressing his willingness to do Rabin's bidding, told Israeli television they would crush the opposition.

In the preamble of the DOP, Israel recognized "mutual legitimate and political rights" but not the *national* rights of Palestinians or other rights enshrined in U.N. resolutions. Moreover, in the exchange of letters, Israel recognized the PLO but not the Palestinian people, and the so-called mutual recognition was asymmetrical and nonreciprocal in that the Palestinians were presumed to be the party that had done wrong, and were expected to apologize for their legal resistance to a military occupation. Nothing was said about the Israeli practices, which have been described as crimes of state in the Nuremburg sense.

Regarding the issue of withdrawal, the DOP provided for Israeli *withdrawal* from the Gaza Strip and Jericho Area, but only for *redeployment* from population centers in the West Bank. Moreover, this partial and limited withdrawal did not abolish the military government. The fact that Israel did not acknowledge its status as occupier implied that its military government had remained as the body vested with sovereignty under international law, even in Jericho and Gaza.

Prior to the signing of the DOP, Israeli chief of staff Mordechai Gur and Prime Minister Rabin expressed their interpretation of the clauses that dealt with withdrawal and redeployment. Their statements revealed no ambiguity whatsoever. Gur said: "This is redeployment not withdrawal. Anything that happens, the IDF [Israel Defense Forces] will be there."[17]

Rabin's statement on this subject was even more explicit:

> The forces of the Israeli army will be redeployed on locations determined only by us, unlike the Camp David agreements, which mandated a withdrawal of the Israeli armed forces. In the agreement we reached, we didn't consent to use the formula "withdrawal of Israeli army forces" except when it applied to the Gaza Strip. In application to all other places, the only term used is "redeployment."[18]

Third, the source of authority was clearly the occupation regime. The Palestinian Council was given legislative power, but only relating to the six areas in Article VI and in Annex II of the DOP. That excluded the Israeli settlements and the network of roads connecting these settlements with each other and with Israel proper. It also excluded Jerusalem and military locations. Article VII-5 of the DOP's "Specific Understandings and Agreements" solidified Israel's claims as final authority: "The withdrawal of the military government will not prevent Israel from exercising the powers and responsibilities not transferred to the Council." The Palestinian Council, unlike a real legislature, was allowed to exercise powers and responsibilities only in the spheres "transferred" to it by the agreement. Its powers are purely "delegated," not by the Palestinian people or their representatives, but by the occupation regime.

Moreover, the so-called self-government arrangements described in the DOP could only be altered or amended during the final status talks. Hence the Palestinians were unable to adopt their own constitution and enact their own laws, inasmuch as they were required to conform to the spirit and the letter of the DOP. Article IX insured that the Israeli military orders of the previous twenty-seven years and the relevant Jordanian laws remained in effect unless they were amended by both Israel and the Palestinian Council, thus giving Israel veto power.

That the occupation regime remained as the source of authority was reconfirmed in the subsequent agreement signed in Cairo by Israel and the PLO on May 4, 1994.[19] The Cairo Agreement, also known as "Gaza-Jericho First," enabled the PLO to set up a governing apparatus with a police force and a judiciary in Gaza and Jericho, but it did not end the occupation (despite the confusing language in Article VII-5 of the DOP: "After the inauguration of the council, the Civil Administration will be dissolved, and the Israeli military government will be withdrawn"). One of the principal authors of the DOP and the Cairo Agreement, Joel Singer, a legal adviser to the Israeli foreign ministry, addressed this mattter quite candidly. The Palestinian entity, he said, "will not be independent or sovereign in nature, but rather will be legally subordinate to the authority of the military government."[20]

The level of jubilation that greeted the Oslo and Cairo agreements in the West was truly out of place, if not bizarre. "Self-government," as the sole concern of the negotiations in the immediate term, was seen by the Palestinians as the necessary link toward independence, whereas Israel viewed it as a way to repackage the occupation under a different label. That outcome was in fact assured by the accumulated effect of U.S. Middle East policy during a period of more than twenty-five years.

From Oslo to Cairo and Beyond: The Cairo Agreements

The three Cairo agreements that followed Oslo I (February 9, April 4, and May 4, 1994) secured Palestinian acquiescence in Israeli unilateral acts taken in the course of the occupation. The agreements on the questions of jurisdiction, security, economics, and settlements, for example, offered insight into the outlook for the future, when the final status of the Occupied Territories was expected to be resolved. These agreements demonstrated that the "Gaza-Jericho First" model, under which the Palestinian Authority was set up in Gaza and the Jericho Area, was not likely to produce any improvements during the next phase. After all, there was no ambiguity about the fact that, during the interim period, the status of the Gaza Strip and the Jericho Area were going to be identical to that of the West Bank, despite the dissolution of the civil administration and the redeployment of the Israeli Army.

When the various interpretations of the DOP regarding the control of border crossing, the relative size of the Jericho Area, and the question of security were finally resolved in Cairo on February 9, 1994, Rabin felt vindicated while Arafat appeared despondent. Rabin had only to invoke Article VIII of the DOP: "Israel will continue to carry the responsibility for defending against external threats, as well as the responsibility for overall security of Israelis." The serious implication of this article was actual Israeli control of the border and symbolic Palestinian presence. The Orientalist experts of Israel's colonial departments came up with the tools: flags, guards with uniforms, immigration officials armed with ineffectual entry stamps, and even special arrangements for "VIP crossing." While Israeli officials screened all passengers crossing the Jordan River via a three-wing terminal, Palestinian officials were given a peripheral role in inspecting passengers through the Palestinian wing. Meanwhile, Israeli officers were responsible for Palestinian travelers, Israelis, and all others destined to the West Bank. Palestinian refugees wishing to return home would not be helped by so-called Palestinian immigration officers holding ineffectual entry stamps. Refugee issues were to be decided by a tripartite committee consisting of Israel, Jordan, and the PA, and all decisions were to be reached "by agreement," which gave Israel an automatic veto.

The security reasoning that Rabin used to confirm Israeli control of crossings in Cairo I was later claimed to confirm Israeli responsibility for overall security, even in Jericho and Gaza during the interim phase. This is what Cairo II had in fact resolved, and what Rabin had announced on the BBC in April 1994: "Only one party must retain overall responsibility for security. Israel will retain sole responsibility for security in Hebron … [and] throughout the Gaza Strip as well as in that area of Jericho where the Palestinian self-administration body will be established."

Consequently, the entry of the Palestinian police into Gaza and Jericho in May 1994 did not relieve Israel of that "responsibility." Rabin stated, "While there is redeployment, on the one hand, we continue to bear overall responsibility for whatever happens in the Gaza Strip."[21] He made it crystal clear that a vacuum of power would not be allowed, and therefore no Palestinian police units would be deployed until they are "thoroughly ready to undertake their responsibility to uphold law and public order." Clearly, security and public order meant, in effect, security of Israel and Israelis. The Hebron massacre in February 1994 demonstrated how lax security procedures were in relation to Palestinians. The mass killer, Dr. Baruch Goldstein, was able to enter a presumably guarded mosque with sufficient arsenal to kill and maim dozens of worshipers before he was finally subdued and killed by survivors of the massacre.

Cairo II had already closed the files of the Hebron massacre. In the absence of an impartial investigation, and given the revelations that Israeli soldiers and police are not allowed to shoot at settlers, even if the settlers are shooting at Palestinians with the intent to kill, the security provisions of Cairo II revealed how one-sided that concept was. Not only did the PA assume the role of Israel's enforcer, but it also deprived itself of enforcing security for its own constituents. Every demand that was raised by the PLO in the wake of the massacre (international protection, dismantling of Hebron settlements, and placing settlements immediately on the interim phase agenda) was dismissed as posturing.

Again, Israeli responsibility for overall security was reconfirmed in 1994 when a token force of 160 observers from Norway, Denmark, and Italy were declared a substitute for the international force requested by the Palestinians. Rabin assured his constituents that the Temporary International Presence in Hebron (TIPH) did not constitute a "force," not even "entirely an observer group," since some of them were assigned administrative duties at the Hebron municipality. This group was hemmed in by unusual constraints: it had no military or police functions; its only weapons consisted of pistols, which could be used only in self-defense; its freedom of movement was restricted by Israel; the renewal of its mandate was subject to an Israeli veto; and it was not made responsible to the U.N. secretary-general, but to the Joint Hebron Committee (JHC), consisting of two Israelis and two Palestinians.

Given Israel's long-standing policy against the admission of any international commissions or forces into the Occupied Territories, there was no reason to assume that the Hebron massacre would change that policy, particularly when it was designed to serve a strategic goal. A more gruesome massacre in Jenin in 2002 by Sharon was treated in the same way, except *all* forms of international presence were denied. From the very inception of the occupation in 1967, Israel has been able to sidetrack all actions and initiatives by the United Nations, particularly when Israel determined that they would infringe on its implicit or explicit claims of sovereignty in the Occupied Territories.

The strategy of manipulating the two-stage concept was also applied by Israel in Cairo I to establish another precedent for (and to gain PLO acquiescence in) a long-standing position on settlements. Again, playing on the concept of security in Article VIII of the DOP, Israel made a startling achievement regarding settlements in Gaza. Sixteen settlements occupying twelve square miles, which seemed dispensable to Israel during the Washington rounds, not only obtained a new lease on life, but were also provided with an additional fifteen square miles of land as a "security zone" and a measure of contiguity.

The Trappings of Statehood

Consistent with Cairo I and II, Cairo III, which was signed on May 4, 1994, was replete with make-believe elements of statehood. Just as Cairo I invented the symbolic entry stamps and token immigration officers, Cairo III invented such ornaments as "laissez-passers" in place of real passports and postal stamps issued by the "Palestinian Authority." But Yasir Arafat was made to understand categorically that his five-year-old title, "president of Palestine," would be dropped and exchanged for the earlier title "chairman of the PLO," in view of the fact that Israel had recognized the PLO and not Palestine or its people in the September 1993 exchange of letters. Later, he was allowed to use the title *ra'is* (head, president, or chief), a vague formulation.

Likewise, the Palestinian monetary authority, which was created in the Paris Protocol on April 28, 1994, was presumed to be something of a central bank, but the Palestinians were denied the right to issue their own currency. Meanwhile, the phrase "economic cooperation," which appears frequently in the DOP, was utilized by Israel to insure the continued dependency of the Palestinian economy on that of Israel. "Cooperation" was hardly the description of a relationship between an economy with a $63 billion gross domestic product (GDP) and another with a mere $2.5 billion GDP, two-thirds of which was derived at the time from work in Israel. This kind of cooperation was intended to safeguard against Palestinian economic independence and to reinforce the myriad restrictions on political independence in such a way that the area between the Jordan River and the Mediterranean could only accommodate a single nation. The peace treaty between Jordan and Israel, signed on October 27, 1994, together with the Cairo Agreement of May 4, 1993, confirmed Israel's control of external security along the Jordan River. Likewise, together with the Israeli-Egyptian Peace Treaty of 1979, the Cairo agreement confirmed Israel's control of external security along the old Palestine-Egypt border in the southwest. Thus, in return for recognition of Israel's right to exist, the Palestinians were simply allowed to live in scattered portions of the West Bank and in Gaza as residents in greater Israel but not as citizens in the future state of Palestine. This was the pattern set by the Cairo agreements, making the DOP the legal foundation for *all* subsequent agreements.

Early Empowerment: The Burden, Not the Responsibility

On August 24, 1994, Israel and the PLO signed the fourth major agreement since the signing of the DOP. It was an agreement on the Preparatory Transfer of Powers and Responsibilities in the West Bank, better known as "Early Empowerment"—not to be confused with the limited "self-rule" extended by the Cairo Agreement to Gaza and Jericho.[22] In the Gaza-Jericho transfer, Israel retained control over external security and ultimately over internal security. Under "Early Empowerment" in the West Bank, it retained total control over *all* types of security and all responsibility for public order.

Israel's de facto sovereignty was protected by numerous provisions that relegated the PA to a mere functionary apparatus, existing and operating in total legal and political subordination to the Israeli occupation regime. Any powers delegated to the PA or new responsibilities were carefully circumscribed to guard against any misinterpretation or exaggeration of the limited transfer. The spheres that were affected by this transfer were education and culture, health, social welfare, tourism, and direct taxation. With regard to legislation in the five spheres, the agreement granted the PA "secondary" authority.

The basic premises that governed the "Early Empowerment" agreement were the following:

First, continuity of the Israeli occupation. No substantive change was effected or contemplated in the status of the West Bank. Occupation law remained in force, and Israel retained an effective veto over any amendments to the existing military orders and regulations (Article VII). Unlike the situation in Gaza, where the civil administration had been dissolved, in the West Bank both the civil administration and military government remained intact and retained their security functions. To underscore the importance of these functions, Article VI-4 obligated the PA to inform the occupation regime about any "planned" large-scale public events and "mass gatherings" related to certain topics in any geographic areas. Thus, the freedom of assembly, were it to be exercised by students, welfare recipients, or disgruntled taxpayers, for example, could be suppressed by the Israeli military with open and legal PA participation. Likewise, the PA was obligated to inform the occupation authorities if any person wounded by any kind of weapon was admitted to any hospital, and to report "any death from unnatural causes" (Annex II-8). The PA was further expected to provide for the transfer of "the corpse of any deceased from unnatural causes, for an autopsy in the Institute of Forensic Medicine" located in Israel proper (Annex II-9). The head of the civil administration, General Gadi Zohar, described the agreement this way: "We are transferring the control of issues but not of territory." [23]

Second, consolidation of the apartheid system. The existence of two separate entities with separate legal standards for the indigenous population and for the Israeli settlers was not only preserved; it was legitimized with a legal framework and Palestinian approval. Moreover, that legal separation was solidified by the formalization of a hierarchy with categories, including West Bank, Gaza and Jericho Area, settlements, Jerusalem, and Israelis. The last three were totally excluded from the PA jurisdiction, while the status of the West Bank remained separate from that of Gaza

and Jericho. For example, Article VII-9 decreed that "legislation regarding the West Bank shall be published as a separate part of any publication
of legislation regarding the Gaza Strip and the Jericho Area issued by the
Palestinian Authority."

The confirmation of legal separation in the West Bank implied a system of "separate but not equal" institutions and conditions for Palestinians. Borrowing from the discourse of extraterritoriality, a relic of
European relations with the Ottoman Empire and the Manchu Dynasty
during the nineteenth century, the agreement empowered Israel to use
force as a measure for collecting land taxes from Palestinians, but prohibited the PA from using any force to collect income tax from Israelis under
its jurisdiction (Appendix B-5). Consistent with extraterritoriality and
with Menachem Begin's dictum of "autonomy for the people, not for the
land," enunciated during the 1978 Camp David talks,[24] the taxing authority was to be split between Israel and the PA, with the former continuing
to tax the entire Palestinian land within the PA's sphere, while the PA
could only collect income tax and Value Added Tax (VAT) (Article XI
and Annex V). Moreover, the agreement empowered Israel to collect income tax not only from Israelis working in the settlements, but also from
Israelis working in the West Bank, providing that the "business or service" in which they worked "accrues or derives an annual turnover ... ex-
ceeding $7,000 U.S." (Annex V-3-6). Needless to say, the PA was not
granted a corresponding privilege.

Third, the exemption of Israel from all liabilities, obligations, and
omissions with regard to acts occurring prior to the transfer: Consistent
with the unusual provisions of the Cairo Agreement of May 4, 1994, Israel was again exempted from legal responsibility for acts committed during its more than twenty-seven years of brutal occupation. Thus the
families of civilian victims of Israel's death squads and the numerous
owners of the vast tracts of land that Israel expropriated during all these
years were denied the right to redress grievances against Israel. Worse
yet, any such grievances of financial claims against Israel, were they to
arise, were required to be "referred to the Palestinian Authority" (Article
IX-1-a and b). And in the event that an award was made against Israel and
subsequently paid by Israel, the PA was obligated to "reimburse Israel the
full amount of the award" (Article IX-1-e). These provisions were tanta-

mount to a blanket amnesty granted by the victim to the perpetrator, even prior to a peace agreement.

The numerous impasses which occurred from 1993 onward were not over means but over ends, as well. Apparently, when the Palestinian negotiators initialed the DOP at Oslo, their hope was that the *spirit* of the agreement, as they conceived it, would ultimately overcome disagreements over the *letter*. It was a groundless hope, at best, which reflected a political naivete and unwarranted optimism. In reality, these agreements and their antecedents represented an attempt to normalize the occupation and to consolidate the unilateral and illegal acts undertaken by Israel in the course of the occupation. Accordingly, Oslo engendered a historically unprecedented situation of occupation by consent.

From Oslo I and Early Empowerment to Oslo II

A major stumbling block to extending the Gaza-Jericho agreement to the West Bank, as provided for in the DOP, was Israel's reluctance to jeopardize its numerous settlements there. Having scored a "legal" victory regarding the status of settlements in the Cairo agreements, as has already been described, Israel balked on further deployment without ensuring the security of these settlements, whose inhabitants already numbered at this point 150,000 in the West Bank and another 150,000 in villages adjacent to Jerusalem. The result was a new stalemate, which required a newly altered and expanded version of the DOP, known as the Interim Agreement on the West Bank and Gaza of September 24, 1995, and commonly referred to as "Oslo II." A major factor in that stalemate was Israel's insistence that Articles V and VI of the DOP made a distinction between Gaza and Jericho, where there was a requirement to "withdraw" Israeli forces, on the one hand, and the West Bank, where there was a requirement only to "redeploy" from certain areas and not from the entire area, on the other hand. A legal facade was also built upon the notion that the omission of the definite article "the" from all reference to the West Bank (using instead the phrase "West Bank") was deliberate. That formulation by the Israeli authors of the DOP was clearly intended to leave open the possibility that there would be areas of the West Bank, in addition to those connected with the permanent status issues, that would not fall under the jurisdiction of the Palestinian Council. That was also the basis for the division of the West Bank in Oslo II into three zones—A, B, and C—in which Israel and the PA had a division of functions. Accordingly, only the cities (Area A, comprising 3 percent of the total area in the West Bank) experienced a transfer of civil authority, in which Arafat's police replaced Israeli troops and a Palestinian bureaucracy inherited the Israeli "Civil Administration." In these cities, where 26 percent of the population of the Occupied Territories lived, the Palestinian Authority was granted full responsibility for internal security, public order, and civil affairs. One exception was Hebron, the only Palestinian city having an Israeli settlement in the downtown area. Hebron's status was deferred, as was the fate of about 450 villages designated as Area B, comprising 27 percent of the West Bank, and the roughly 70 percent of the West Bank comprising public land, settlements, and Israeli army camps designated as Area C. In Area B, which contained 70 percent of the Palestinian population, the council was given responsibility for maintaining public order, while Israel retained overriding security responsibility to protect the settlements. In Area C, Israel retained full responsibility for public order, security, and civil affairs related to territory (planning, zoning, archaeology, etc.).

This hierarchy of functions and responsibilities made it unlikely that the arrangements for Gaza and Jericho would be duplicated in the West Bank. Unlike "withdrawal" from Gaza and Jericho, the extent of Israeli redeployments in Areas B and C was left open-ended, but the timing was defined—eighteen months after the convening of the Palestinian Council (September 1997). That deadline, however, was impeded by disagreement over settlement building and responsibility for suicide bombings, Israel's ideological tool to insure the impasse. Meanwhile, redeployment from Area A was carried out in the winter of 1996, leaving Hebron intact. After one full year, during which Israel had failed to redeploy any troops from any section of Area B or from Hebron, while Area C remained under total Israeli control, an agreement was finally reached in January 1997.

Notes

1   The text of the Israel–PLO Draft Agreement of Palestinian Self-Rule appeared in the *New York Times*, September 14, 1993.
2   The exchange of letters between Arafat and Rabin appeared in the *New York Times*, September 1, 1993.

3   *Jerusalem Post*, January 13, 1991.
4   *Washington Post*, February 9, 1993.
5   Agence France-Presse, February 8, 1993.
6   *Houston Chronicle*, February 7, 1993.
7   *New York Times*, February 4, 1993.
8   *New York Times*, February 4, 1993.
9   *New York Times*, January 29, 1993.
10   *New York Times*, February 4, 1993.
11   Agence France-Presse, February 7, 1993.
12   Text of Security Council resolution in *Journal of Palestine Studies* 21: 3 (Spring 1992): 148.
13   Letter to Warren Christopher signed by Aryeh Neier, executive director of Human Rights Watch, and Patricia Derian, member of the board of Middle East Watch, February 4, 1993.
14   *Mideast Mirror*, July 5, 1993.
15   "Report on Lebanon," *Middle East Watch* 5 (September 7, 1993): 2.
16   *Yedioth Ahronoth*, September 7, 1993.
17   *New York Times*, September 3, 1993.
18   *New York Times*, September 3, 1993.
19   Text of the Cairo Agreement of May 4, 1994, in *Journal of Palestine Studies* 23: 4 (Summer 1994): 118–26.
20   Joel Singer, "The Declaration of Principle on Interim Self-Government Arrangement: Some Legal Aspects," *Justice* (February 1994): 6.
21   See excerpts from Rubin's speech to the Knesset on May 11, 1994, in *Journal of Palestine Studies* 24: 1 (Autumn 1994): 141–43.
22   Text of the agreement in *Journal of Palestine Studies* 24: 2 (Winter 1995): 109–26.
23   *Al-Hamishmar*, July 15, 1994.
24   Shlaim, *The Iron Wall*, pp. 363–65.

CHAPTER 7

UNRECIPROCAL RECIPROCITY

NETANYAHU'S OSLO

The defeat of Prime Minister Shimon Peres and his Labor Party in the Israeli elections in June 1996 and the ascendancy of Benjamin Netanyahu to power sent shock waves throughout the Middle East, the United States, and Western Europe. The consensus was that the "peace process" had been dealt a severe, if not fatal, blow. After all, it had been widely assumed that the diplomatic developments of the previous three years had constituted a milestone in the history of the Arab-Israeli conflict, and that more than a quarter century of U.S. diplomatic efforts had finally paid off. But Netanyahu's opposition to the Oslo Accords was a matter of public record. Peace had become so popular in Israel that Netanyahu, the opponent of the "peace" candidate, had to repeatedly pay lip service to Israel's commitment to its international agreements and to "peace."

Israel's Gains from the "Peace Process"

Israeli relations with the United States had never been closer than during the closing years of the twentieth century. Never before had Israel had such carte blanche from Washington—to confiscate Arab land, build settlements, enlarge Jerusalem, terrorize the Lebanese, pauperize Palestinians, and sustain such transgressions with U.S. taxpayer funds, U.N. Security Council vetoes, and Congressional standing ovations.

Not only had Israel been able to shed the pariah image of the previous three decades, but it had been transformed into a special state, an oracle in the field of security and "antiterrorism." Its expertise in security affairs, technology, health services, and irrigation was being sought regularly by countries in Asia, Africa, and Central Asia, most of which did not even have consular relations with Israel prior to Oslo. Even municipalities in the United States were dispatching law enforcement teams to study Israeli practices of repression. Oslo had also won Nobel prizes for Shimon Peres and Yitzhak Rabin, both of whom could have faced international tribunals for their roles in the 1996 Qana massacre in Lebanon and Israel's death squads, respectively.

The "peace process" had also been good for business, as more and more Israeli companies entered new markets in hitherto closed areas. By 1995, Israel was able to boast one of the highest GDP growth rates among Western economies: 7.1 percent per year. Its per capita GDP was on a par with Great Britain: nearly $16,000 per year, up from $3,400 twenty years earlier, placing it twentieth among two hundred countries in the world. Since 1990, the economy had grown by more than 40 percent, while unemployment had sunk below 6 percent. Israel was spending less than 10 percent of its GDP on defense, compared to 30 percent in the 1970s. Inflation had decreased from 17.6 percent in 1990 to 8.1 percent in 1996. The "peace process" opened numerous export markets for a country with a limited domestic market and whose growth could only be enhanced by expanding exports. Since 1990, Israel's exports have grown by 54 percent, to $30 billion. Foreign investments tripled in three years, and close to $4 billion in foreign investments have been attracted since the beginning of 1995.[1]

No longer willing to devote precious resources to the military at unacceptably high levels, Israel became able to assure security and regional hegemony through the utilization of advanced technology and minimal reliance on traditional repressive techniques that required foot soldiers and thus overburdened its limited human resources. One of the world's most developed economies was being created in a society that had been sustained by U.S. grants,[2] slavelike Palestinian labor, and land and water acquired mostly through conquest. This economic trend was enhanced by the deal between Israel and the Palestinian Authority. The Oslo process and the creation of the PA were therefore part of Israel's strategic planning for the twenty-first century.

Diplomatic intercourse with the Arab world was the direct result of the "historic handshake." Israel negotiated full diplomatic representation with Egypt and Jordan and quasi-diplomatic relations with more than a half dozen Arab countries, not to mention relations with numerous Islamic states for the first time since the creation of Israel. Moreover, Oslo had separated the Palestinian struggle from broader Arab-Israeli issues. Peace with Syria, for example, was no longer dependent on Israeli compliance with U.N. resolutions on Palestine. Peace with the less steadfast Arab states was not even dependent on Israeli compliance with Security Council Resolution 242 as it applied to Syria, or with Security Council Resolution 425 as it applied to Lebanon, not to mention Jerusalem, refugees, settlements, or water.

The PLO had been transformed, thanks to Oslo, from the liberation movement of the Palestinian people to Israel's warden and gendarme in the Palestinian ghettos and Bantustans of Gaza, Jenin, Jericho, Nablus, and Ramallah. The agreement, in which the division of responsibility was not territorial, enabled Arafat to assume responsibility for the maintenance of order and repression of the Palestinians so that Israel, which retained effective sovereignty, could continue to rule over the West Bank and Gaza. PLO institutions, such as the Palestine National Council (PNC), the Palestinian people's parliament-in-exile, have been used to legitimize the Zionist enterprise and its various conquests. Resistance to an illegal military occupation was reclassified as random terror, the suppression of which by Arafat's police force, now acting as Israel's enforcer and subcontractor, became an obligatory condition for continuing the talks and the meager U.S. subsidy provided to the PA. This new reality came alive in the famous April 1996 amendments to the Palestinian National Covenant by the PNC at a special session held in Gaza at the request of Israel and the United States. These amendments removed and modified articles in the historic Covenant, which rejected Israel as a Zionist exclusivist state and called for the liberation of Palestinian territory.

Overall, "peace" for Israel came to mean prosperity, prominence, hegemony, normalization, and the effective fragmentation of Palestinian society, thus retarding its struggle for independence and statehood. If Israel had never had it so good, why would Netanyahu then kill the goose that laid the golden egg? His campaign rhetoric and post-campaign statements were designed to extract from the "peace process" bigger and better dividends by exploiting the spate of suicide bombings in early 1996 and by blackmailing Palestinian leader Yasir Arafat. As for the United States, Netanyahu knew beforehand that Clinton's opposition to his candidacy did not constitute an opposition to his policies. Recent history showed that the Clinton administration was a follower rather than a leader in the Middle East. Even if the administration were to stand up for its guardianship rights over the "peace process," an unlikely venture, Israel's domestic proxies and tributaries in the United States, who were then (and are even more so now) entrenched in key Congressional committees, had the means not only to render the attempt superfluous, but to make it a lesson in the breach of faith, especially during an election year.

Netanyahu's "New Framework"

How was Netanyahu, then, to reshape this "peace process," and what did he intend to achieve? Were his goals or only his means different from those of Peres? An analysis of his post-campaign speeches, interviews, and statements by key advisers shortly after the elections reveals that there was a plan of action already in place. Contrary to what U.S. officials were telling Arab leaders, the new Israeli government did not need time to transform the campaign rhetoric to real policy. Although Netanyahu was not known as a particularly rigorous or systematic policy maker, his government did have a fairly detailed statement of policy guidelines.

Washington's plea for prudence on the part of Arab leaders, and Mubarak's initial assurances that the real Netanyahu was yet to emerge, either reflected calculated political strategies or extreme political naivete. Netanyahu's campaign promises were, in fact, meant to be translated into public policy, a framework for which had already been delineated. Netanyahu's policy reflected three dominant themes relating to Israeli security interests, Palestinian concerns, and the nature of peace.

Israel's Security Interests

Israel's overall interest was defined as security, itself described by Netanyahu as one of the pillars of peace. Security had three main aspects: first, a strategic dimension, based on the principle that Israel must be in a position to guarantee its own security with its own forces stationed along the Jordan River, the Golan Heights, and the Rafah border. In this scenario, while Arafat's police apparatus has a crucial role to play in guarding Israel's security, Israeli forces must remain forever in a position to exercise all options, including hot pursuit into the so-called autonomous zones (still official policy today). The "external security" clause in Oslo I, which was a bone of contention between Rabin and Arafat in late 1993, was meant to insure that all points of entry and exit, a matter of sovereignty, were firmly in Israel's hand, with the Palestinian Authority performing only a window-dressing role.

For Netanyahu, "external security" and "demographic security" were integral. Control of the former was a necessary condition for ensuring the latter, argues Dore Gold, the American academic (described as Netanyahu's Kissinger) who serves as Prime Minister Sharon's top adviser, since the Palestinians should not be in a position to change the demographic balance of "Judea and Samaria" (Israel's name for the West Bank).[3] Ironically, Gold, who immigrated to Israel from Connecticut and acquired citizenship under the "Law of Return," considers the return of indigenous Palestinian refugees, a right protected by international law, untenable. For him, a Jewish majority is synonymous with demographic security, and both would be guaranteed by precluding a sovereign role for the Palestinians on the borders. Hence a Palestinian state, which would have its own immigration policy, is impermissible.

The three other dimensions of security—settlements, water, and "greater Jerusalem"—were, likewise, effectively, nonnegotiable. The "Guidelines of the Government of Israel," published on June 17, 1996, conferred a permanent status on the Jewish settlements in the West Bank, Gaza, and the Golan Heights similar to those in Israel proper (the Galilee and the Negev), all of which then were considered of "national importance to Israel's defense and an expression of Zionist fulfillment."[4] Placing all settlements, whether in Arab territory occupied in 1948 or in 1967, in the same category was an ominous signal that the distinction between Israel proper (1948) and occupied territory (1967) had been rendered irrelevant. Jewish settling in what was seen as the "land of Israel"—that is, mandated Palestine—was regarded as part of the free movement of persons and goods.

According to Gold's interview with *Yedioth Ahronoth* on June 4, 1996, and to the "Guidelines" of Netanyahu's government, water supplies from the Golan Heights and from "Judea and Samaria" were also vital to state security and must therefore remain under Israeli control.[5] Israel's well-known and long-standing policy on the status of Jerusalem, which stood at variance with international law and the will of the international community, was reaffirmed by Netanyahu, to a resounding ovation by the U.S. Congress, in a joint session on July 10, 1996.[6]

Israel's concept of security rendered the whole phenomenon of final status negotiations, considered as the litmus test of Arafat's gamble, totally superfluous. The issues of borders, sovereignty, water, settlements, and Jerusalem had already been determined by the requirements of "strategic and demographic security," as well as by Biblical imperatives.

Palestinian Concerns

Palestinian "concerns" could only be met insofar as Israel's security permitted. Gold had resurrected a phrase used by Netanyahu when he was deputy foreign minister in Shamir's government in 1990: "maximum autonomy" for the Palestinians with Israel maintaining "maximum security" for itself. That maximum autonomy, however, did not stop the enlargement of Jewish settlements. It did not insure withdrawal from Hebron, and did not grant the Palestinians territorial contiguity within a decent portion of the West Bank.

The Nature of Peace

Netanyahu's "real peace," as articulated before the U.S. Congress, at the National Press Club, and on CNN's "Larry King Live" show, was presumed to rest on two other pillars besides security. These were "reciprocity" and "democracy," both of which were considered to be lacking on the Arab side. The Palestinian Authority was seen as lax in adhering to the terms of the Oslo agreements and as nonreciprocal in its dealings with Israel. Reciprocity, as defined by Netanyahu, would require Arafat to dismantle Hamas, keep the intelligence network of Jibril Rajoub (Arafat's head of Preventive Security) out of greater Jerusalem, keep the PA out of Jerusalem's school curricula and zoning regulations, and stop using Orient House as a virtual Palestinian embassy where international visitors were received by Palestinian officials.[7] These are some of the "violations" invoked by Netanyahu as unacceptable *fait accompli* and inconsistent with his criterion of reciprocity. The reciprocity charade took center stage in Netanyahu's verbal strategy during his various public appearances in the United States in July and October 1996. What that really meant was that despite a diplomatic facade, Oslo would remain effectively on hold until the PA adhered "fully" to what Netanyahu and his U.S. congressional supporters designated as "compliance requirements." The list was so broad that it was almost impossible not to find some justification for cutting the Palestinian Authority's subsidy.

As an example of informal coordination between segments of Congress and Netanyahu's government, the Subcommittee on International Operations and Human Rights of the House International Relations Committee decided to hold hearings on the Palestinian Authority record of human rights on July 23, 1996, ostensibly due to the broad international opposition to its imprisonment and ill-treatment of Dr. Eyad Sarraj, the commissioner-general of the Independent Palestinian Commission for Citizens' Rights. The barely hidden agenda of the hearing was to accentuate the PA's presumed lack of "compliance" with Oslo.

Democracy and Human Rights

Netanyahu's third pillar of "real peace" was democracy and human rights, a mere public relations ploy designed to achieve two objectives. The first was to enable Israel to delay and obstruct Palestinian autonomy in pursuit of yet more concessions from the Arabs. In his July 1996 address to the joint session of the U.S Congress, Netanyahu lectured on the relationship between democracy and aggression, saying that democracies, of which there was only one in the Middle East, do not initiate aggression. The implication was that, while a serious move toward "real peace" must not necessarily await the transition of the Arab world to democracy, Israel, the "sole democracy," which does not initiate aggression, must not be rushed and cajoled into peace with the Palestinians, Syrians, and Lebanese as if they were normal partners. The Palestinian Authority and Syria would have to "dismantle" Hamas and Hizbollah, but that would not bring about the dismantlement of Israel's occupations. For as long as the occupier was presumed to be a democracy, military occupations would not constitute aggression, a rather strange logic.

Netanyahu's second objective was to capitalize on the antiterrorist mood that gripped the U.S. in the wake of the bombings in Dhahran and Atlanta, and after the crash of TWA Flight 800 (much as it has today in the wake of the attacks of September 11, 2001). His U.S. listeners were treated to expert advice from the quintessential victim and conqueror of terrorism. He spoke of a broad front of terror that included the usual suspects: Iran, Syria, and Libya, all considered tyrannical and lethal. The United States should lead a movement to stop the "nuclearization of terrorist states," he said, drawing analogies with U.S. deterrence of Soviet power during the Cold War, except now he urged Congress to consider "immediate and effective prevention" rather than "deterrence."[8] The fact that Israel is the only nuclear power in the Middle East, and the only one which does not adhere to international inspection, did not seem to embarrass Netanyahu.

Reassessment in Action: The Real Strategy

The indiscriminate shooting at Palestinians demonstrating against the Netanyahu government's decision in September 1996 to open an archaeological tunnel through part of the Muslim quarter of Jerusalem threatened to destroy whatever remained of an ailing peace process. The sight of Israeli tanks and U.S.-supplied Apache and Cobra helicopter gunships utilized in the suppression of demonstrations, causing more than seventy deaths and many injuries in but four days, threatened to serve as an indictment of both the peace sponsor and the peace partner, and to reverse whatever perceived progress had been made under the Labor government.[9] In fact, the broad criticism directed against Netanyahu had less to do with human rights and more to do with the potential effect of his intransigence on politics and economics in the Middle East. Netanyahu was simply seen as being bad for business.

The Waqf did not consent to the September 23 opening of the tunnel by Netanyahu's soldiers beneath the steps of a medieval Muslim School (Al- Umariyeh) located on the Via Dolorosa, one of the principal streets in the Old City. Not only was that an illegal act, but it was also an overt attempt to alter the historical and cultural character of the city unilaterally. For the Palestinians, it was a violation of the letter and spirit of the Oslo agreements, which designated Jerusalem as an issue in the final status negotiations, not to mention the international law of belligerent occupation, which requires an occupying power to refrain from making fundamental changes in occupied territories. It was also an overt challenge to Palestinian national claims and an illegal assertion of Israeli sovereignty over East Jerusalem.

That move by Netanyahu and the Likudist mayor of Jerusalem, Ehud Olmert, came in the midst of increased tension in the West Bank and particularly in and around Jerusalem caused by the expropriation of more Arab land for bypass roads serving the Jewish settlements. The failure to

redeploy Israeli troops from Hebron, scheduled for March 1996, and to release political prisoners—coupled with Israel's demolition of Palestinian
homes and an economic blockade which was estimated to cost the Palestinian economy about $7 million per day—helped fuel the tensions that
erupted at the opening of the tunnel.[10]

Almost immediately, the Netanyahu government accused Arafat of
fomenting the violence. The director of Israel's press office said, "We're
not going to give Arafat any opportunity to say that he has achieved diplomatic gains through the use of violence, because the next time he is unhappy he will turn the screws and that is unacceptable."[11] In full accord
with that view, Netanayhu went to Washington for a meeting with Arafat
and Clinton and returned without ever making a single concession. Undoubtedly, he felt vindicated, believing that Clinton offered him continued assurances of carte blanche. He told the press he would go back and
engage in "nonstop negotiations," which was consistent with his belief that
negotiations, per se, were meant to insure the perpetuation of the status quo,
exemption from compliance, and denial of Palestinian sovereignty.

But Netanyahu's verbal strategy was beginning to wear thinner in the
aftermath of the tunnel issue. His government, which was primarily ac-
countable to a domestic constituency of fundamentalist Jews, the settler
movement, and hawkish generals and politicians, was effectively trying
to renegotiate Oslo II, on Hebron and other issues, rather than implement
its provisions. Even the implementation of Oslo II would have fallen short
of the requirements of a durable and credible peace: occupation law
would still be the supreme law of the land, and the PA-controlled areas
would still be a collection of fragmented dots on the West Bank map, surrounded by thriving Israeli settlements connected to each other and to Israel proper through an infrastructure of bypass roads constructed on
Palestinian land.

The U.S. role, which was previously defined by Bush and Baker as
"catalyst for peace," had been scaled down by Clinton to mere "facilitator."
This was the capacity in which Arafat and Netanyahu were summoned to
the White House on October 1, 1996. The achievement of that summit
was an announcement that the parties would go home and engage in
around-the-clock negotiations. While Clinton did not have to expend political capital, Netanyahu went back with his tunnel decision intact, while
Arafat, whose empty threat to make an abrupt departure was rather typical,

returned empty-handed to a bereaved and captive community laboring under a crippling economic siege. Netanyahu's tough posture appeared vindicated given the absence of a framework, a timetable, or any commitment except for more talks.

Why a Hebron Agreement?

It is worth recalling that Prime Minister Shimon Peres had used the spate of suicide bombings during winter 1996 as a pretext to delay redeployment as required by Oslo II. After that, Netanyahu began his rule in June 1996 with widely known reservations about the whole "peace process" and a declared intent to renegotiate the agreement in line with his campaign slogan—"peace with security," a euphemism for sweeping annexation. With the Hebron agreement signed on January 16, 1997, the die was cast.[12] The incremental pattern of this rather unique conflict resolution had already been set. What was different, however, between the Hebron impasse, which produced a sort of Oslo III, and the previous impasse, which had produced Oslo II, was that "Oslo III" derived largely from Likud's antipathy to the whole Oslo process. Netanyahu was simply opposed to establishing a timetable for troop redeployment from rural areas (Area B) of the West Bank. Under Oslo II, a three-stage redeployment was to have taken place between March 1996 and September 1997. When pressed for a deadline for completion of that redeployment, Netanyahu offered the end of 1999. King Hussein and Dennis Ross (Clinton's special envoy and former right-hand man for James Baker), however, persuaded him to change this date to mid-1998, which still gave him a year beyond the agreed deadline. In that respect, the only concession that Netanyahu made was to scale down his unilaterally expanding demands, which exceeded agreed upon arrangements.

In return, Arafat agreed to yet another list of new concessions, some of which inflicted major damage to a position already battered by Oslo I and Oslo II. Netanyahu told the Israeli parliament, the Knesset, on January 16, 1997, that the Hebron agreement was a vast improvement over Oslo II. Two components of Israel's negotiating strategy (security and reciprocity) received yet broader construction, bringing the Oslo process even closer to the Israeli position.

Security as a Determinant of Redeployment

Netanyahu's triumph in the Hebron agreement was largely related to Arafat's acquiescence in the U.S. decision to cede to Israel, in writing, the right to determine the extent of territory and number of forces that would be affected by the required redeployment in Area B during the interim phase. That was made clear by Secretary of State Warren Christopher, who stipulated that Israel itself would determine the extent of redeployment in order to protect its own security. Thus, Israel was no longer committed to withdrawing troops from occupied Arab territories as called for by U.N. Resolution 242. Warren Christopher's letter of assurance to Netanyahu truly was a landmark in the rapidly changing U.S. policy under Clinton. Christopher, who talked tough to Arafat (according to his own revelations in an interview with *USA Today* on Januray 17, 1997), threatening that he would recall Dennis Ross unless Arafat accepted the U.S. proposals, assured Netanyahu that Arafat had been advised of what U.S. policy really was.[13] Christopher's position impressed and stressed was summarized rather aptly by a proud member of the Israeli cabinet, Natan Sharansky: "[T]he nature of future deployment—three are due by mid-1998—is to be determined by the government of Israel, and will not be subject to negotiations with the Palestinians."[14] No less proud than Sharansky was the conservative *New York Times* columnist A.M. Rosenthal, who issued his own reminder: Netanyahu could not have agreed to the mid-1998 deadline "unless it was made clear that Israel would designate 'military locations' it would not give up."[15] This major gain for Israel was codified in Christopher's Letter of Assurance, in which, in his own words, he "advised Chairman Arafat of U.S. views on Israel's process of redeploying its forces, designating specific military locations." What had Arafat been advised of by Christopher prior to his signing the Hebron agreement? These main points are spelled out in an Israeli public document, accessible through the Israeli foreign ministry's website. It is entitled "Further Redeployment," dated January 19, 1997. The relevant portions read as follows:

> [T]he further redeployment process will take place in territory of West Bank (but not necessarily all the West Bank) and that, in those areas in which it will take place, it will not include settlements, military locations and borders, nor those areas required for the implementation by Israel of its overall responsibility for Israelis and borders. The extent and

location of these areas is to be determined by Israel in the light of its security concerns.[16]

The Israeli position and Christopher's acceptance of it were also confirmed in Oslo II, which provided that Israeli military forces would redeploy to "specified military locations." These locations were not defined in the agreement, but were to be defined by Israel. This understanding was confirmed by Warren Christopher in his letter to Netanyahu in which he wrote of Israel's process of redeploying its forces and "designating specified military locations."[17] The Clinton administration had effectively enunciated a new policy, which considered Israel's territorial needs and security requirements as intertwined, and their relationship as determined by Israel. It had thus endowed Israel with the express power to redeploy in accordance with its security requirements as it "identifies" them itself during the interim phase, rather than according to its DOP obligation, let alone U.N. resolutions.[18]

"Reciprocity" as a Determinant of Redeployment

The second major gain for Israel in the Hebron agreement is what the U.S. "Note for the Record" refers to as "reciprocity," a term introduced into the lexicon of Mideast diplomacy by Netanyahu.[19] After he assumed power in June 1996, Netanyahu continued to accuse Arafat of failing to live up to his commitments, thus justifying his own refusal to implement the terms of an agreement that he had explicitly opposed. Whatever Netanyahu pledged to do would be contingent on Arafat's fulfillment of Israel's expanding list of requirements, as determined by Israel. Indeed, the reciprocity clause in the Hebron agreement had a brand new list of "Palestinian responsibilities" that would have to be met before Israel could be expected to fulfill its open-ended obligations: the Palestinian National Covenant would have to be disavowed; all resistance activities ranging from terror to political commentary (euphemistically described as "incitement and hostile propaganda") must be stopped and any suspected violators must be apprehended, prosecuted, or transferred to Israel; the size of the Palestinian police force must be trimmed; and the Orient House in East Jerusalem could not be used as a quasi-foreign office for the PA. This alleged reciprocity was applied to Jerusalem in one way, as it did not enjoin Israel from changing the geographic and demographic character of the city and its environs. In fact, after the Hebron signing and on the eve of his February 1997 visit to Washington, the prime minister reiterated his determination to build settlements around Jerusalem in a speech to a right-wing coalition of Knesset members: "Israel is acting as the sovereign authority in Jerusalem, and according to its understanding, and does not require the permission of any outside body for construction, development and road paving there; and there is no link or connection to any negotiations on other issues."[20]

Diplomatic Paralysis: 1997

No sooner had the Hebron "classifications" been made and signed than new diplomatic trouble emerged. Two incidents in particular had ignited new crises, creating a diplomatic paralysis during most of 1997. First, Israel announced plans in March to construct a new settlement on the site of Jabal-Abu Ghunaym (known as Har Homa in Israel), south of East Jerusalem. Second, two suicide bombings occurred in West Jerusalem on July 30 and September 4. Palestinian suspension of the talks was followed by Israeli suspension. The major issue on the Palestinian side was the settlements. The major issues on the Israeli side were "security" and the PA's "obligation" to meet its stated commitments. Madeleine Albright, the new secretary of state, commanded the two parties to stop taking actions that antagonized each other and to come to terms with the issues that faced them. Otherwise, she did not wish to waste her time by "treading water."[21]

The only tangible result to emerge from Albright's much publicized trip was an agreement by the PA and Israel to have their representatives meet with her while attending the U.N. General Assembly meetings in New York. Her call, however, for a time-out from unilateral actions was repudiated by Netanyahu, who pledged to build more settlements on the thirtieth anniversary of the Efrat settlement, on September 26, 1997. But behind Israel's conditions regarding security and reciprocity and Arafat's issues of the settlements, prisoners, the Gaza airport, and safe passage, there stood a bigger and more substantive issue: the lack of difference between Likud and Labor on the final outcome, which precluded Palestinian sovereignty in any portion of historic Palestine. In actuality, the conventional wisdom that Netanyahu had derailed Rabin's peace train stood in contradiction with the realities of Israeli politics. For example, the concept of limited autonomy, adopted by the Knesset in 1977 and dubbed the Begin Plan, was the centerpiece of Likud's Camp David. It also became the essence of Labor's Oslo agreements, and together they seem to be promoting the ongoing atomization of the West Bank. Meanwhile, Labor's Allon Plan, based on the classical Zionist doctrine of "separation," was not far apart from the various schemes by Likudist leaders such as Menachem Begin and Ariel Sharon, which had seemingly promoted a "mixture of population," rather than strict separation.[22]

Slicing both the West Bank and Gaza into three separate zones was in fact Labor's solution to Likud's earlier dilemma: how to insure that its absorption of the Occupied Territories (which contrasted with Labor's formula of separation) did not lead to a binational state, in which Arabs and Jews would coexist in equality. Now, the Arab population lives in subordinated enclaves within a Jewish state. Oslo II provided Israel with the land without the people, thus meeting Labor's requirement of ethnic purity and separation, in conformity with classical Zionism, and at the same time, accommodating Likud's proclivity for penetration deep into Arab population centers. At last, Labor's presumed "territorial settlement" and Likud's "functional settlement" were reconciled (though on terms which favored Likud's model of unequal "population mixture"). The increased decoupling of Gaza from the West Bank and the corresponding easier communication between the West Bank and Jordan suggested at that time a possible Israeli convergence toward the early 1970s formula advanced by Moshe Dayan, known as "functional compromise." According to that formula, Israel would maintain sovereignty over the West Bank, while the Palestinians would   administer their internal affairs under Jordanian control. Netanyahu's policies, therefore, did not repudiate his predecessors' "peace," but only the process. Whereas Rabin and Peres succeeded in enlisting their adversary's meaningful participation in the new governance structure, Netanyahu, who had to cater to the ideological right-wing and the fundamentalist sector, was less sensitive to Arafat's lust for the trappings of statehood.

The revelations by Yossi Beilin, the deputy foreign minister in the Labor government, about a Palestinian state, with its capital in the village of Abu-Dis, were a case in point.[23] Labor was willing to allow Arafat to take home something he could call a state. The fact that the settlements and Area C (70 percent of the West Bank) would firmly negate statehood was simply overlooked. Netanyahu, on the other hand, was unwilling to accommodate even the diplomatic ambiguities necessary to give Arafat the illusion of self-determination.

Netanyahu's Oslo: The Wye River Venue

Like all its predecessors since the first Oslo agreement, the Wye River Memorandum, signed at an official ceremony at the White House on October 23, 1998, was vintage Israeli maneuvering, conceived and structured to serve Israeli interests. It surpassed all of its predecessors, however, in two respects. First, it held the Palestinian Authority to a set of rigorous "security" commitments that—if carried out in full—would render decades of Palestinian struggle for liberation a mere exercise in random violence. Second, it committed the United States to pay for settlement-related projects—heretofore considered by Washington as a "complicating factor" in the "peace process" and previously seen as "obstacles to peace" and even "illegal." In addition, there was an understanding, beyond the formal agreement, which committed the United States to enhance "Israel's defensive and deterrent capabilities" and to upgrade strategic alliance between the two countries.[24] For Prime Minister Benjamin Netanyahu, the Wye Memorandum bridged the gap between his well-known public opposition to the Oslo process and Rabin's embrace of it. At the Wye Plantation in rural Maryland, the 1993 DOP was sufficiently adapted to Netanyahu's wishes that he could publicly refer to Arafat as "my partner" and, at the same time, boast to his constituents, as well as to his critics, upon his return from Washington: "We plugged many of the holes in the Swiss cheese of Oslo."[25]

Wye River was, in fact, Netanyahu's own Oslo. His nemesis, Leah Rabin, the slain prime minister's widow, expressed vindication: "This is a full recognition of Yitzhak's path.... Greater Israel was buried in this agreement, and the formula of land for peace has been accepted by all."[26] It was a far cry from her earlier comment, in which she said that Netanyahu's charged rhetoric had created the climate that inspired her husband's assassination. Ironically, her remarks were echoed by Arafat's close aide Al-Tayeb Abdel-Rahim, who said, "The agreement symbolizes the final downfall of Zionist ideology, which views the West Bank as part of historical Biblical Israel."[27]

A substantive conflict over Oslo between Netanyahu and Rabin had never existed in reality. The real differences between them lay in the price that each one would exact from Arafat for further redeployment, and for the trappings of statehood. In reality, the Wye Memorandum was no more than a long-overdue mechanism to implement a transient aspect of a five-year interim phase. At the broader level, it deepened the damage wrought on Palestinian rights by Oslo I and II by trying to criminalize all forms of opposition to these agreements. It demanded of the Palestinians an effective renunciation of a part of their history and a virtual apology for more than a half century of struggle for national liberation. Furthermore, it put them on notice that any form of resistance was now punishable under CIA supervision. This, indeed, was the price set by Netanyahu for redeployment from a small percentage of West Bank land, despite the fact that Israel had failed to make three required redeployments between the spring of 1997 and mid-1998.

The redeployments that were to have been completed by mid-1998 were to take place in three installments totaling 13 percent during the second week, between the second and sixth week, and between the sixth and twelfth week. Every single redeployment was contingent on PA compliance with specific "security" and "reciprocity" requirements, subject to CIA verification. Thus, the first redeployment of a mere 2 percent from C to B and a change of status from B to A, affecting 7.1 percent, was to take effect only after a Palestinian "security work plan," shared with the United States, had been accepted by bilateral and trilateral security committees and implemented by the PA. In addition, that redeployment was also pegged to a reaffirmation by the PLO Executive Committee and Central Council of Arafat's letter of January 22, 1998, to President Clinton concerning the nullification of certain provisions of the PLO National Covenant (specifically Section 11-C-2). That redeployment had, in fact, taken place on November 19, 1998, after much procrastination by Netanyahu and his cabinet, which attempted to add new conditions to the Wye deal. For example, the renunciation of the Palestinian Covenant would have to emerge from a formal meeting of the more than 600 members of the Palestine National Council in which a majority vote would be reached. The PA did meet two requirements for the first redeployment on November 19: It issued a police order prohibiting the possession, importation, and manufacturing of arms, and set a deadline for turning illegal weapons in to the authorities. Secondly, it issued a decree outlawing "incitement against brotherly or foreign states to which the PLO is a signatory."

The second redeployment of 5 percent from Area C to B was linked to the renunciation of the Covenant by a meeting of the PNC, the Central Council, the PLO Executive Committee, the PA cabinet, and the "Legislative" Council, combined, as well as to weapons collections by the PA and the completion of "anti-incitement" measures. The third redeployment would transfer 1 percent from Area C to A and 5 percent from C to B. It would also reclassify 7 percent of Area B, under joint control, as being in Area A, following additional compliance by the PA in the area of "security."

Perhaps one of the most humiliating aspects of this agreement for the Palestinians was the scarcely veiled incongruity of the security needs and "security actions" described in Section II of the Memorandum. There was no uncertainty, however, about who must take the "security actions." Section II-A enumerates a long list of exclusively Palestinian obligations. Apparently, Netanyahu's concept of reciprocity was a euphemism for blackmail: partial autonomy in a small portion of a small section of Palestine, which was conquered in 1967, in exchange for Palestinian obligation to disavow all forms of resistance and to outlaw opposition to this process of dispossession.

The Palestinians, in other words, must atone, reform, and prove their innocence in order to restore partial control over 12 percent and direct control over 1 percent of the West Bank, itself 22 percent of historic Palestine.

Human Rights

Admittedly, the performance of these obligations was bound to involve the violation of fundamental human rights. And yet, a token human rights clause required the Palestinian police to perform these obligations with "due regard to internationally accepted norms of human rights and the rule of law." That was clearly an oxymoron because the "security actions" detailed in the Memorandum constituted repression, censorship, and denial of basic freedoms, such as freedom of association and of the press, among others. These actions required a work plan to be developed by the PA and shared with the U.S. based on "zero tolerance for terror." In addition, the PA was expected to apprehend specific individuals on Israel's wanted list (a list of Palestinian activists who resist the occupation, considered by Israel to be common criminals) and to transfer them to Israel (but not "extradite" them, due to the connotation of sovereignty associ-

ated with that term). The PA's decree against incitement, required by the
Wye Memorandum, was delivered to the Israelis as Order No. 3: "Emphasizing National Unity and Preventing Incitement." Not only was there no
definition of the term "incitement," but there was also no distinction between incitement and legitimate political dissent. The decree cites as pre-
cedents a repressive British Mandate law of 1936 and a Jordanian law of
1960. In pursuance of eliminating "incitement," the PA was required to participate in a trilateral committee (with the U.S. and Israel) whose members
included "specialists" in media, education, and law enforcement areas.

Even prior to the signing and ratification of this agreement by the appropriate Palestinian bodies, Arafat's police conducted an arrest campaign against Islamic opposition in the West Bank. On October 23, 1998,
two days prior to the signing, eleven journalists were arrested in Gaza by
the PA Criminal Investigation Department.[28] Moreover, a leading cleric
and president of the Sharia Court of Appeals, Sheikh Hamed Al-Bitawi,
was detained by the Palestinian Security Services after he criticized the
Wye Agreement.

The overzealous demeanor of the PA security apparatus was in no in-
stance better displayed than when Military Intelligence attacked the Fateh
District Offices (maintained by young activists loyal to Arafat but not en-
amored by Oslo's security entanglements) in Ramallah on October 23,
1998, in order to arrest suspects named in the Israeli "transfer" list. During the melee, a sixteen-year-old Fateh activist was killed.

Given the PA's poor record on human rights, it seemed plausible that
its "security" commitments under the Wye agreement would encourage it
to violate these rights even more. After all, Israel's further redeployments
were linked to these obligations. Moreover, Israel itself had shown little
regard, if any, for the human rights of the Palestinian people under occupation. For example, torture, which has routinely been used as an interro-
gation tool in Israel's prisons, was, in fact, allowed by its High Court of
Justice. That court described the practice euphemistically as "moderate"
or "enhanced physical pressure."[29] Moreover, what Amnesty International describes as "extra-judicial execution" is another practice carried
out by Israel's death squads also known as Special Forces.[30] According to
the Palestinian nongovernmental organization LAW (The Palestinian Society for the Protection of Human Rights and the Environment), there
were 285 such killings in the Occupied Territories in the period from Jan-

uary 1994 to September 1998.[31] Most of the victims were dissidents who would qualify as "inciters to violence" under the Wye rules.

The CIA, as the third party to the Wye implementation process, was no more respectful of human rights, which is not surprising given its record in Honduras, Guatemala, Chile, and elsewhere. Under the Wye rules, the CIA, through bilateral and trilateral watchdog committees with the PA and Israel, was expected to act as an umpire, verifying that the PA was in fact engaged in arresting, holding trials, collecting arms, criminalizing incitement (political dissent), and acting in good faith to carry out its Wye obligations. The PA's head of Preventive Security, Jibril Rajoub, welcomed the CIA as "a needed witness to balance Israel's claims of noncompliance by the Palestinians."[32] Hosam Khader, a representative in the Palestinian Council from Balata refugee camp, showed a much more prescient understanding of this relationship when he said, "I am afraid our entire security apparatus will become an extraterritorial department of the CIA."[33]

Although incitement was treated with a semblance of symmetry in the Wye Memorandum, it surely was not expected that the PA would be able (assuming it was willing) to hold Israel responsible for acts of incitement against Arabs inside Israel and in the Occupied Territories by settler organizations and the right-wing entrenched in Netanyahu's cabinet. According to Meron Benvinisti, a former Israeli deputy-mayor of Jerusalem and an authority on the West Bank, on the eve of Netanyahu's departure to the Wye meeting, the "media in Israel launched a wave of incitement that was fed and stage managed by official spokespersons."[34] The issue was a series of fires that hit Israel, which were attributed by the head of the Jewish National Fund, among other officials, to "terrorists," a code word in Israel for Arabs. In that regard, Benvinisti wrote:

> Didn't we learn in school that the Arabs were responsible for defoliating the Jewish landscape, that they neglected it for centuries, and that it was only when the Jewish people returned to its homeland, that the landscapes were restored, the swamps dried and the hills covered with forests. The children of the desert are continuing their tradition of destruction, and people who burn down trees obviously do not deserve a homeland.[35]

The asymmetrical nature of the agreement was further demonstrated with regard to the policy of possession, manufacture, or importing of weapons. Settlers routinely don automatic weapons issued to them by the government, and they do not hesitate to use them against unarmed Palestinians. Israel's record of arresting and punishing "individuals suspected of abetting or perpetrating acts of violence and terror" (II-A-1-e) in the Occupied Territories leaves much to be desired. After an initial arrest of an Israeli killer, bail is easily arranged, a quiet release is effected, and the case is usually forgotten.

Wye as Seen by Its Architects

The Wye agreement was the most unreciprocal of the Oslo Accords and its derivatives. Yet, Clinton declared it as "good for Israel's security," and good for the political and economic well-being of the Palestinians.[36] Netanyahu declared the day of signing as "a day when Israel and our entire region are more secure."[37] Arafat declared it a significant step toward the realization of "an independent nation having a lot of democracy" and of "the Palestinian dream of geographic unification" between the West Bank and Gaza, in addition to the promise of security, "particularly for the Israeli people."[38] Netanyahu accurately identified the emphasis which the Wye agreement gave to Israel's security:

> We are more secure today because, for the first time since the signing of the Oslo Accords, we will see concrete and verifiable commitments carried out. Our Palestinian partners will join us in fighting terrorism. They will follow a detailed and systematic plan to fight terrorists and their infrastructure; to jail killers that have so far roamed at large; to stop vitriolic incitement; and above all, finally, after thirty-five years, to cancel the articles in the Palestinian Charter which call for the destruction of Israel.[39]

Netanyahu's concern for Israel's security was also expressed by President Clinton, who emphasized Palestinian willingness to accommodate that concern: "The commitments made by the Palestinians were very strong, as strong as any we have ever seen. They include continuous security cooperation with Israel and a comprehensive plan against terrorism and its support infrastructure."[40]

What was really chilling about the signing ceremony was the underlying assumption that peace had been hindered by Palestinian violence. Clinton thanked Arafat for "turning away from violence toward peace." Arafat responded, unwittingly, by pledging to "never go back to violence and confrontation." It was almost a replay of his useless renunciation of terrorism, performed on December 14, 1988, as Reagan's price for a "substantive dialogue with the PLO," which turned out to be a farce.[41]

Sounding oblivious to the horrendous Israeli infringements on Palestinian security, Arafat directed the following remarks to the Israeli people:

> I will do everything I can so that no Israeli mother will be worried if her son or daughter is late coming home, or any Israeli would be afraid when they heard an explosion. It is true that nobody can secure 100 percent results of security for all Palestinians and all Israelis.[42]

Netanyahu, who had his own scandals, and Sharon, who was disgraced for his complicity in the massacre of hundreds of Palestinian civilians in Sabra and Shatila refugee camps in September 1982, emerged as the victors at Wye Plantation. In fact, when Sharon arrived late in Maryland (reportedly to avoid shaking hands with Arafat at the opening ceremony), he was armed with the same map that he had drafted as defense minister in 1982 (and which he would continue to try to implement as prime minister in 2002).[43] By appearing in Maryland, on their own terms, Netanyahu and Sharon had already named their price. From Clinton they expected the usual monetary compensation, presumably to enable Israel to relocate military bases and shooting ranges, to fortify settlements, and build bypass roads. And yet, despite the unilateral and illegal nature of these acts, subsidized by the U.S. taxpayers, one of Israel's numerous demands from the Palestinians was that they refrain from taking any "unilateral measures" such as declaring a state prior to final status talks. From Arafat, they obtained virtual acquiescence to Israel's version of the Palestinian national struggle.

The grotesque imbalance between the Memorandum's "give" and "take" had an additional implication at the regional level. The Arab world had effectively made a reassessment of the policy of normalization with Israel at the Doha Conference in 1997 in Qatar. After three economic conferences in Casablanca, Cairo, and Amman, many Arab countries decided to boycott Doha when it became obvious that the bilateral track was lagging far behind the multilateral track. The absence of Saudi Arabia and Egypt from Doha, despite strong U.S. pressure, was an indication that Netanyahu's unwillingness to implement Oslo II and its belated Hebron corollary had finally provoked a feeble Arab response.

At the international level, the Wye agreement introduced a new element into the U.S.-Israel strategic alliance by establishing a joint planning

committee to recommend new areas of cooperation and to study new technology transfers to Israel and ways to coordinate strategy against regional
influentials. The target of this updated strategic relationship was Iran,
which had successfully tested an 800-mile-range missile and which refused to accept U.S. hegemony in the Gulf as a given.

Emphasizing the Wye agreement's significance, Dore Gold, Israel's
U.N. representative, told the *New York Times* that it pushed the strategic
relations of the two countries beyond "the baseline" established during
the Cold War.[44] Meanwhile, by the end of Netanyahu's term, neither the
Hebron agreement's October 1997 deadline for further redeployment, nor
the May 4, 1999, deadline for a permanent status agreement had been met.

Notes

1   See *The Economist* (U.S. edition), July 26, 1997, and August 11, 2001.
2   See several articles on U.S. aid online at http://www.wrmea.com/html/
    us_aid_to_israel.htm.
3   *Boston Globe*, June 6, 1996.
4   "Guidelines of the Government of Israel," Israeli Government, Ministry of
    Foreign Affairs, June 17, 1996, http://www.mfa.gov.il/mfa/go.asp?
    MFAH00hm0.
5   *Yedioth Ahronoth*, June 4, 1996.
6   *New York Times*, July 11, 1996.
7   Most of these goals were achieved during Sharon's rule in 2001–2002.
8   Prime Minister Benjamin Netanyahu, "Remarks to a Joint Session of
    Congress," July 10, 1996, Federal News Service.
9   *Daily News*, September 30, 1996.
10 *Guardian* (London), March 4, 1997.
11 *Boston Globe*, September 30, 1996.
12 Naseer H. Aruri, "Oslo's Muddled Peace," *Current History* (January
    1998): 7–12.
13 *USA Today,* January 17, 1997.
14 *New York Times*, January 17, 1997.
15 *New York Times,* January 17, 1997.
16 "Further Redeployments: The Next Stage of the Israeli–Palestinian Interim
    Agreement," Israeli Government, Ministry of Foreign Affairs, January 19,
    1997.
17 "Further Redeployments," Ministry of Foreign Affairs.

18   This was expressed in a letter written by Secretary of State Christopher to
      Prime Minister Netanyahu at the time of the signing of the FRD.
      http://www.mfa.gov.il/mfa/go.asp?MFAH00qo0 or http://www.palestine-un.org/
      peace/p_j.html.

19   *New York Times*, January 17, 1998. The U.S. "Note for the Record" was
      prepared by U.S. Ambassador Dennis Ross and its full text can be found at
      http://www.likud.nl/ref14.html.

20   Eight high-ranking former U.S. officials, mainly secretaries of state and
      national security advisers, sent a letter to Prime Minister Netanyahu
      expressing the view that settlement building was "inimical to the peace
      process and even dangerous." See *Journal of Palestine Studies* 26: 3
      (Spring 1997): 162–63.

21   *USA Today*, September 16, 1997.

22   The Allon Plan is discussed in an article by Yigal Allon, former deputy
      prime minister of the predominantly Labor government after the June war:
      Yigal Allon, "Israel: The Case for Defensible Borders," *Foreign Affairs* 55:
      1 (October 1976); for a discussion of the similarity between Labor and
      Likud's visions, see Sheila Ryan, "Plans to Regularize the Occupation,"
      Occupation: Israel Over Palestine, ed. Naseer H. Aruri (Belmont, MA:
      Association of Arab-American University Graduates, 1983), pp. 339–75.

23   Associated Press, July 31, 1996.

24   See Chapter 3.

25   From his remarks at the airport upon returning from the Wye meeting. *New
      York Times*, October 26, 1998.

26   *New York Times*, October 26, 1998.

27   Khaled Amayreh, "On The Seventh Day," *Al-Ahram Weekly* 401 (October
      29–November 4, 1998).

28   "Wye: A Charter for Human Rights Violations," Press Release, Palestinian
      Society for the Protection of Human Rights and the Environment, October
      26, 1998, http://www.lawsociety.org/Press/press/1998/oct_26.html.

29   B'Tselem (The Israeli Information Center for Human Rights in the
      Occupied Territories), "Legislation Allowing the Use of Physical Force
      and Mental Coercion in Interrogation by the General Security Service,"
      Position Paper, January 2000; "Sheer Brutality: The Beatings Continue,"
      Information Sheet, August 1997; "Standard Routine: Beatings and Abuse
      of Palestine by the Israeli Security Forces During the Al-Aqsa Intifada,"
      May 2001. Online at http://www.btselem.org.

30   Naseer H. Aruri, "Israeli Death Squads Amid Mideast Talks," *Christian
      Science Monitor*, December 29, 1993.

31 "Israeli Reciprocity and Palestinian Security," Press Release, Palestinian Society for the Protection of Human Rights and the Environment, October 17, 1998.
32 *New York Times*, October 23, 1998; Associated Press, October 22, 1998.
33 *The Economist* (London), October 1, 1994; *U.S. News & World Report*, May 4, 1998.
34 *Ha'aretz*, October 15, 1998.
35 *Ha'aretz*, October 15, 1998.
36 Press Release, the White House, Office of the Press Secretary, October 23, 1998.
37 Press Release, October 23, 1998.
38 Press Release, October 23, 1998.
39 Press Release, October 23, 1998.
40 Press Release, October 23, 1998.
41 *Financial Times* (London), December 15, 1988.
42 Press Release, October 23, 1998.
43 For an analysis of Sharon's plan, see Ryan, "Plans to Regularize the Occupation," pp. 369–74.
44 *New York Times*, November 2, 1998.

CHAPTER 8

JERUSALEM AND A CHANGING AMERICAN POLICY

The Annexation of Jerusalem

Defying U.N. resolutions on Jerusalem and the entire Palestine question, the Israeli Knesset adopted three legislative acts on June 27 and 28, 1967, extending Israeli law to the occupied eastern sector of the city and enlarging the municipal boundaries of "united" Jerusalem.[1] On July 4, 1967, the U.N. General Assembly adopted Resolution 2253, calling upon Israel to "rescind all measures already taken [and] to desist forthwith from taking any action which would alter the status of Jerusalem."[2] The Security Council also adopted Resolution 252 in 1968, declaring invalid the measures taken by Israel to change the status of Jerusalem.

As far as the United Nations was concerned, the legal status of Jerusalem was the one governed by General Assembly Resolution 181-II of November 29, 1947, which called for the partition of Palestine into a Jewish state and an Arab state, and for the establishment of the city of Jerusalem "as a *corpus separatum* under a special international regime [which] shall be administered by the United Nations."[3] This resolution continues to constitute international legality with regard to the city, and no subsequent resolution has altered that status. In fact, the international status of Jerusalem was reconfirmed in General Assembly Resolution 194-III of December 11, 1948, which Israel violated when the Knesset proclaimed the city as Israel's capital on January 23, 1950. Israel also ignored Security Council Resolution 242 of 1967, which called on Israel to withdraw to the lines of June 4, 1967, making the annexation official on July 30, 1980.

The Israeli argument, however, has always been based on the denial of the existence of the Palestinian people and the assertion that no other state can produce a legal claim to Palestine equal to that of Israel.[4] Israeli jurists pressed the argument that the Jordanian occupation of the city in

1948 was an act of aggression, hence illegal, and that, by accepting the "illegal" act, the Palestinians relinquished their right to establish a Palestinian state under U.N. General Assembly Resolution 181-II. Moreover, they maintain that Jordan "again" committed aggression in June 1967 and lost Jerusalem, leading to the dissolution of its special status under Resolution 181-II. According to Israel, therefore, that resolution was "overtaken by events."[5] This spurious thesis remains at the core of the continuing colonization of the Occupied Territories, including Jerusalem, because Israel has never viewed them as occupied. It was the basis for the Israeli measures that altered the status of Jerusalem, and which themselves were the prelude to the de facto annexation of the West Bank.

On December 17, 1967, Israel dropped the term "West Bank" from official usage and adopted the Biblical name "Judea and Samaria" to refer to these Palestinian lands. To reconfirm that change, Israel introduced another measure on February 19, 1968, according to which the occupied territory was no longer referred to as "enemy territory."[6] These measures exemplify Israel's ability and willingness to manipulate the law in pursuit of its colonial ambitions. They also reflect its tenacity in defying the world community and international public opinion. Gradually, but persistently, Israel was able, over a period of quarter of a century, to sway the U.S. position toward its own.

Jerusalem in the U.S. Political Arena

Ever since Israel annexed Jerusalem and enlarged its boundaries, nineteen days after its occupation, the status of the Occupied Territories, including Jerusalem, has been a matter of major controversy. Its status becomes a U.S. campaign issue at least once every four years, when presidential candidates exploit it in pursuit of votes and campaign contributions.

An important controversy over the status of Jerusalem took place in the American political arena on March 3, 1990, when President George Bush was questioned about a statement made by Secretary of State James Baker in congressional testimony two days earlier. Baker had said that he would seek assurances that $400 million, requested by Israel for housing new immigrants, would not be used in the Occupied Territories. Actually, Baker was testifying about foreign aid in general before the House Appropriations Subcommittee on Foreign Operations, and he also enraged Israel and its domestic supporters by suggesting an across-the-board reduction of aid in order to help new U.S. clients in Nicaragua and Panama and to bolster the new anti-Communist regimes in Eastern Europe.[7] The impact of that suggestion would have fallen heaviest on Israel, being the top recipient of U.S. aid. Together with the implied threat to reopen the Jerusalem file, Baker's statement was bound to mobilize U.S.-Israeli supporters against the administration. In fact, when President Bush was asked during a news conference in Palm Springs, California, whether he would tie U.S. aid for the resettlement of Soviet Jews to Israel's willingness to refrain from housing them in West Bank settlements, he went out of his way to assert that Jerusalem would also be included in that ban:

> My position is that the foreign policy of the United States says we do not believe there should be new settlements in the West Bank or in East Jerusalem. And I will conduct that policy as if it's firm, which it is, and it will be shaped in whatever decisions we make to see whether people can comply with that policy. And that's our strongly held view, and we think it's constructive to peace—the peace process, too—if Israel will follow that view. And so there is division in Israel on this question, incidentally. Parties are divided on it. But this is the position of the United States and I'm not going to change that position.[8]

Not unexpectedly, the added emphasis on Jerusalem by the president, absent throughout the Reagan era, was assaulted by the major American Zionist organizations, the Israeli government, and U.S. legislators. The president, however, was simply reiterating official U.S. policy and reaffirming the U.S. obligation under the Fourth Geneva Convention of 1949.

Paradoxically, however, the U.S seems to have maintained two asymmetric positions on Jerusalem: a *presumed policy* and a *symbolic position*. President Bush was, in effect, rebuked mostly for having indirectly questioned his predecessor's presumed policy, which was to push the U.S. symbolic position to the sidelines while giving unqualified support to Israel's policy that "Jerusalem must never again be divided." President Bush was apparently guilty of attempting to deviate from an unwritten U.S.-Israeli agreement to violate international law. His critics, who were doing AIPAC's bidding, paid no attention to the legal issues that governed the status of Jerusalem. Senate majority leader George Mitchell, Democrat of Maine, for example, who was a former judge and a top recipient of pro-Israel political action committee (PAC) funds, played a leading supportive role in the battle waged by Israel and AIPAC over Jerusalem.

The Symbolic Position

The United States tacitly agreed with the majority of world nations by abstaining in the vote on U.S. General Assembly Resolution 2253 of July 4, 1967, calling on Israel to rescind the annexation and enlargement of Jerusalem's boundaries in violation of Resolution 181. The United States again abstained on U.N. General Assembly Resolution 2254 of July 14, 1967, which "deplore[d] Israel's failure to implement General Assembly resolution 2253," and "reiterate[d] its call to Israel ... to rescind all measures ... which would alter the status of Jerusalem." The U.S. implied association with that broad consensus was strengthened when Security Council Resolution 242 of November 22, 1967, calling for Israeli withdrawal to the boundaries of June 4, 1967, became a cornerstone of official U.S. Middle East policy.

U.S. association with the international consensus on this issue, however, underwent serious transformation and came to a dead halt when President Reagan ventured into the area of jurisprudence with the original, albeit dimwitted, opinion that Israeli settlements were "not illegal."[9] Meanwhile, Israel managed to keep the question of settlements in the enlarged boundaries of Jerusalem—that is, on Arab land confiscated since June 1967—outside the general discourse on settlements. Thus the Jewish settlers in that area were not included in the contrived statistics on settlers, which stood at 140,000, up from 112,000 when Rabin was elected in 1992 and double the number in 1990. It was also in 1990 that Shamir claimed that less than 1 percent of the new immigrants were settled in the Occupied Territories, when in fact 11 percent had settled in occupied Jerusalem. (The actual number of settlers at that time approached 310,000.) For the first time ever, the Jewish population of East Jerusalem exceeded that of the Arab population, with the near-term outlook favoring rapid Jewish population growth.[10] It is interesting to note that there was no Jewish population whatsoever in East Jerusalem in June 1967.

Slowly, but steadily, as U.S. adherence to the withdrawal clause of U.N. Resolution 242 changed its focus away from the letter of the resolution, and as the U.S.-Israeli special relationship was institutionalized and eventually transformed into a strategic alliance, the issue of Jerusalem became largely dormant. The American association with international legality was reduced to the symbolic level, occasionally upheld during U.N. rituals, which had almost no substantive effect on the real situation.

As U.S. ambassador to the United Nations in 1971, George Bush had a chance to participate in the formalities on Jerusalem. On September 25, 1971, he reaffirmed Ambassador Charles Yost's 1969 statement that Jerusalem is "occupied territory and thereby subject to the provisions of international law governing the rights and obligations of an occupying power."[11] He also decried Israel's failure to acknowledge its obligations as contrary to the "letter and spirit" of the Fourth Geneva Convention, and cautioned against adverse effect on the "eventual disposition of the occupied section of Jerusalem." Although the Bush statement was strong and forthright, it nevertheless contributed to the process leading toward a presumed U.S. policy:

> But an Israeli occupation policy made up of unilaterally determined practices cannot help promote a just and lasting peace any more than that cause was served by the status quo in Jerusalem prior to June 1967, which I want to make clear, we did not like and we do not advocate reestablishing.[12]

The Presumed Policy

The statement by Ambassador Bush made it clear that the United States was dissatisfied with the division of Jerusalem and preferred unification. But while U.S. policy makers continued to reject Israeli sovereignty over the city and to hold that its final status must be negotiated, they looked the other way while Israel was taking physical and "legal" steps that systematically foreclosed on any possibilities of future negotiations. When Israel dissolved the East Jerusalem Municipal Council on June 29, 1967, expelled the Arab mayor, Rouhi Al-Khatib, expropriated Arab land surrounding Jerusalem, demolished Arab homes, and built an expansive network of suburbs in accordance with its own master plan for the "Greater Jerusalem Area,"[13] the United States limited its response to occasional statements upholding its symbolic position. It did the same when Israel employed the euphemism "controlled territories" to avoid the internationally recognized obligations of an occupying power. It paid no attention when Prime Minister Levi Eshkol declared Jerusalem, "by the grace of the unfolding of Jewish history," to be the "whole and sovereign capital" of Israel.[14] Nor did the United States threaten to reassess its economic, military, or diplomatic underwriting of Israel when Israel moved ministerial and other government offices to East Jerusalem, placing the United

States in the position of aiding and abetting serious violations of international law. Moreover, the 1969 and 1974 Israeli-sponsored elections in the city demonstrated the separateness between the two parts of the city. No Arab candidates and less than 10 percent of the eligible Arab voters took part, and yet the United States continued to cling tenaciously to a facade of unity as the logical alternative to division.

By contrast, the March 1990 statements by Baker and Bush unleashed tremors that seemed to disrupt the harmonious atmosphere that had prevailed under Reagan. These statements simply called in the symbolic position as a means of pressure to resuscitate a peace process facing a death sentence by its original author: Yitzhak Shamir. No one, of course, was under any illusion that Bush's statement entailed the possibility of a change in the U.S. policy on Jerusalem. The issue was whether the presumed policy would be allowed to continue with no inhibitions or encumberances whatsoever. In short, President Bush's comment was seen as a possible interruption of ten years of U.S. acquiescence in Israeli plans for Jerusalem.

The Challenge and the Outcome

The statement by the elder President Bush triggered the inevitable battle in the American public opinion arena. The lineup of forces pitted Shamir's caretaker government, the U.S. Zionist lobby, and the U.S. Congress against the president of the United States. Israel's ambassador to the United States, Moshe Arad, leveled severe criticisms of George Bush in a speech to the United Jewish Appeal on March 13, 1990, saying that Bush's statement harmed the peace process, at least in the short run, because of the political crisis it triggered in Israel.[15] Another embassy official, Oded Aran, expressed anxiety about the future of U.S.-Israeli strategic cooperation, nurtured carefully during eight years of Reagan's presidency. He said that there was a lurking threat to the Arrow missile project, a joint U.S.-Israeli enterprise.[16]

Shamir's defiance of Bush was expressed in a statement to American-Jewish fundraisers on March 4, 1990, in which he said "there are no settlements in Jerusalem ... it is part of Israel and it will never be divided again."[17] It was also dramatized in the April 2, 1990, decision to begin the construction of four settlements on confiscated Arab land north of Jerusalem.

Congress and the Jerusalem Controversy

President Bush was the target of some powerful salvos delivered by Senate Majority Leader George Mitchell. "Heavy-handed blunder" was the way Senator Mitchell referred to Bush's comment. Mitchell accused Bush of undermining the "peace process" through "insensitivity or conscious provocation," of having contributed to the fall of the Shamir government, and of casting "doubt upon America's intentions and role in promoting peace in the Middle East." He added:

> There was simply no reason to suddenly thrust into the forefront of debate the issue of Jewish Israelis' rights to live in East Jerusalem.... [C]ertainly the status of East Jerusalem must be decided as part of a negotiated, comprehensive peace. But the president's comments served no purpose but to impede progress toward establishing the very process needed to resolve this issue.[18]

The campaign against Bush swept the U.S. Senate in the aftermath of the majority leader's harsh rebuke. Senator Daniel Patrick Moynihan, Democrat of New York, who had sponsored numerous pro-Israel resolutions with Senator Jesse Helms and others, dutifully pushed concurrent Resolution 106 through the Senate, securing approval by voice vote on March 22, 1990. (A similar resolution declaring Jerusalem as Israel's capital was also adopted by the House on April 24, 1990.[19])

Giving full credence to the Israeli position on Jerusalem, which stood at variance with the accepted view throughout the international community, Resolution 106 begins thus: "Whereas the state of Israel has declared Jerusalem to be its capital." Disregarding any need for accuracy, it proceeds:

> whereas from 1948 to 1967, Jerusalem was a divided city and Israeli citizens of all faiths were not permitted access to holy sites in the area controlled by Jordan;

> whereas since 1967 Jerusalem has been a united city administered by Israel and persons of all religious faiths have been guaranteed full access to holy sites within the city.

The Congressional view of Jerusalem, which paralleled the official Israeli position and was at variance with the U.S. government position, was made clear in the fifth clause:

> whereas ambiguous statements by the government of the United States concerning the right of Jews to live in all parts of Jerusalem raise con-

cern in Israel that Jerusalem might one day be redivided and access to religious sites in Jerusalem denied to Israeli citizens.

The Senate and the House then "resolved that the Congress acknowledges that Jerusalem is and should remain the capital of the state of Israel; [and] strongly believes that Jerusalem must remain an undivided city."

Media Assault

Joining in the campaign against Bush were the major Jewish-American organizations and the *New York Times,* as well as the *Washington Post.* William Safire's diatribe against Bush left no distinction between responsible journalism and hollow propaganda:

> Mr. Bush, by extending his anathema on "settlements" to a portion of Israel's capital, is the first to raise the prospect of a divided Jerusalem. Mr. Bush pretends that his bombshell, which brought down the Likud government, is no change in U.S. policy; that legalistic half-truth fools nobody.[20]

Raising a domestic political issue which was above all about votes and campaign contributions, Safire did not hesitate to present the issue in existential terms. Again, he injected the worn-out label of anti-Semitism and the potential for genocide against Jews:

> Come the first pogrom, which God forbid, who in the Bush White House will accept responsibility for failing to facilitate the new exodus while there was little time? Who among supporters of Israel will step forward on some future Passover and admit they were so caught up with the "peace process" that they refused to confront the real possibility of a death process?[21]

A.M. Rosenthal insured that he wouldn't be out-Israelized by Safire by creating his own facts while equating Israel's position with international law: "There have been no Jewish 'settlements' in Jerusalem, as Mayor Teddy Kollek noted. The very use of the word 'settlement' to describe Jews moving into Jewish neighborhoods in Jerusalem is insulting."[22]

The *Washington Post's* news stories on the controversy, though more subtle than Safire's prose, sounded more like editorials than news reporting.[23]

Bush Caves In

Initially, Bush had insisted that his remarks were consistent with the U.S. position of twenty-two years, which is that the United States defined the Occupied Territories as including all the land seized by Israel in 1967. But, shortly afterward, he dispatched a letter to the Israeli mayor of Jerusalem, Teddy Kollek, saying "there is no intention on our part to focus now on the final status of Jerusalem."[24] Although it turned out in the end to be too late for making amends with the American Jewish community, that letter won him praise from the director of the Anti-Defamation League of B'nai B'rith, who said, "The president put this issue on the front burner through his statement in California, and now, with this letter, he is putting it on the back burner."[25]

The president's fence-mending also included an earlier assurance which he communicated to Seymour Reich, then the president of the conservative Conference of Presidents of American Jewish Organizations, on March 5, 1990, that "U.S. policy toward Jerusalem is unchanged."[26]

Israel's friends on Capitol Hill, who tried to send a strong message with their concurrent Resolution 106, proceeded with another resolution two years later (May 26, 1992) calling upon the president to "congratulate Israel" on the twenty-fifth anniversary of the "reunification" of Jerusalem. Concurrent resolutions S-316 and H-113 made the claim, again, that the Israeli occupation authorities had guaranteed full access for Palestinian Muslims and Christians to Jerusalem, ignoring the fact that Palestinians from all over the Occupied Territories were barred from entering the city during the twenty-fifth anniversary festivals. A year later, Jerusalem was closed to all Palestinian men under the age of forty, except workers carrying special passes. The age limit was later raised to fifty. This arbitrary closure was then even further tightened through Sharon's draconian measures, and yet broad support in the U.S. Congress for Israeli-administered "freedom of movement" and for religious freedom continues.

The Jerusalem Question During Clinton's Presidency

By the time Bill Clinton assumed the presidency in January 1993, "Greater Jerusalem," which covered nearly one-fourth of the entire West Bank, had a settler population of 170,000.[27] An Israeli committee consisting of representatives of the Jerusalem municipality and the ministries of housing and the interior had set up a special commission of planners to prepare a new master plan for metropolitan Jerusalem by 1993. The area then included about forty settlements, in addition to the annexed eastern sector of the city. These settlements extend in all directions, reaching

Ramallah in the north, a position halfway between Hebron and Bethlehem (Gush Etzion) in the south, and Ma'ale Adumim settlement in the east. In 1993, the municipal boundary of Ma'ale Adumim was expanded all the way to Jericho. These settlements, in essence, annex to Jerusalem, and therefore to Israel, the area extending from Ramallah to Jericho to Bethlehem.[28] Moshe Amirav, a former member of the Jerusalem City Council, described the area in 1991 as "one metropolitan area."[29]

The commission was working on plans for transportation, commerce, housing, industry, health, education, water, and sewage. A guiding principle of its work was that "Metropolitan Jerusalem" will be a "single district" for its entire population, and "regardless of any political agreements, the free movement of people, goods, services and capital will be assured." It is significant that the commission's mandate extended over a sizable area of the West Bank, over which Israel had no statutory authority. The trends in planning at that time made it crystal clear that the deferral of Jerusalem to a "final status" issue in the negotiations between Israel and the PLO was a ruse. Israel was not planning a meticulously constructed metropolis with an expensive and sophisticated infrastructure, only to hand a share of it to the Palestinians on a silver platter after final status talks were concluded. The fate of the city had, in fact, been sealed since it was occupied in June 1967.

Both of Jerusalem's mayors, the Laborite Teddy Kollek, who served for twenty-eight years until 1993, and the Likudist hardline mayor, Ehud Olmert, are on record saying that the status of Jerusalem is not negotiable. Kollek was reported to have told President Clinton that Jewish claims in Jerusalem were unique: "In another few years, we in Jerusalem will celebrate 3000 years since the construction of the city by King David, whereas the Palestinian claim is less than one generation old."[30] This view has, in fact, been supported by every Israeli prime minister since 1967.

In October 1993, the Jerusalem City Council approved a plan to build a housing project on the Mount of Olives in East Jerusalem. Meanwhile, Mordechai Gur, then deputy defense minister, announced that the settlement city of Ma'ale Adumim (population 17,000), whose boundaries had been expanded by 12,000 acres eastward to Jericho, was included in "Greater Jerusalem, and that it would accommodate 50,000 residents on top of the 50,000 targeted in the present plan."[31] Israel's policy has been to consolidate settlements in East Jerusalem and all around the city in order to give Jerusalem a unique character distinguishing it from the West

Bank. Jerusalem then would become Jewish physically, ethnically, and politically. The closure of the city to Palestinians from the West Bank and Gaza, ongoing since March 1993, was intended to reinforce that plan and to hasten foreclosure on the future of the city.

This has been the strategy behind the pattern of grouping the ever-expanding settlements around Jerusalem into blocs. The Ma'ale Adumim bloc, approved in November 1993, comprises seven settlements and cities, which, according to its mayor at that time, would create a band of housing for 70,000 Israelis between the East Jerusalem settlement of Pisgat Ze'ev and the Jericho enclave created for the Palestinians under the 1993 DOP.[32] The Gush Etzion bloc is in the south and the Giv'at Ze'ev bloc strategically extends Jerusalem in a northwest direction. Gush Etzion had approval for plans targeting 50,000 inhabitants before 2000, while the target for Giv'at Ze'ev is no less than 30,000.[33]

A more recent project is the development of the Abu-Ghoneim region (known in Hebrew as Har Ha'Oma), which is located at the northern border of the Arab town of Beit Sahour, south of Jerusalem. This region also includes a hill east of Abu-Ghoneim (Abu-Alsokhour) and a plain to the east of the city (Khirbat al-Mazmouriyah). Most of this area, which constitutes approximately 500 acres, belongs to families in the Arab town of Beit Sahour and the village of Um-Tuba. It was part of the Bethlehem district, but Israel included all of it in the extended borders of Jerusalem after the 1967 occupation. The plans for Abu-Ghoneim call for the building of a settlement with all the required infrastructure on expropriated land for approximately 35,000 Jewish settlers. The completion of this project would finalize the encirclement of the original city with Jewish settlements on *all* sides and would alter the demographic balance decidedly in Israel's favor in East Jerusalem. Not only will it be the final step in Judaizing East Jerusalem, but it will also represent an advanced stage in the Judaization of Bethlehem. Bethlehem would become as vulnerable to the Etzion bloc of settlements as Hebron has been to Kiryat Araba, from which the Brooklyn settler Goldstein and his accomplices launched the Hebron massacre in February 1994.

The fact that the Abu-Ghoneim colonization took place after the signing of the Cairo Agreement on May 4, 1994, was just another indication that the DOP was a mere pause on Israel's path of conquest. The Cairo agreement granted Israel zoning authority that it used to continue the expansion of its settlements and to discriminate against Arab residents in need of housing.[34] The Abu-Ghoneim area represents the only path for solving a chronic shortage of housing for the Palestinian residents of Beit Sahour and Um-Tuba. Their requests to build on their own land in the area have all been rejected by the Jerusalem municipality and the Israeli government, despite the dire need for housing and the overly crowded conditions in Um-Tuba. Palestinian residents throughout East Jerusalem suffer from severe housing shortages, and at the same time the expropriation of their privately owned lands continues unabated.

While Arafat consented to deferring the issue of Jerusalem for the final stage, Israeli bulldozers and cranes have been put to work on the most ambitious project to complete a three-ringed encirclement of Palestinian communites in east Jerusalem. There is the expanding outer ring of Ma'ale Adumim, Gush Etzion, and Giv'at Ze'ev; the intermediate ring of Ramat Shufat, Sheikh Jarrah, and Jabal al-Mukabber and Wad al-Jouze; and the inner ring surrounding the old city, which covers Silwan, Ras al-Amoud, and the Mount of Olives. The plan aims to reduce the 450,000 Palestinians of the West Bank section of "Metropolitan Jerusalem" to a scattered minority in separate enclaves in and around the de facto Israeli "capital." The new infrastructure of highways bypasses them and renders them marginal. Much of this construction had took place during the Clinton presidency, and Israel's actions received much cheering from the U.S. Congress, as well as unambiguous support from the administration.

The Shift in U.S. Policy

Since 1967, official U.S. policy has been that East Jerusalem is part of the Occupied Territories. That policy, however, which was already watered down in 1990, underwent a serious change under the Clinton administration. The first visible sign of a shifting U.S. policy on Jerusalem appeared in the State Department's Declaration of Principles of June 30, 1993, which hinted broadly that it considered the Occupied Territories as "disputed." The Bush II administration had eventually reached an accord on the $10 billion worth of loan guarantees without obligating Israel to halt its settlement activity. U.S. officials were no longer scrutinizing expenditure on settlement activity in and around Jerusalem. In fact, after the "historic handshake" on the White House lawn between Arafat and Rabin, on September 13, 1993, all discussion of settlement building in East Jerusalem ceased. Israel's housing minister, Benjamin Ben-Eliezer—now Sharon's defense minister—after meeting with top officials from the Clinton administration in Washington in November 1993, admitted that the subject had never even come up in their talks: "They didn't ask and I didn't tell them," he said, according to AIPAC's newsletter *Near East Report.*[35]

The Clinton administration had embraced Israel's position on Jerusalem to the extent that settlement construction was effectively excised from the broad agenda. Clinton's assistant secretary of state for Near Eastern and South Asian affairs, Robert Pelletreau, enunciated a marked shift in U.S. policy not only toward Jerusalem but also toward settlements in general. According to Geoffrey Aronson, a well-informed settlement expert, the U.S. was "no longer maintaining its historical policy of opposing unilateral actions—such as Israeli settlements—that are aimed at determining the final status of Jerusalem. Indeed, Pelletreau refused to characterize settlement per se as a unilateral action prejudicial to Jerusalem's final status."[36] In addition, the U.S. began in March 1993 to overlook the expansion of settlements, mainly taking place around Jerusalem, due to what Israelis described as "natural growth."

Bill Clinton was the first president who actually moved toward translating campaign rhetoric on Jerusalem into policy. He told American Jewish leaders on March 13, 1994, that he opposed any reference to Jerusalem as occupied territory and that he would adhere to his campaign promise to support the Israeli view of Jerusalem as the "eternal capital."[37] Vice President Al Gore, who developed close ties to the Likud Party and to Christian Zionists in the United States when he was a member of the U.S. Senate, told AIPAC's annual policy conference on the same day the following: "I want to assure you at this critical moment, that the president and I have not forgotten the meaning of Jerusalem."[38]

The March 1994 session of the U.N. Security Council, which took place in the wake of the Hebron massacre, was considered as the litmus test for Clinton and Gore with regard to Jerusalem. The original draft resolution that was presented, which condemned the massacre, seemed acceptable to all members of the council and, incidentally, to the Rabin government and the Clinton administration. As a sign of changing times, Rabin had reportedly demanded that AIPAC and the Conference of Presidents of Major Jewish Organizations "neither protest the inclusion of Jerusalem in [the resolution] nor try to mobilize support in Congress for an American veto of the resolution."[39]

Apparently, Rabin and Clinton accepted the original draft as the price for resuming peace talks in the wake of the massacre and the declared PLO suspension of its participation in the talks. The "peace process" was too much of a good deal for them to pass up, and another condemnatory U.N. resolution would simply be an addition to a long list of ineffectual U.N. documents, thanks to the U.S. diplomatic shield. Nevertheless, Rabin was unable to control the American Zionist lobby, and Clinton was unable to control Congress. Despite Rabin's reported urgings, AIPAC's annual conference adopted a position, contrary even to that of its own president, Steven Grossman, in favor of condemning the U.N. resolution. There was considerable lobbying on Capitol Hill by pro-Israeli organizations, and Congress, in defiance of Clinton and Rabin, called on President Clinton to veto the resolution. The Senate passed a resolution on March 17, 1994, by voice vote and attached it to an unrelated banking bill. It urged the administration to veto any U.N. resolution that "states or implies that Jerusalem is 'occupied' territory."[40]

Letters were also sent by eighty-one senators and twenty-nine representatives urging a veto. The senators asked the president to oppose "biased and counterproductive language" in the U.N. resolution: "Clearly, the United States understands that Jerusalem is a 'final status' issue to be negotiated between the parties. The United States must not be party to attempts to prejudice this issue through United Nations Security Council resolutions." The House letter to Clinton of July 25, 1994, left very little doubt where the signers really stood on the issue: "Jerusalem is the indivisible capital of Israel and must remain united under sole Israeli sovereignty."

Both the House and the Senate moved to prohibit any new offices or official meetings in Jerusalem to deal with the Palestinian Authority, which was created by the "Gaza-Jericho First" accord on May 4, 1994. Their objective was clearly to outlaw any Palestinian symbols of sovereignty in Jerusalem and to render any Palestinian claims to Jerusalem illegitimate. To that end, they asked the Clinton administration not to open offices in Jerusalem to manage aid to the Palestinian Authority in Gaza and Jericho.

It was rather significant that the House signatories of the letter cited Israeli legislation on Jerusalem as a basis for U.S. policy, thereby ignoring not only international law, but also U.S. policies:

> We note that the government of Yitzhak Rabin has approved new legislation that will prohibit both the PLO and the Palestinian Authority from maintaining offices and conducting business in Jerusalem. In light of these developments, we are very concerned about actions by the U.S. government that could give any credibility to Palestinian claims on Jerusalem.... Jerusalem is the capital of only one country, Israel, and we urge you to implement a policy that does not in any way support a Palestinian claim to the city.[41]

When the vote on the controversial resolution finally came before the Security Council, U.S. ambassador Madeleine Albright insisted that the resolution be voted on paragraph by paragraph, a rather unprecedented procedure. She abstained from voting on two Jerusalem paragraphs and threatened to veto future U.N. resolutions that had similar language. Reaffirming the new policy enunciated in the State Department's Declaration of Principles of June 30, 1993, she said:

> We simply do not support the description of territories occupied by Israel in the 1967 war as "occupied Palestinian territory." In the view of my government, this language could be taken to indicate sovereignty—a matter which both Israel and the PLO have agreed must be decided in negotiations on the final status of the territories.[42]

To demonstrate this shift in U.S. policy on Jerusalem, Albright said that she would have vetoed the entire resolution had the reference to Jerusalem as occupied territory appeared in the operative paragraph:

> [W]e sought a paragraph-by-paragraph vote ... because we wanted to record our objections to language introduced there. Had this language appeared in the operative paragraph ... let me be clear—we would have exercised our veto. In fact, we are today voting against a resolution in the Commission on the Status of Women precisely because it implies that Jerusalem is occupied Palestinian territory.[43]

In fact, Albright made good on her threat to use the U.S. veto on May 17, 1995, thus enabling Israel to seize land illegally in the vicinity of Jerusalem. Meanwhile, all fourteen other members of the Security Council supported a draft resolution describing the Israeli intent to seize 140 acres of Arab land in the adjacent villages of Beit Hanina and Beit Safafa as merely "unhelpful." [44]

Albright had earlier taken another important step toward changing U.S. policy in Israel's favor when she sent a letter to all member states of the U.N. General Assembly in August 1994 suggesting that the Assembly session, scheduled to open in September, drop from its Middle East resolutions language dealing with matters still to be negotiated. That would include resolutions on Jerusalem and all other issues classified by the Oslo process as final status issues. Her letter stated: "We ... believe that resolution language referring to 'final status' issues should be dropped, since these issues are now under negotiations by the parties themselves."[45]

Congress and the executive branch undertook further actions to bolster Israeli plans for Jerusalem, including the elimination of any Arab political presence—manifest or implied—in the city. In late July 1994, after a Congressional outcry and Israeli government pressure, the Clinton administration withdrew plans to open an Agency for International Development branch office in East Jerusalem, which would have overseen the disbursement of funds to the Palestinian Authority. Other Congressional actions against the Palestinians included a harassment campaign against Arafat, ostensibly because he had used the term "jihad" in his call for the liberation of Jerusalem. Senator DeConcini, for example, demanded that President Clinton:

> [make] very clear that the U.S. is not part of a peace accord, a peace process, or a statement of principles that talks about the liberation of Jerusalem. That is not part of the agreement. It is my understanding that, under the accords, the status of Jerusalem would be discussed, but it is not part of the agreement that there would be any pullout by the Israelis.[46]

The Clinton administration, which needed no prodding on the question of Jerusalem, went a step further in September 1994 by applying financial leverage against the PA in order to gain concessions for Israel on the status of Jerusalem. On September 13, 1994, Arafat was compelled to drop his insistence that some international donor assistance be allocated for Palestinian institutions in East Jerusalem. The agreement, which was reached by Arafat and Shimon Peres, after serious pressure from the United States, the European Community, and Japan, stipulated that neither Israel nor the PLO shall bring before the donor community those political issues that are of disagreement between them, and must deal with such issues between themselves, based on the DOP and subsequent agreements.[47]

The Jerusalem Embassy Relocation Act

In 1991, the U.S. voted for U.N. Resolution 694, which referred to "all the Palestinian territories occupied by Israel since 1967, including Jerusalem." Only four years later, Jerusalem ceased to be occupied territory and was recognized by the U.S. Congress as the "capital of Israel." Both Bill Clinton and George W. Bush made campaign pledges to move the U.S. embassy in Israel to Jerusalem if they were elected.[48]

Although the move has not occurred yet, Congress adopted the Jerusalem Embassy Relocation Act on October 23, 1995, by a vote of ninety-three to five in the Senate and 374 to thirty-seven in the House.[49] The act stipulated that Jerusalem should remain a "united city in which the rights of every ethnic and religious group are protected" and that it should be recognized as the "capital of Israel." It also declared that the U.S. embassy should be established in Jerusalem no later than May 31, 1999. In order to insure compliance by the executive branch, the act stipulated that 50 percent of the money used to acquire and maintain official U.S. buildings abroad could not be spent in fiscal year 1999 if the embassy was not opened in Jerusalem by the target date. It also required the secretary of state to report every six months on the progress made toward opening the U.S. embassy in Jerusalem. Despite all these restrictions, however, the president was allowed a certain loophole to permit some maneuverability. He could waive the 50 percent spending restriction beginning in October 1998 for six-month periods, and then only if he determined and reported to Congress that such a suspension was necessary to protect the national security interests of the United States.

Both presidents Clinton and Bush II made use of the waiver authority in order to placate the Arab world, yet Congress has been sending signals and making hints that the move is long overdue. On June 12, 2001, President Bush suspended for six months the process of moving the U.S. Embassy to Jerusalem on the basis that he had determined that the suspension was "necessary to protect the national security interests of the United States," adding, however, that his administration "remains committed to beginning the process of moving our embassy to Jerusalem."[50] Bush again suspended the process for six more months on December 18, 2001, and the U.S. embassy remains to this day, but perhaps not for long, in Tel Aviv. For on September 30, 2002, Bush signed legislation that requires the administration to identify Jerusalem as the capital of Israel.[51]

Bush had no choice but to sign, in view of the fact that the Jerusalem issue was a small part of the Foreign Relations Authorization Act for 2003, which gives the administration more than $4 billion for conducting the affairs of the State Department, thus making it impossible to veto the resolution and still engage in any diplomatic activity. The new legislation added three mandatory stipulations which change the way the United States treats the city.

First, it bars the administration from spending any money on the U.S. consulate in Jerusalem unless the consulate is placed under the jurisdiction of the U.S. ambassador to Israel. The U.S. consul-general in Jerusalem, who deals mainly with Palestinians, now reports directly to the State Department. Second, any U.S. government document which lists countries and their capitals will have to identify Jerusalem as the capital of Israel. Third, in official U.S. documents, such as passports, birth certificates and nationality certifications, U.S. citizens born in Jerusalem, such as this author, may insist that the documents record their place of birth as Israel.

For four decades since the establishment of Israel in Palestine, U.S. policy on Jerusalem held that the status of Jerusalem cannot be unilaterally decided by Israel or any other country. That policy, however, has been gradually, but consistently, eroding since the advent of the Clinton era, when Congress and the president seemed in agreement that "every country designates its own capital, and that Israel has so designated Jerusalem, the spiritual center of Judaism."[52] Not only does this assertion fly in the face of international law, but it also violates the principles of religious plurality and tolerance and promotes the acquisition of territory through unbridled force. Ironically, the new legislation, which violates numerous U.N. resolutions, already cited above, coincides with the drum beats of a war against Iraq, presumably because of alleged violations of U.N. resolutions.

Notes

1   Ibrahim Dakkak, "The Transformation of Jerusalem: Juridical Status and
     Physical Change," in *Occupation: Israel Over Palestine*, 2nd ed., ed. Naseer
     H. Aruri (Belmont, MA: Association of Arab-American University
     Graduates, 1989), pp. 139–71.

2   *The Status of Jerusalem*, prepared for and under the guidance of the
     Committee on the Exercise of the Inalienable Rights of the Palestinian
     People (New York: United Nations, 1979), pp. 17–18.

3   *The Status of Jerusalem*.

4   The late prime minister Golda Meir, who was born in Russia and grew up in
     the United States, summed up this position thus: "There is no such thing as
     a Palestinian … it was not as though there was a Palestinian people in
     Palestine considering itself *as* a Palestinian people and we came and threw
     them out and took their country away from them. They did not exist."
     London Sunday Times, June 15, 1969.

5   "Testimony of Yehuda Zvi Blum," *Hearings Before the Subcommittee on
     Immigration and Naturalization of the Committee on the Judiciary,* U.S.
     Senate, Ninety-fifth Congress, October 17 and 18, 1977 (Washington:
     Government Printing Office, 1978), pp. 25–26, 35. A number of scholars have
     argued that the Israeli thesis is a rationalization of unilateral acts undertaken
     illegally and not a bona fide legal judgment. See, for example, Seth Tillman,
     "The West Bank Hearings," *Journal of Palestine Studies* (Winter 1979): 21,
     27; also "Testimony of W.T. Mallison," in *Hearings Before the Subcommittee
     on Immigration and Naturalization*, pp. 46–56; Henry Cattan, "The Status of
     Jerusalem," *Journal of Palestine Studies* (Spring 1981); Kathleen Kenyon,
     Digging Up Jerusalem (London: Ernest Benn, 1974); M.A. Amiry,
     Jerusalem: Arab Origin and Heritage (London: Longmanns, 1978).

6   Raja Shehadeh, *The West Bank and the Rule of Law* (New York:
     International Commission of Jurists and Law in the Service of Man, 1980).

7   *Boston Globe,* March 2, 1990. Senator Bob Dole wrote an article in the *New
     York Times*, January 21, 1990, proposing that 5 percent of the monies allocated
     to the top recipients of U.S. aid (Israel, Egypt, Turkey, the Phillipines,
     Pakistan) be reallocated to Eastern and Central Europe. On May 1, 1990, Dole
     rose in opposition on the Senate floor to loan guarantees for Israel and cited the
     generous pattern of U.S. aid since the early 1970s. He filled twenty pages of
     the *Congressional Record* with studies by the respected Congressional Research
     Service detailing congressional generosity toward Israel over the years, and
     other material critical of aid to Israel. See Donald Neff, "The U.S. and Israel:
     Tilting at a Windmill," *Middle East International* (May 11, 1990): 9.

8   *New York Times*, March 4, 1990.

9   President Reagan's response to the establishment of three Israeli settlements
       on January 26, 1981, was the following: "As to the West Bank, I believe the
       settlements there—I disagreed when the previous administration referred to
       them as illegal, they are not illegal. Not under the U.N. resolution that leaves
       the West Bank open to all people—Arab and Israeli alike, Christian alike."
       House Committee of Foreign Affairs, *The Search for Peace in the Middle
       East: Documents and Statements, 1979–82*, p. 228.

10   Palestinian Geographic Centre, "Integrated Geographical Information
       System Base Project No. 1," *Survey of Israeli Settlements in the West Bank
       and Gaza Strip: Figures and Analysis* (Palestinian National Authority,
       Ministry of Transportation, 1995). For reliable data on settlements, see also
       Report on Israeli Settlements in the Occupied Territories, a bimonthly
       publication of the Foundation for Middle East Peace. See also Geoffrey
       Aronson, *Settlements and the Israel-Palestinian Negotiations: An
       Overview* (Washington, D.C.: Institute for Palestine Studies, 1996).

11   *New York Times*, September 26, 1971.

12   *New York Times*, September 26, 1971.

13   Dakkak, "The Transformation of Jerusalem," pp. 67–68, 72–73, 83–86.

14   *Israel Government Year Book, 1968–1969* (Jerusalem: Central Office of
       Information, Prime Minister's Office, S739), p. 9.

15   *Washington Post*, March 6, 1990.

16   Jerusalem Press Service (Washington D.C.), March 6, 1990.

17   Jerusalem Press Service, March 6, 1990.

18   Jerusalem Press Service, March 6, 1990.

19   *Congressional Record*, April 24, 1990; *Washington Post,* April 25, 1990.

20   *New York Times*, March 26, 1990.

21   *New York Times*, March 26, 1990.

22   *New York Times,* March 8, 1990.

23   *Washington Post*, March 14, 1990.

24   *Washington Post,* March 15, 1990.

25   *Washington Post*, March 15, 1990.

26   *Washington Post*, March 6, 1990.

27   Aronson, *Settlements and the Israel-Palestinian Negotiations*, p. 23.

28   John Tyler, "Finishing Jerusalem," *Challenge* (Jerusalem) 28
       (November–December 1994): 15–16.

29   Aronson, *Settlements and the Israel-Palestinian Negotiations*, p. 23.

30   "Plans Gaining Momentum for Metropolitan Jerusalem," *Report on Israeli
       Settlements In the Occupied Territories,* 3: 2 (March 1993).

31   Aronson, *Settlements and the Israel-Palestinian Negotiations*, p. 24. See
       also Jan de Jong, "The Secret Map of Non-Negotiable Jerusalem,"
       Challenge 28 (November–December 1994): 12.

32 *Jerusalem Post,* November 11, 1993.

33 de Jong, "The Secret Map of Non-Negotiable Jerusalem," p. 12.

34 Raja Shehadeh, "A Legal Analysis of the Gaza–Jericho Agreement," *Journal of Palestine Studies* 23: 4 (Summer 1994): 20–21.

35 *Near East Report,* November 15, 1993.

36 Geoffery Aronson, "U.S. Policy Shifts on Settlements," *Report on Israeli Settlement In the Occupied Territories* 4: 6 (November 1994): 6.

37 *Mideast Mirror,* March 14, 1994.

38 *The Jewish Advocate,* March 18–24, 1994.

39 Leon Hadar, "Muddling Through in the New World Disorder—And in the Middle East," *Journal of Palestine Studies* 23: 4 (Summer 1994): 68.

40 Donald Neff, "Embracing Israel's Claims at the U.N.," *Middle East International* 472 (April 1, 1994): 4.

41 See Lucille Barnes, "Indyk Nomination a Puzzler for Helms," *Washington Report on Middle East Affairs* (March 1995): 45–46.

42 See Albright's March 18, 1994 speech to the Security Council in *Journal of Palestine Studies* 23: 4 (Summer 1994): 151–52.

43 *Journal of Palestine Studies* 23: 4 (Summer 1994): 151–52.

44 Donald Neff, "The Thirtieth Veto to Shield Israel," *Middle East International* 501 (May 26, 1995): 152–53.

45 See the excerpts from Albright's letter to U.N. ambassadors, August 8, 1994, in *Journal of Palestine Studies* 24: 2 (Winter 1995): 152–53.

46 *Congressional Record,* May 23, 1994.

47 *Jerusalem Post,* September 14, 1994.

48 Bush told Zionist Organization of America's Morton Klein during the campaign that he would not discuss moving the embassy to Jerusalem because to do so "might screw up the peace process" (*Forward,* July 16, 1999). He also told William Safire that "peace has to be negotiated between the parties" (*New York Times,* April 15, 1999). Yet, a spokeswoman for his campaign, Mindy Tucker, called *Forward,* a Jewish American newspaper, saying that what he really meant was that he "intends to move the embassy to Jerusalem" and "will set the process in motion" as soon as he becomes president (*Forward,* July 23, 1999).

49 For a text of the law, see http://www.us-israel.org/jsource/Peace/Jerusalem_Relocation_Act.html.

50 Available at http://www.usembassy-israel.org.il/publish/peace/archives/2001/june/0613b.html.

51 Reuters, September 30, 2002.

52 From the Preamble of the Jerusalem Embassy Relocation Act of 1995.

CHAPTER 9

THE UNITED STATES AND THE PALESTINE REFUGEE QUESTION

A Historical Overview

Since the 1948 Palestinian Catastrophe (*al-Nakba*) and its concomitant creation of the Palestinian refugee crisis, the issues of return, compensation, and restitution have taken a back seat to discussions surrounding the overall question of Palestine. During the better part of the past five decades, the issue of refugees has been marginalized, despite the fact that Israel's admission to the United Nations was made contingent on its compliance with U.N. General Assembly Resolution 194 of December 1948.[1] General Assembly Resolution 273 of May 11, 1949, made Israel's admission conditional on an unambiguous commitment by Israel to "unreservedly" respect U.N. resolutions pertaining to the Arab-Israeli conflict, including Resolution 194. Article 11 of that resolution stated that Palestinian refugees "wishing to return to their homes and live at peace with their neighbors should be permitted to do so at the earliest practicable date, and that compensation should be paid for the property of those choosing not to return and for loss of or damage to property, which, under principles of international law or in equity, should be made good by the governments or authorities responsible."[2]

Obviously, Israel was admitted to the United Nations without complying with its obligations to Palestinian refugees, thus keeping alive and exacerbating the refugee crisis we face today. General Assembly Resolution 194 has been ritualistically reaffirmed numerous times. Israel's noncompliance impelled the General Assembly to adopt other resolutions calling on Israel to meet its obligations to the refugees. For example, Resolution 3236 of November 22, 1974, upheld the "inalienable right of the Palestinians to return to their homes and property from which they have been displaced and uprooted."[3] And in 1997, Resolution 52/62 reaffirmed that the "Palestine Arab refugees are entitled to their property and to the income derived therefrom, in conformity with the principles of justice and equity."[4]

With the emergence of the PLO and resumption of armed struggle during the 1960s, the issue of the refugees, rather than becoming the central human dimension of the revolutionaries' struggle to reverse the Nakba, was relegated to a humanitarian, charitable issue better left to organizations such as the United Nations Relief and Work Agency (UNRWA).[5] The armed struggle thesis posited that the refugees would be naturally accommodated in the future democratic secular state, which was, at the time, the stated goal of the PLO.

The 1967 war exacerbated the refugee crisis by creating a new generation of refugees. At the same time, the refugee crisis completely disappeared from the PLO agenda. The overarching objective of the PLO was global recognition of its status as sole legitimate representative of the Palestinian people. Subsequently, through the 1960s and 1970s, PLO legitimacy and Palestinian self-determination became intertwined and almost indistinguishable goals. Moreover, once it became the anchor of Palestinians scattered throughout the diaspora, the PLO perceived discussion of the plight of the refugees as a distraction from the "important" issues. True, the refugees remained a humanitarian concern, especially for showcasing the "social" institutions of the PLO in Lebanon. Yet from the perspective of political rights, the refugee question continued to lack any political content and force.[6]

After 1972, as the armed struggle further gave way to a new form of diplomatic work, the refugee question became dormant. The new definition of "struggle" formulated in Arab summit conferences in Algiers, Rabat, and Cairo encouraged the PLO to promote itself with a program of "self-determination" in a mini–Palestinian state in the West Bank and Gaza. In return for supporting the "new" PLO, with its watered-down objectives, the Arab governments demanded an unwritten *quid pro quo*. The PLO would drastically scale down its guerilla operations and cease its rhetoric about a democratic secular state in all of historic Palestine. In return, not only would the PLO be "rewarded" with Arab diplomatic support in far-flung countries, but the Arab governments would also increase economic assistance to the organization.

For the next two decades, this unwritten agreement, and the search for a "two-state solution," was to consume the combined energies of Palestinians and Arabs. The PLO quest for international recognition as the sole legitimate representative of the Palestinian people and as a solid bargaining partner for the creation of a mini-state, claimed the largest portion of Arab and Palestinian resources. This came at the expense of refugee rights and interests. And while the PLO achieved its goal of becoming the focal point of the Palestine question, ironically, in 1993, it became the first Arab party to sign an agreement that effectively deferred internationally recognized refugee rights. More drastically it agreed at the meetings in 2000 at Camp David not to insist on the right of return.

The joint Arab-Palestinian pursuit of the two-state solution was never taken seriously by the United States and Israel, yet it was exploited by them repeatedly in their own attempts to marginalize the refugee issue and remove it from the active diplomatic agenda.

U.S. Policy and the Refugees

In 1948, more than 800,000 Palestinians (about 83 percent of the population) became refugees. An additional 235,000 Palestinians became refugees as a result of the 1967 war. Today there are five million refugees; 3.7 million are registered with UNRWA, and 1.3 million are unregistered.[7]

U.S. Palestine policy in the 1940s can be described as inconsistent, if not altogether incoherent, vacillating between acknowledging self-determination for the Palestinians and, at the same time, justifying its denial by colonial-settler Jews and a Palestinian Jewish minority. Until 1947, the State Department acknowledged the rights of Palestinians to self-determination. The U.S. government, however, lobbied strongly for the U.N. partition plan, which denied that right, having proposed in 1947 the establishment of a Jewish state in 55 percent of Palestine and an Arab state in 43.5 percent, despite the fact that the Jews constituted less than one-third of the population and owned no more than 6 percent of the total land. But by 1948, the U.S. began to float the idea of replacing the partition plan (General Assembly Resolution 181 of 1947) with a U.N. trusteeship under Chapter XII of the U.N. Charter. When the partition plan failed to materialize, and the Zionist militias prevailed over the Palestinian resistance and the Arab fighters who came to their defense, U.S. policy began to shift toward support of a Jordanian takeover of the 22 percent of Palestine that did not fall under Israeli control. Jordan was also encouraged to absorb most of the refugees who were the victims of Zionist ethnic cleansing in 1948.

At the same time, the United States took an active part in drafting General Assembly Resolution 194 of December 11, 1948, which stated that those "refugees wishing to return to their homes and live in peace with their neighbors should be permitted to do so at the earliest practicable date." That resolution, which also called for compensation and restitution, established a U.N. agency to secure implementation, to help in economic rehabilitation, and to provide legal protection. That agency was the United Nations Conciliation Commission on Palestine (UNCCP).[8]

Israel's response was predictably negative. Despite the fact that Israel's admission into the U.N. was made contingent on its implementation of Resolution 194, Israel simply created its own condition (that a comprehensive settlement in the region had to precede any discussion of the refugee question), and the United States accommodated that position. There were disagreements along the road, and at certain times it seemed as if the U.S. was threatening Israel with a major reassessment of its policy, but at the end of the day, Israel was able to get away with making its own rules.

Allowing Israel to set the pace in the Middle East had, in fact, begun during the Truman administration. Despite expressing some misgivings about Israel's handling of the refugees, Truman approved an Israeli plan to repatriate about 100,000 Palestinians on the basis of family reunification. And it was Truman who attempted to settle about 100,000 Palestinian refugees in Iraq. Resettlement of the refugees in Arab countries became effectively an American policy goal, despite a *pro forma* endorsement of Resolution 194 on an annual basis at the General Assembly. That pattern was largely set by the inability of U.S. decision makers to perfect a formula that would reconcile the strategic imperatives of U.S. policy with the requirements of domestic politics. For the most part, succeeding U.S. administrations tried in vain to reconcile the global and the domestic imperatives, and, ultimately, Israel prevailed.

By late March 1949, the Truman administration announced that the refugee problem was "a likely channel for Soviet exploitation" that could jeopardize the "stabilization of the Near East," which was "a major objective of American foreign policy."[9] Yet the administration failed to reflect that concern in the imperatives of its Middle East policy, which remained virtually dependent on Israel's voluntary compliance.

By the time Lyndon B. Johnson inherited the presidency, the refugee question had ceased to be a matter of real concern for U.S. policy makers. In fact, the Israeli position of "resettlement" was incorporated into the platform of the Democratic Party on which Johnson was elected in 1964. The important new reality affecting U.S. policy toward the refugee question was the war of 1967 and the new issues created by that war. The defeat of Arab armies in only six days elevated the role of Palestinian resistance to new heights, and shifted the focus away from the refugee issue, now deemed a charitable, humanitarian matter.

From this moment on, any proposals emanating from Washington addressed the refugee question in a merely ritualistic manner. The impact of that approach was to relegate the whole Palestine issue to the sidelines while trying to find an acceptable Arab-Israeli formula based on land for peace. Consequently, the Palestinian right of return was subordinated to resolving issues that divided states in order to minimize the chances of a wider conflict with global ramifications.

A new chapter in the marginalization of the Palestinians' right of return came under President Jimmy Carter. He began his reassessment of Middle East policy with a specific reference to the Palestinian people, "who suffered so much and who were in need of a home." But his 1978 Camp David peace redefined the refugees' right of return, in the words of the late Fayez Sayegh, as a *selective* privilege of readmission.[10] Carter's proposed "self-governing authority," together with Egypt, Israel, and Jordan, was empowered to decide on the modalities for admission of persons displaced from the West Bank and Gaza in 1967. As for the 1948 refugees, Camp David merely called for a "just solution," with no mention of what that might entail. The Palestinian dimension of Carter's Middle East policy was abandoned in favor of a separate peace between Israel and Egypt, and the step-by-step approach of Nixon's secretary of state, Henry Kissinger, was effectively restored.

Despite the passing of more than a decade in which the PLO gained acceptance as the representative of the Palestinian people, whose struggle for national self-determination was supported by a global consensus based on U.N. General Assembly resolutions, Ronald Reagan considered Palestine as a problem of mere refugees. It was only after the PLO was evacuated from Lebanon in September 1982 that he made a cursory amendment of that view. He also considered the PLO a terrorist organization, enrolled in the service of the "evil empire."[11]

From the outset of his administration, Reagan exempted Israel from most of the responsibility for the plight of the refugees, having assigned Jordan 80 percent of the burden of redress, with Israel assigned 20 percent. His calculus reflected a well-known revisionist Zionist assumption that the Palestinian state designated by the United Nations was Jordan, notwithstanding the fact that the United Nations had divided Palestine, west of the River Jordan, in 1947 into a Palestinian Arab state and a Jewish state. According to revisionist Zionist thinking, the former Palestine mandate included Trans-Jordan, which amounts to 80 percent of the whole. The only reference that Reagan made to the question of refugees in his 1982 plan was the statement: "The departure of the Palestinians from Beirut dramatizes more than ever the homelessness of the Palestinian people. Palestinians feel strongly that their cause is more than a question of refugees. I agree."[12]

Despite that superficial agreement, however, Reagan ordered his U.N. ambassador to vote "no" on a General Assembly resolution three weeks later (September 24, 1982) that condemned the perpetrators of the massacre of Sabra and Shatila, and resolved that the Palestinian people should be enabled to return to their homes and property, in accordance with previous resolutions. The United States was joined by one other state: Israel.

With the advent of the first Bush administration, all attention was focused on Iraq and subsequently on the Madrid conference of October 1991, with much of the emphasis being placed on an Israeli-Palestinian deal based on Camp David's notion of Palestinian autonomy. Throughout the four years that Bush and Baker were at the helm, a rather deceptive confrontation between them and Prime Minister Shamir gave the impression that the U.S. and its strategic ally were on a collision course, despite the fact that Israel was able to supply the framework for a settlement, later described by Baker as " the only game in town." That "game" had nothing for the refugees, except the implied resettlement policy adopted by the U.S. since Nixon.

As was the case with so many other issues, Clinton continued the refugee policy of Bush and Baker, but went farther than any other previous president in embracing Israel's conditions. The Oslo arrangements con-

cluded during his tenure were badly flawed, and the gridlock they produced was utilized by Israel to further its strategic objectives. By the
summit meeting at Camp David in July 2000, the most that refugees could
realistically hope for was limited and regulated repatriation to the Palestinian entity, but not to their homes and certainly not to property in pres-
ent-day Israel. That routing would only have been open to token numbers,
and strictly in accord with what Israel would be willing to designate as
"family reunification."

Palestinian Civil Society

Despite the exceedingly numerous meetings held between Palestinian and Israeli negotiators during the seven years of Oslo, the input of the
community of five million Palestinian refugees has never been sought or
solicited. When the right of return began to resurface as a top item on the
Palestinian people's agenda around 1999–2000, the role of the Palestinian
Authority was minimal. In fact, the issue was placed on the public agenda
not by the PA or by the PLO, but by various segments of Palestinian civil
society. In particular, it was grassroots organizations—older ones and
ones recently formed in the refugee camps, inside Israel, and in the Palestinian diaspora—that seized the initiative by restoring the right of return
to a central place in the discourse about Palestine.[13] As an example, on
September 16, 2000, two demonstrations attended by several thousand
activists were held simultaneously in Washington and London to promote
the right of return. During the same period, similar demonstrations, most
of which coincided with the eighteenth anniversary of the massacres at the
Sabra and Shatila camps in Lebanon, were also staged in the Lebanese
refugee camps and in Palestine. Numerous conferences, workshops, and
rallies were held in and outside the region, bringing together community
leaders, activists, and scholars to discuss various strategies for reviving
the right of return. Such gatherings, mass rallies, symposia, and public
protests are likely to be repeated in various cities and refugee camps in the
region and around the world, until the right of return is dealt with in a fair
and legal manner in any future settlement.

Israel and the Refugee Question

If there were ever the slightest hope that the refugees could possibly
attain even a modicum of their internationally recognized rights within

the context of the Oslo framework, such hopes have been absolutely dashed. Under the unwritten rules of the "peace process," suspended in 2002 by Sharon and Bush, it would be considered a sign of intransigence if Arafat or any of his negotiators were to bring up the right of return, Resolution 194, or the November 29, 1947, partition resolution.[14] For Israelis across the ideological spectrum, including members of the so-called peace camp, the return of refugees constitutes a clear and present danger, a real demographic threat. Since they insist that their state remain exclusively Jewish—juridically and otherwise—such a position, although illegal and immoral, is nevertheless consistent with the Zionist framework of the state. The Palestinian refugees' right of return is not only absent from the public Israeli agenda and from the consciousness of the Israeli Jewish public, it is also opposed by Israel's peace movement. For example, thirty-three prominent members of the Israeli Jewish peace movement addressed a message to the "Palestinian leadership" in a front-page advertisement in *Ha'aretz*, saying in part:

> We recognize the true and urgent need to resolve the problem of the 1948 refugees, and we recognize the part of the State of Israel, also, in the creation of the problem. The refugees will have the right to return to their homeland, Palestine, and settle there. But, we want to clarify that we shall never be able to agree to the return of the refugees to within the borders of Israel, for the meaning of such a return would be the elimination of the state of Israel.[15]

One of the signatories, Amos Oz, wrote an article in the *New York Times* in which he praised Barak's government for offering to let the Palestinians govern themselves, as he put it, while describing the Palestinian Authority as the real "obstacle for peace" because it had raised the issue of the right of return:

> Implementing the Palestinian "right of return" would amount to abolishing the Jewish people's right to self-determination. It would eventually make the Jewish people no more than an ethnic minority in the country, just as fundamentalist Islam would have it.[16]

The Israeli public seems united in its rejection of international law as it pertains to the rights of the Palestinian refugees. And yet, of all the issues to be addressed in the so-called final status negotiations—borders, Jerusalem, settlements, water, refugees—the question of the refugees is certainly the most arduous.

Israel's approach to the "peace process" before Sharon assumed power in 2001 was to some degree based on the notion that the conflict began in 1967 and not in 1948. Paradoxically, the 1967 borders, known as "the green line," have continually been eroded by the insatiable appetite of successive Israeli governments for settlements. That ever-elusive "green line" has, in effect, ceased to exist.

Internal Refugees

Refugees also include those who live in the area on which the Jewish state was established in 1948. They are internal refugees, refugees who can see their land, but can't live on it or make use of it. They are what Israel refers to as "present absentees." Many of them live in "unrecognized villages." These villages exist, but cannot be found on any official map. They receive no municipal services whatsoever, despite the fact that their inhabitants are Israeli citizens who pay the same taxes as everyone else. They are not entitled to water and electricity, schools and health facilities, or paved roads. The present absentees and the citizens of the unrecognized villages certainly qualify for the status of refugees. Displaced Palestinians who are citizens of the state of Israel number between 150,000 and 200,000. They constitute a significant sector of the Palestinian community carrying Israeli citizenship in the Galilee, Negev, and in what are known as the "mixed" cities (that is, cities where there isn't Jewish hegemony, such as the Haifa and Lydda areas).[17]

According to Ori Nir, about half of Nazareth's Arab residents are internal refugees and their descendants, while more than half of Umm al-Fahm's residents belong to this group. Nir cites the work of Hebrew University professor Hillel Cohen, who put the number of the abandoned villages at 162.[18]

Conscious of Arafat's propensity for making repeated concessions, these internal refugees have organized themselves and refused to have the PA assume responsibility for their future. According to Nir, attorney Wakim Wakim, secretary of the National Council for the Defense of the Rights of Displaced Persons in Israel, did not wish to have the PA incorporate the case of the internal refugees into the "peace" talks. Instead, his organization wanted the internal refugees to wage their own legal, public, and political struggle within the framework of the state of Israel:

We don't want a situation to arise in which we end up being forgotten and not included in an arrangement on the refugee problem. On the other hand, if such an arrangement is one in which the Palestinian leadership makes concessions about our basic rights, we wouldn't want any linkage between the diplomatic negotiations and our struggle as Israeli citizens.[19]

More than a year after Wakim expressed this lack of confidence in the Palestinian leadership, Yasir Arafat reaffirmed an earlier concession on the right of the return in an op-ed in the *New York Times:*

In addition, we seek a fair and just solution to the plight of Palestinian refugees who for fifty-four years have not been permitted to return to their homes. We understand Israel's demographic concerns and understand that the right of return of Palestinian refugees, a right guaranteed under international law and United Nations Resolution 194, must be implemented in a way that takes into account such concerns. However, just as we Palestinians must be realistic with respect to Israel's demographic desires, Israelis, too, must be realistic in understanding that there can be no solution to the Israeli-Palestinian conflict if the legitimate rights of these innocent civilians continue to be ignored. Left unresolved, the refugee issue has the potential to undermine any permanent peace agreement between Palestinians and Israelis. How is a Palestinian refugee to understand that his or her right of return will not be honored but those of Kosovar Albanians, Afghans, and East Timorese have been?[20]

It must also be kept in mind that new refugees are being created on an ongoing basis as Israel's campaign of ethnic cleansing, underway since 1967 in and around Jerusalem, continues to escalate. Residency cards are confiscated at will; building permits are all but absolutely denied to Palestinians in all parts of the West Bank, which includes "Greater Jerusalem," a concept that has no juridical meaning and would appear to be a euphemism for Jewish land expansion and ownership via expropriation, eminent domain policies, and other methods of land theft. Palestinian homes are being demolished on a wholesale basis. The bulldozer is a more lethal instrument of war against the Palestinian people (in 1948 Palestine as well) than any other.

The Refugees and the Beilin–Abu-Mazin Agreement

In the aftermath of the Israeli-Palestinian Interim Agreement on the West Bank and Gaza, concluded on September 24, 1995 (known as Oslo II), which divided the West Bank into three zones (A, B, and C), Israel and the

PA began to study possible modalities for a framework for the final status issues as mandated by the DOP. A secret agreement was forged between Arafat's next in line (Mahmoud Abbas, known as Abu-Mazin) and Yossi Beilin, a Meretz bloc leader close to Shimon Peres, which envisaged solutions to the refugee question, among other final status issues. That agreement, however, was pushed to the sidelines due to the failure of Shimon Peres in his bid for reelection in the spring of 1996. The resurfacing of the agreement and the publication of the full text in *Newsweek* in September 2000 came in the wake of the unsuccessful Camp David II talks in July 2000.

Dated October 13, 1995, the "Framework for the Conclusion of a Final Status Agreement Between Israel and the Palestine Liberation Organization" was regarded by its two authors as the document paving the way for a "lasting and comprehensive peace."

It was deemed essential in the sense that it declared "null and void any agreement, declaration, document or statement which contradicts this Framework Agreement." Presumably, it *ipso facto* nullifies not only U.N. Resolution 194, but also all other international instruments and provisions of refugee law, human rights law, and humanitarian law in which refugee rights are enshrined, including Article 13 of the Universal Declaration of Human Rights and the 1949 Fourth Geneva Convention. The former provides that, "Everyone has the right to leave any country, including his own, and to return to his country." Moreover, the Beilin–Abu-Mazin agreement also negates fundamental rights guaranteed by the International Covenant on Civil and Political Rights, which provides that "no one shall be arbitrarily deprived of the right to enter his own country"; and the International Convention on the Elimination of All Forms of Racial Discrimination, which also provides that a state may not deny, on racial or ethnic grounds, the opportunity "to return to one's country."

Surely, it does not take much legal research to discover that what Abu-Mazin carelessly signed on behalf of the five million refugees relinquishes fundamental rights that are well-established in numerous international instruments. Such instruments are well-known to international lawyers and international law students everywhere. It is hard to imagine that they are not known to Abu-Mazin.

Section 1 of Article VII of the Framework commits the Palestinian side to reconsidering the refugees' rights under international law in light of the changing realities on the ground since 1948:

> Whereas the Palestinian side considers that the right of the Palestinian refugees to return to their homes is enshrined in international law and natural justice, it recognizes that the prerequisites of the new era of peace and coexistence, as well as the realities that have been created on the ground since 1948, have rendered the implementation of this right impracticable. The Palestinian side, thus, declares its readiness to accept and implement policies and measures that will insure, insofar as this is possible, the welfare and well being of these refugees.

Clearly, it must not have occurred to Abu-Mazin, himself a refugee, now accustomed to luxurious living, that the "welfare and well being" of "these refugees," who constitute 63 percent of the eight million Palestinians in the world (five million), include their right of return, like all other refugees.

In Section 2 of Article VII, Israel acknowledges " the moral and material suffering caused to the Palestinian people as a result of the war of 1947–1949," but in practice Israel accepts neither legal nor moral responsibility for that "suffering." In conformity with Oslo I, which transfers all responsibility for injuries sustained during the Israeli occupation to the PA, this framework places the burden of redress on the PA. According to the agreement, the right to compensation and restitution, another Israeli responsibility under international law, was to be dealt with by a specially created International Commission for Palestinian Refugees (ICPR). The commission would be charged with responsibilities to fundraise, distribute payments, adjudicate claims disputes, and to develop "rehabilitation and absorption programs." Its decisions would be final and subject to no appeal.

The ICPR would, in effect, shield Israel from its obligations under international law and look elsewhere for means of redress. It would also protect Israel from any international litigation process. The Palestinian "state," truncated as it may be, the Arab states, and international donors are, in effect, summoned by this agreement to assume Israel's obligations. Not only is this obstruction of the judicial process unusual and improper, but its mechanism could never provide the refugees reasonable redress. Their right of return to their homes and property will have been forever surrendered, and the most Israel would be willing to do is to admit into Israel proper fewer than 100,000 refugees, strictly on "humanitarian basis" and under "full peace conditions" (peace, that is, as defined by the victor).

Former Israeli prime minister Ehud Barak confirmed the gist of the framework as he was departing for the negotiations of Camp David II. He assured his constituents in a published message that Israel's many red-lines included the right of return: "Israel will not recognize any moral or legal responsibility for the Palestinian refugee problem."[21]

Just as President Clinton was preparing to hand over the presidency to George W. Bush, he proposed that both sides recognize the right of Palestinian refugees to return either to "historic Palestine" or to "their homeland."[22] Conversely, however, under the Clinton proposal, there was no specific right of return to what is now Israel. Instead, the refugees would have been forced to choose to go to the "state of Palestine" (that is, the areas in one of the proposed "land swap" schemes under discussion at that time) or to be resettled in Arab and/or other countries.

Toward Convening a Congress of Return and Self-Determination

Tampering with the legal framework of Palestinian rights has raised a profound question for the Palestinian people: What can the Palestinians do in order to escape the fate of other native people who have been subjected to genocide and were forced onto reservations, Bantustans, and other forms of quarantined and marginalized areas? To avoid becoming perpetual captives in isolated Gaza, or remaining forever a disenfranchised community, or wandering in the diaspora living on the sufferance of hostile Arab governments, Palestinians have already considered taking a variety of actions to protect their rights. Through numerous conferences and meetings, they have reaffirmed the legal framework establishing the right of return, despite the fact that this right has been almost completely surrendered on their behalf, without their consultation or authorization. The state of legal limbo imposed on Palestinian refugees must be terminated, and their internationally guaranteed rights must be reaffirmed.

To that end, an assemblage of the representatives of the five million living in the diaspora and the two million in the West Bank and Gaza should begin to undo the implied surrender, reclaim their national rights, and declare all acts denying them these rights, whether in transitional arrangements or final status talks, null and void.

The Congress of Self-Determination and Return, as it may be called, is a minimal step that the Palestinian people can take as they embark on rectifying the wrongs of Oslo. Whereas concluding the DOP involved less than a half dozen confidants of Arafat, meeting in secret with Israelis outside the parameters of public scrutiny, the Conference of Return would be an open forum for all Palestinians from all walks of life, meeting within the rules of accountability. It would be a culmination of a grassroots effort with decisions by local committees and regional groupings, moving from the bottom up in a democratic process and in an egalitarian spirit. It would be a nonpartisan, nonideological, nonsectarian project, aiming to manifestly uphold the right of return and self-determination. These rights, enshrined in the Universal Declaration of Human Rights, U.N. Resolutions 194 and 3236, and long supported by an international consensus, must be placed high on the active agenda of any peace talks.

The conference would serve as a constituent assembly to remedy the legal vacuum that plagues the Palestinian nation. For neither the PNC in its present form, nor the Legislative Council representing the West Bank and Gaza, is qualified to adequately fulfill that function. The PNC was last reformed in 1991 and repackaged in the spring of 1996 to suit specific requirements conflicting with Palestinian rights and injurious to Palestinian interests. The Legislative Council, on the other hand, is a product of the DOP and its derivative agreements.

The omission from the DOP of the right of return, within the meaning of Resolution 194, is the singlemost serious impediment to genuine redress of the refugees' grievances. How can a council representing two million Palestinians in the so-called self-rule areas—leaving the bulk of the Palestinian population, most of whom are refugees, out—negotiate momentous issues with Israel, under Israeli occupation and according to utterly inequitable conditions imposed by Israel itself? It is not unreasonable to assume that an independent PLO, rather than the Legislative Council and Arafat's executive, must be charged with negotiating the question of the refugees. Despite serious damage inflicted on the PLO by the Oslo affair, it is still the only valid representative of the entire Palestinian people, including the refugees. It is still the national embodiment of Palestinian nationalism. Care, therefore, must be exercised to insure that PA agreements with Israel are not perceived as being those of the PLO, as has been the case with Oslo and the Beilin–Abu-Mazin agreement.

Moreover, the representative character of the Legislative Council is limited to a single segment of the Palestinian people, that which is based in the West Bank and Gaza. It is the only sector of the Palestinian nation for which Israel was seemingly willing to accept some obligation, albeit in return for giving Israel total exemption from all responsibilities for breaches and crimes committed against the Palestinian people. Under the present rules of the game, the Legislative Council and Arafat's executive would not be able to deal substantively with the right of self-determination and the right of return. Israel views the DOP as granting the Council neither judicial nor legislative powers.

The question of return is further marginalized by the fact that it has already been considered by the DOP as a regional matter affecting *all* refugees, including Jews who left property in Arab countries. That is why both Camp David and the DOP call for a committee consisting of Israel, Jordan, Egypt, and the Palestinian Council to settle that problem, with Israel retaining an effective veto.

The proposed Congress of Return would be inclusive, comprehensive, and people-oriented, rather than elitist. Its legitimacy would be derived from the entire Palestinian nation and from the relevant international declarations and U.N. resolutions, which the United States and Israel are feverishly trying to render superfluous. The Congress would be able to undo the negations of Madeleine Albright and voice an eloquent reply to her decree that the U.N. resolutions are "contentious and obsolete."[23] Representatives of the Palestinian people from all walks of life—from the refugee camps of Lebanon, Jordan, and Syria; from the West Bank and Gaza; from Israel proper; from the United States, Australia, and elsewhere—would reaffirm their rights under these resolutions. They would reestablish the right of a reconstituted PLO to resolve the refugee question with Israel. They would declare in unison that they—not the handful of operatives who have met in Oslo, Cairo, Taba, and other such places—have the right to determine which rights they will claim and which, if any, they will relinquish. It would be an experience that would initiate the process of redress, of real confidence building, of democratization, and of giving real voice to the voiceless.

Notes

1   General Assembly Resolution 194 (III), United Nations Document A/810
     at 21 (1948); see also W.T. Mallison and S. Mallison, *An International Law
     Analysis of the Major United Nations Resolutions Concerning the Palestine
     Question*, U.N. Doc.ST/SG/ser.F/4 (1979).
2   See partial text in *Occupation: Israel Over Palestine*, ed. Naseer H. Aruri
     (Belmont, MA: Association of Arab-American University Graduates,
     1983), pp. 94–95.
3   *Occupation: Israel Over Palestine,* pp. 95–96.
4   On restitution, see Atif Kubursi, "Valuing Palestinian Losses in Today's
     Dollars," *Palestinian Refugees: The Right of Return*, ed. Naseer H. Aruri
     (London: Pluto Press, 2001), pp. 217–51; also Susan Akram,
     "Reinterpreting Palestinian Refugee Rights under International Law, in
     Palestinian Refugees, ed. Aruri, pp. 165–95.
5   See http://www.un.org/unrwa.
6   The marginalization of the refugee issue in PLO-Arab dealings and the
     "peace process" is outlined in an earlier work by the author: "Towards
     Convening a Congress of Return and Self-Determination," in *Palestinian
     Refugees*, pp. 260–71.
7   Salman H. Abu-Sitta, *The Palestinian Nakba 1948: The Register of
     Depopulated Localities in Palestine*, 2nd ed. (London, PRC, 2000). See
     also Abu-Sitta, "The Right of Return: Sacred, Legal and Possible," in
     Palestinian Refugees, p. 195.
8   Akram, "Reinterpreting Palestinian Refugee Rights," pp. 166–67.
9   *U.S. Policy on Palestine: From Wilson to Clinton*, ed. Michael Suleiman
     (Normal, IL: Association of Arab-American University Graduates, 1995);
     Fred H. Lawson, "The Truman Administration and the Palestinians," *Arab
     Studies Quarterly* 12 (Winter/Spring 1990): 1–2
10   Fayez A. Sayegh, *Camp David and Palestine: A Preliminary Analysis*
     (New York, Americans for Middle East Understanding, 1979).
11   See address by George Shultz, "Terrorism and the Modern World," U.S.
     Department of State, Bureau of Public Affairs, *Current Policy* 629
     (October 24, 1984).
12   See Naseer H. Aruri et al., *Reagan and the Middle East* (Belmont, MA:
     Association of Arab-American University Graduates, 1983).
13   Among these organizations are the BADIL Resource Center for Palestinian
     Residency and Refugee Rights in Bethlehem; A'idun ("We Will Return")
     in Lebanon and Syria; SHAML, the Palestinian Diaspora and Refugee
     Centre in Jerusalem; and Al-Awda (The Return) in the United States.
14   Mallison and Mallison, *An International Law Analysis*.

15   *Ha'aretz*, January 2, 2001.
16   *New York Times*, January 6, 2001.
17   *Ha'aretz*, January 8, 2001.
18   *Ha'aretz*, January 8, 2001.
19   *Ha'aretz*, January 8, 2001.
20   *New York Times*, February 3, 2002.
21   *Yedioth Ahronoth*, July 11, 2000.
22   See Chapter 10.
23   *Journal of Palestine Studies* (Winter 1995): 152–53

CAMP DAVID, THE INTIFADA, AND THE END OF OSLO

The Al-Aqsa Intifada of September 2000 revealed the inherent flaws of Oslo and what had been touted since 1993 as the "peace process." It also exposed the fraudulent nature of this process, and the bad faith in which the negotiations and brokering have been conducted, effectively creating a post-Oslo juncture in the Middle East. By the end of November 2002, more than 2,000 Palestinians were killed, and more than 20,000 sustained serious injuries. By the same time, more than 700 Israelis were killed, and much of the civilian infrastructure of Palestinian society and the PA security apparatus lay in ruins.[1]

With the failure of the Camp David Summit in July 2000, any lingering illusions that peace would be the end result of this hopelessly defective process were completely shattered. Oslo was meant to serve Israeli ends, and Camp David served as Barak's exit strategy.

The Death of Oslo

By 2002, any pretense that the Oslo process, which was mortally wounded at Camp David, could still be revived became ludicrous. Israel's last three prime ministers, including Sharon, have been openly opposed to Oslo. Yet, the Israeli mainstream has never failed to recognize its benefits for Israel. For example, Uri Savir, one of the Israeli architects of Oslo, expressed the view that Israelis needed "more Oslo," not less.[2] The Palestinian people, by contrast, could see no potential for Oslo to fulfill the aspirations of the exiled, the occupied, or the Palestinian minority in Israel proper. For the millions of Palestinians in the diaspora, Oslo came to mean an end to the promise of restitution and a right of return, replaced by offers of only meager compensation raised by the international community and token "family reunifications." For the Palestinians inside Israel,

Oslo meant that they would have to accept, for all time, their status as sec-ond-class citizens, as the cutters of wood and haulers of water. Oslo shat-tered any dreams of reintegrating the Palestinian nation.

Oslo was the first diplomatic arrangement that allowed Israel to make tangible colonial achievements with a minimum reliance on its armed forces. It enabled Israel to recruit its victims to police themselves and keep the natives in line. The colonial power's dirty work was thus transferred to its new subcontractor—the Palestinian Authority. But the Intifada has dealt a severe blow to this seven-year-old "diplomatic" pretense. Oslo has run its course (indeed, it did so some time ago).

Major international human rights organizations, such as Human Rights Watch, Physicians for Human Rights, and Amnesty International, as well as the U.N. General Assembly, have criticized Israel for using le-thal force to quell demonstrations. Amnesty International, known for its measured responses and slow action, even accused Israel in November 2000 of "cruel, inhuman or degrading treatment" of Palestinians.[3] Am-nesty International went even further by accusing Israel of having com-mitted "war crimes" in Jenin and Nablus, and naming Shaul Mofaz, a former army chief of staff slated to become defense minister in early No-vember 2002, as one who could be charged.[4] Such universal condemna-tion went unnoticed by a complicit U.S. media, which managed to cover up not only Israeli crimes against civilians living under military occupa-tion but U.S. actions aiding and abetting these crimes. The Clinton admin-istration used its U.N. Security Council veto repeatedly to shield Israel from worldwide condemnation. It supplied Israel with the Cobra helicop-ter gunships and other instruments of death that have been used with im-punity against Palestinian refugee camps and urban areas. Instead of holding hearings about the possible violation of the Arms Export Control Act, which limits the use of U.S.-supplied weapons to defensive purposes, the U.S. Congress adopted a number of resolutions blaming the victims for the violence in the area.

Oslo has become a symbol of diplomatic paralysis and economic im-poverishment for the Palestinian people, an instrument that enabled Israel to extend the colonization of Palestinian land. In fact, the number of Jew-ish settlers has increased from 110,900 at the start of the Oslo process in 1993 to 198,000 in 2001, not including Jerusalem and vicinity.[5]

Palestinians simply sat and watched the expropriation of their land and resources for settlements and bypass roads built for Israelis only. These roads connect the settlements to each other and to Israel proper, while at the same time atomizing Palestinian society. Oslo provided a cover for these conquests. While people around the world watched a diplomatic charade that was packaged by the U.S. media and Israel's propaganda apparatuses as "peace" negotiations, Israel bulldozed Palestinian homes, expanded settlements, and built more "facts on the ground."

Was the Collapse of Camp David II Inevitable?

President Clinton seemed determined not to leave office without cleansing his historical legacy, which had been badly tarnished by several scandals. A breakthrough in the Middle East was seen as the best means to accomplish his mission. Moreover, he was also nudged by Ehud Barak, who was elected prime minister of Israel in May 1999. Barak procrastinated for nearly one year before he decided to proceed directly to final status negotiations as a tactic to avoid Israel's obligations to implement the third stage of its redeployment from the West Bank. These obligations were agreed upon in the 1995 Interim Agreement, which Barak voted against as minister of the interior, and the 1998 Wye Agreement, negotiated by his predecessor, Benjamin Netanyahu. According to Robert Malley and Hussein Agha, Barak, upon taking office, "chose to renegotiate the agreement on withdrawal of Israeli forces from the West Bank, signed by Benjamin Netanyahu, rather than implement it."[6] Thus from the start, Barak was to set the pace, while Clinton, in turn, prevailed on a reluctant Arafat to attend the Camp David conference, assuring him that should the conference fail, neither of the parties would be blamed.[7]

The inevitable failure of Camp David is documented in a book by Charles Enderlin, the Jerusalem correspondent for the France 2 television channel for the past twenty years. Alain Gresh, editor of *Le Monde diplomatique*, informs us that Enderlin was allowed to film the main protagonists and was given access to their personal notes, on the understanding that nothing would be published before the end of 2001.[8] In *Le Reve Brese,* Enderlin questions whether Camp David should even count as a summit, inasmuch as Barak, who could not conceal his disdain for Arafat, refused to negotiate directly with him or meet him alone. Enderlin's assessment was corroborated by Uri Avnery:

[Barak's] closest adviser, Shlomo Ben Ami, recounts that during a state dinner Barak sat "like a pillar of salt," not exchanging a word with Arafat.... At another, similar occasion, when Barak was seated between Arafat and young Chelsea Clinton, Barak demonstratively talked with only with the teenager, ignoring the Palestinian leader.[9]

Both Enderlin and Malley confirmed that the Palestinians were never offered full authority over the Arab district of Jerusalem and the al-Haram al-Sharif area. Full authority was offered over outlying suburbs like the Arab villages of Shufaat and Beit Hanina, north of Jerusalem, but the Arab quarters of Sheikh Jarrah, Ras al-Amoud, and the village of Silwan were accorded only "functional autonomy." The PA was offered only "guardianship" over the area of al-Haram al-Sharif, but the land on which the holy places stood was to be placed under Israeli sovereignty. Barak's curious demand was for sovereignty "beneath the surface" of al-Haram al-Sharif.

With regard to the refugees, Arafat had discussed the return of only a few thousand refugees but never demanded the right of return for all five million.[10] In fact, Malley and Agha point out, the refugee issue was not a major topic of discussion at Camp David, despite the claim by Barak that the refugee issue had dealt the fatal blow to the summit. At first Barak announced that Jerusalem was the culprit, but he later blamed the refugee issue for the collapse of the Camp David meeting.[11] Barak's "generosity" on the refugee issue extended to allowing 4,000 refugees to enter what is now Israel each year within the framework of what he called "family reunions," not the "right of return": "We cannot allow even one refugee back on the basis of the 'right of return'... and we cannot accept historical responsibility for the creation of the problem."[12]

There is more evidence that Barak had no intention of reaching an agreement at Camp David, or at Taba in January 2001, at which the two sides were said to have been brought closer on the issues of territory, Jerusalem, and refugees. According to Menachem Klein, an adviser to Israeli foreign minister Shlomo Ben Ami, Barak told him that he had sent a delegation to Taba solely to reveal "Arafat's true face" and not to conclude an agreement.[13] Avnery wrote in this regard:

> Recently, Barak bragged in an interview on Israeli TV that by making his generous offers to the Palestinians and the Syrians he unmasked both Arafat and Assad, who rejected them.... The Taba talks came to an

end when Barak unilaterally ordered his delegation to break them off. The pretext, this time: elections were too near.[14]

But the blame for the failure of Camp David, and hence of the "peace process" in its entirety, was placed by Clinton on Arafat. Clinton did the opposite of what he had promised Arafat, blaming him unequivocally for the summit's failure, thus paving the way for the Palestinian uprising and massive Israeli repression. Undoubtedly, the warm reception Arafat received upon returning home after the summit failure played right into the hands of Clinton and the media. The average person on the Arab street refrained from applauding what the U.S. and Israel considered one diplomatic breakthrough after another since 1993. Had Camp David succeeded, there would have been celebrations in the United States, but there would have been protest in the West Bank, Gaza, and in various refugee camps throughout the Arab world. Palestinians celebrated the failure of Camp David because it seemed that their leader, Arafat, had finally stood up for Palestinian interests and for once had not caved in to U.S. and Israeli pressure.

Prior to Camp David, the majority of Palestinians had lost faith in the Oslo process. To most Palestinians, Arafat's acccptance of Barak and Clinton's position would have been a total surrender. Yet, for Israel and the United States, Arafat's noncompliance was taken as a signal that he was not the ideal collaborator they had come to expect, hence his demonization and marginalization.

Red Lines at Camp David

It is not uncommon for negotiators to observe certain red lines—in this case, each one of the three negotiators, including the dishonest broker, the United States, had pressed his own. Clinton's red line was to refrain from faulting Israel under any circumstances. In his July 25, 2000 press conference and his July 27, 2000 interview on Israeli television, he placed the blame for failure entirely on Arafat, forfeiting even the pretense of impartiality and violating his solemn promise to Arafat.[15] In an effort to help his wife, Hillary Rodham Clinton, who was seeking a Senate seat in the state of New York, he supported Israel's goal of moving the U.S. embassy from Tel Aviv to Jerusalem, and promised increased military aid to Israel.

Arafat's red lines have dwindled over the years, becoming almost nonexistent. And yet, after surrendering the right of return for the refugees, he resisted going down in history as the Palestinian leader who gave away Jerusalem, at least for the time being. Barak's red lines, on the other hand, were repeated for the umpteenth time on his way to Camp David. In a front-page statement published in *Yedioth Ahronoth*, he addressed his constituents saying:

> Separation—we here and they there; no return to the 1967 borders; Jerusalem united under our sovereignty; no foreign army west of the River Jordan; most settlers under Israeli sovereignty in the final status arrangement; Israel will not recognize any moral or legal responsibility for the (Palestinian) refugee problem.[16]

Barak's red lines were Israel's red lines—those of Rabin, Netanyahu, Shamir, Begin, and Sharon. The Barak plan was now Clinton's "only game in town," and the dishonest broker could only engage in arm-twisting vìs-a-vìs Arafat, whose role, it seems, was to facilitate something of a diplomatic success for his disenchanted "peace partners"—at the expense of the Palestinian people.

Barak's "Generous Offer"

In a June 2002 interview with Israeli historian Benny Morris, Ehud Barak laid the blame squarely on Yasir Arafat for the failure of the Camp David summit. Robert Malley, who was at the summit as an adviser for Bill Clinton, countered this claim.[17] While Barak told Morris that Arafat had sought "Israel's demise," Malley and Agha pointed out that not only did Arafat barely present the right of return issue, but he sent a proposal to Barak after Camp David, in which he made unprecedented concessions, only to be turned down by Barak. The proposal included:

> A state of Israel incorporating some land captured in 1967 and including a very large majority of its settlers, the largest Jewish Jerusalem in the city's history, preservation of Israel's demographic balance between Jews and Arabs, security guarantees by a U.S.-led international presence.[18]

The Palestinian proposal bears a remarkable similarity to Clinton's eleventh-hour proposal made on January 7, 2001, which will be discussed later in this chapter. That in itself should have guaranteed a final settlement, but Barak's red lines stood in the way. Moreover, Barak's disparaging remarks about Palestinians as a people and their culture made it

CONTENTS

Maps Source: Palestinian Academic Society for the Study of International
Affairs, Jerusalem (PASSIA), *The Palestine Question in Maps: 1878–2002*
(Jerusalem: PASSIA, 2002). Maps also available online at http://www.passia.org.

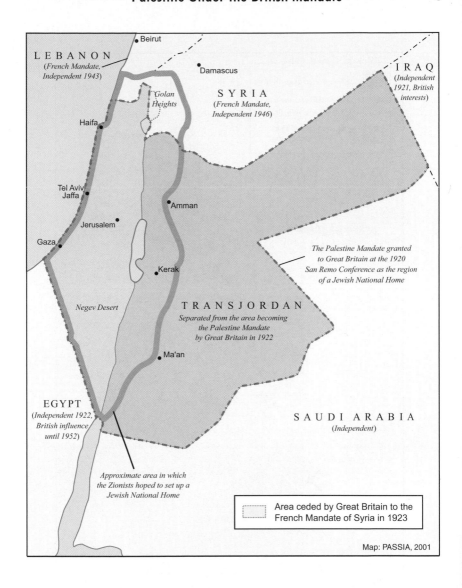

Beirut

LEBANON
*(French Mandate,
Independent 1943)*

Damascus

Golan
Heights

SYRIA
*(French Mandate,
Independent 1946)*

IRAQ
*(Independent
1921, British
interests)*

Haifa

Tel Aviv
Jaffa

Amman

Jerusalem

Gaza

Kerak

*The Palestine Mandate granted
to Great Britain at the 1920
San Remo Conference as the region
of a Jewish National Home*

Negev Desert

TRANSJORDAN
*Separated from the area becoming
the Palestine Mandate
by Great Britain in 1922*

Ma'an

EGYPT
*(Independent 1922,
British influence
until 1952)*

SAUDI ARABIA
(Independent)

*Approximate area in which
the Zionists hoped to set up a
Jewish National Home*

Area ceded by Great Britain to the
French Mandate of Syria in 1923

Map: PASSIA, 2001

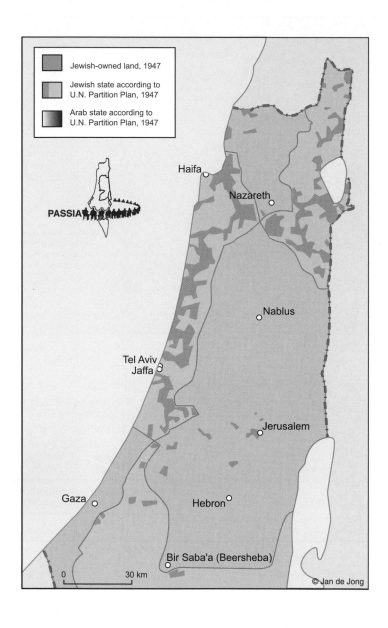

Jewish-owned land, 1947

Jewish state according to
U.N. Partition Plan, 1947

Arab state according to
U.N. Partition Plan, 1947

PASSIA

Haifa

Nazareth

Nablus

Tel Aviv
Jaffa

Jerusalem

Gaza

Hebron

Bir Saba'a (Beersheba)

0   30 km

© Jan de Jong

Jewish-owned land, 1947

State of Israel according to
the Armistice Agreement, 1949

Palestinian villages depopulated in
1948 and 1967 and razed by Israel

The West Bank and Gaza Strip

PASSIA

Haifa

Nazareth

Nablus

Tel Aviv
Jaffa

Jerusalem

Gaza

Hebron

Bir Saba'a (Beersheba)

0   30 km

© Jan de Jong

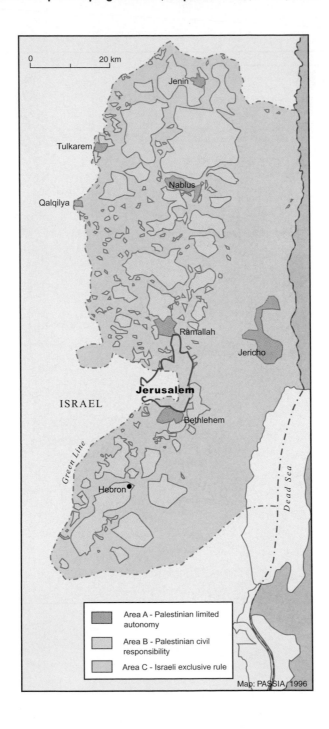

0   20 km

Jenin

Tulkarem

Nablus

Qalqilya

Ramallah

Jericho

Jerusalem

ISRAEL

Bethlehem

Green Line

Hebron

Dead Sea

Area A - Palestinian limited autonomy

Area B - Palestinian civil responsibility

Area C - Israeli exclusive rule

Map: PASSIA, 1996

0   20 km

Jenin

Tulkarem

Qalqilya

Nablus

ARIEL

*MODI'IN
ILLIT*

Ramallah

*GIV'AT
ZE'EV*

Jericho

ISRAEL   **Jerusalem**   *MA'ALE
ADUMIM*

BETAR

Bethlehem

Green Line

Dead Sea

Hebron

Palestinian Autonomous Areas
(Oslo II-Zones A and B)

Projected areas of further Israeli
redeployment

Israeli settlement, projected extent

Designated nature reserve

Israeli settlement

© Jan de Jong, 2001

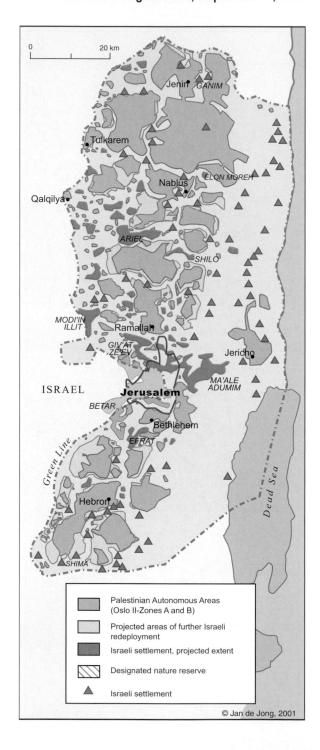

0   20 km

Jenin   *GANIM*

Tulkarem

Nablus   *ELON MOREH*

Qalqilya

ARIEL

SHILO

MODI'IN ILLIT

Ramallah

GIV'AT ZE'EV

Jericho

ISRAEL

MA'ALE ADUMIM

Jerusalem

BETAR

Bethlehem

EFRAT

Green Line

Dead Sea

Hebron

SHIMA

Palestinian Autonomous Areas
(Oslo II-Zones A and B)

Projected areas of further Israeli
redeployment

Israeli settlement, projected extent

Designated nature reserve

Israeli settlement

© Jan de Jong, 2001

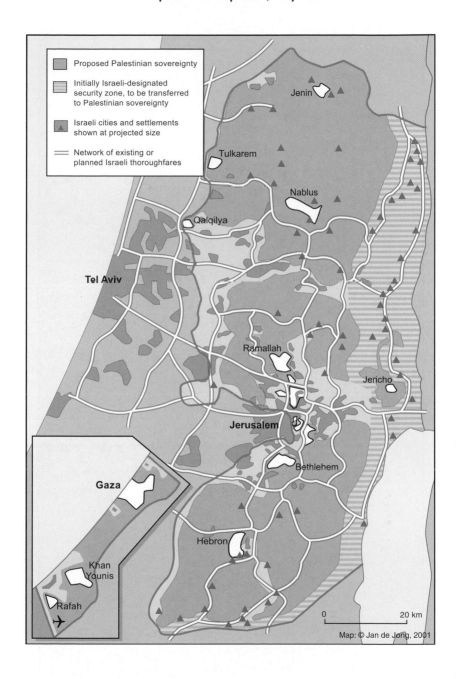

Proposed Palestinian sovereignty

Initially Israeli-designated security zone, to be transferred to Palestinian sovereignty

Israeli cities and settlements shown at projected size

Network of existing or planned Israeli thoroughfares

Jenin

Tulkarem

Nablus

Qalqilya

Tel Aviv

Ramallah

Jericho

Jerusalem

Bethlehem

Gaza

Hebron

Khan Younis

Rafah

0   20 km

Map: © Jan de Jong, 2001

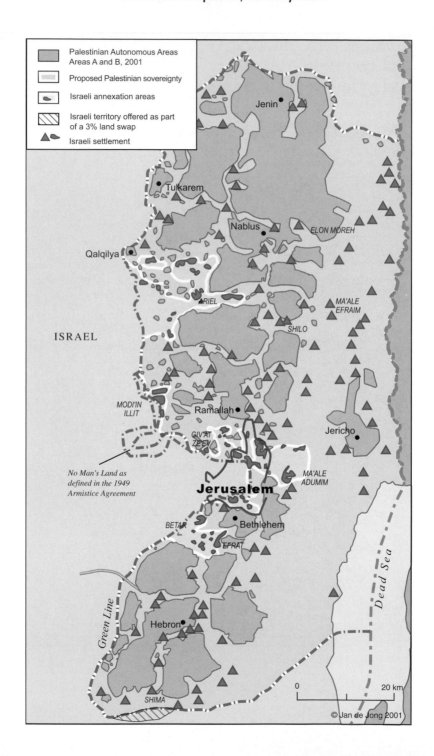

Palestinian Autonomous Areas
Areas A and B, 2001

Proposed Palestinian sovereignty

Israeli annexation areas

Israeli territory offered as part
of a 3% land swap

Israeli settlement

Jenin

Tulkarem

Nablus

ELON MOREH

Qalqilya

ARIEL

MA'ALE
EFRAIM

ISRAEL

SHILO

MODI'IN
ILLIT

Ramallah

GIV'AT
ZE'EV

Jericho

No Man's Land as
defined in the 1949
Armistice Agreement

MA'ALE
ADUMIM

Jerusalem

BETAR

Bethlehem

EFRAT

Dead Sea

Green Line

Hebron

0   20 km

SHIMA

© Jan de Jong 2001

Annexation areas:
41 settlements
65% of settlers

**West Bank
Palestinian Area: 94%**

87 Israeli settlements
35% of Israeli settlers

West Bank division
with number of Israeli settlements
and percentage of settlers,
excluding East Jerusalem

Historical Comparison

Tel Aviv

WEST BANK

Jerusalem

GAZA STRIP

Gaza

Jewish state according to
UN Partition Plan, 1947

Palestinian state according
to UN Partition Plan, 1947

Projected Palestinan state
according to the Israeli
proposal, Jan. 2001

The Sharon Proposal, Spring 2001

Palestinian Autonomous Areas
Areas A & B (41% of West Bank)

Projection of Palestinian sovereign
areas envisioned by Sharon
(43% of the West Bank)

Israeli sovereignty

Israeli settlements / selected
settlement built-up areas

Jenin

Tulkarem

Nablus

ELON MOREH

Qalqilya

ARIEL

MA'ALE
EFRAIM

SHILO

ISRAEL

MODIIN
ILLIT

Ramallah

GIV'AT
ZE'EV

Jericho

No Man's Land as
defined in the 1949
Armistice Agreement

MA'ALE
ADUMIM

Jerusalem

BETAR

Bethlehem

EFRAT

Green Line

Dead Sea

Hebron

0   20 km

SHIMA

© Jan de Jong, 2001

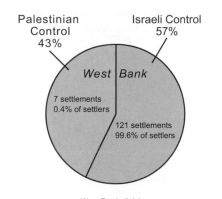

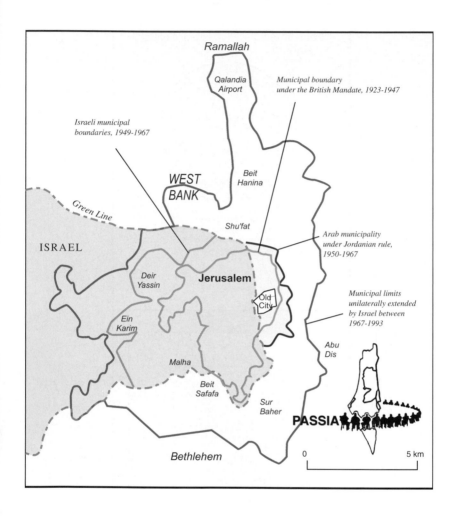

Ramallah

Qalandia
Airport

Municipal boundary
under the British Mandate, 1923-1947

*Israeli municipal
boundaries, 1949-1967*

WEST
BANK

Beit
Hanina

Green Line

Shu'fat

ISRAEL

Arab municipality
*under Jordanian rule,
1950-1967*

Deir
Yassin

Jerusalem

Old
City

Municipal limits
*unilaterally extended
by Israel between
1967-1993*

Ein
Karim

Abu
Dis

Malha

Beit
Safafa

Sur
Baher

PASSIA

Bethlehem

0   5 km

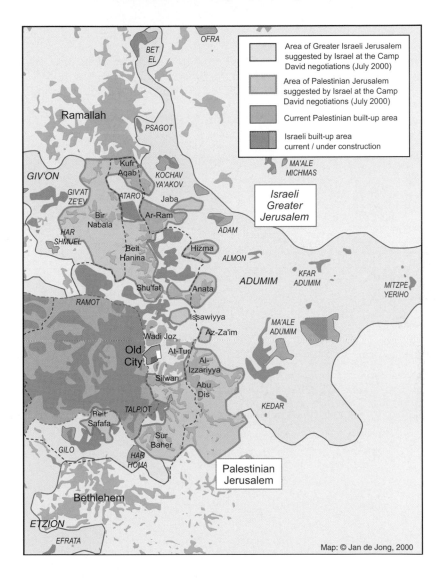

Map: © Jan de Jong, 2000

unlikely that he would reach a principled compromise with them. According to Malley and Agha, he "characterized Palestinian refugees as 'salmon' whose yearning to return to their land is somehow supposed to fade away in eighty years in a manner that the Jewish people's never did even after 2,000 years."[19] He also described Arabs as people who are congenital liars:

> They (the Palestinians, and especially Arafat) are the products of a culture in which to tell a lie ... creates no dissonance. They don't suffer from the problem of telling lies that exists in Judeo-Christian culture. Truth is seen as an irrelevant category.... The deputy director of the U.S. Federal Bureau of Investigation told me that there are societies in which lie detector tests don't work, societies in which lies do not create cognitive dissonance (on which the tests are based).[20]

Uri Avnery commented on Barak's racism thus:

> By condemning Islam and identifying himself with Judeo-Christianity (a dubious concept in itself, since Judaism is closer to Islam than to Christianity), Barak is trying to ride the wave of Islamophobia that is currently sweeping the U.S. and the whole Western world. It reminds one of the words written some 108 years ago by Theodor Herzl, the father of modern Zionism, in his book *Der Judenstaat*, the founding document of Zionism: "For Europe we would constitute (in Palestine) a part of the wall against Asia, we would serve as an outpost of culture against barbarism".... By asserting that all Arabs lie at all times, Barak also constructs a beautiful defense. Whatever the Palestinians say to disprove his account can be dismissed in advance. They always lie, don't they?[21]

In a brief presented to the Center for Policy Analysis on Palestine on March 7, 2001, Malley divided the blame for the failure of Camp David between Israel, the United States, and the Palestinians, noting that, for Palestinians, "it was the culmination of seven long years during which Israel never accepted the legitimacy of their demands and the necessity to undo a historic wrong."[22] From the Israeli point of view, "the Palestinians never accepted the necessity of reconciliation, of partition, even of the existence of the Israeli state itself," a spurious conclusion that fails to stand against the Palestinians' willingness to accept a deal that fell below 22 percent of their national patrimony. But the need that politicians have for symmetry and appearing evenhanded is expected in American political culture.

Malley noted six major mistakes made by the U.S. at Camp David:

1. "We relied ... far too heavily on Barak's timetables and tactics."

2. Barak's offers were "greeted by the U.S. team too often with unwarranted enthusiasm."
3. "We were overly distrustful" of the idea of having third parties, insisting instead on being the sole mediator.
4. "We neglected what was happening on the ground," such as home demolition and settlement expansion.
5. "We were dragged" into inter-Palestinian politics.
6. "We allowed the process gradually to become presidentialized," with Clinton and a small team at the helm.[23]

Barak's mythical "generous offer" consisted of four enclaves bisected by illegally built colonial settlements and bypass roads for Jews only, which would have prevented the Palestinians from ever establishing a viable, independent, and contiguous state in any area between the River Jordan and the Mediterranean Sea. Although the four enclaves (Northern West Bank, Central West Bank, Southern West Bank, and Gaza) may have been called a state, the requirements of a nation-state were sorely missing. It would have been a state without sovereignty, without geographic continuity, and without control over its borders, airspace, and economic and water resources. In fact, it would have consisted of sixty-four clusters or islands in the midst of Israel, a "state" existing within Israel, but not alongside Israel.

According to a recent comprehensive publication by B'Tselem, the settlers now have absolute sovereignty over 41 percent of West Bank territory.[24] Moreover, the often-touted tale of the offer to give the Palestinians 95–99 percent of the West Bank–Gaza territory was hardly examined by U.S. journalists, who accepted it as dogma. In fact, Barak had proposed that sixty-nine Israeli colonies populated by 85 percent of West Bank settlers be annexed as blocs to Israel. Palestinians would thus be expected to relinquish 10 percent of their historic homeland, reducing the offer to 90 percent of the West Bank.[25]

Barak introduced a unique concept called "Temporary Israeli Control" to acquire additional land for an indefinite time, thus reducing the offer by another 10 percent, making it effectively 80 percent of the West Bank. In addition, the percentage game did not take into account that the proposed land swap was based on an exchange at the rate of nine to one, in favor of Israel. According to Malley and Agha, President Clinton "proposed a deal by which Israel would annex 9 percent of the West Bank in exchange for turning over to the Palestinians part of pre-1967 Israel equivalent to 1 percent of the West Bank."[26]

The 95 percent figure also excludes Jerusalem, the Dead Sea, the Jordan Valley, and the settlements. The West Bank and Gaza constitute 22 percent of pre-Israel Palestine, of which Jewish ownership comprised 6 percent in 1948. The generous offer was not 95 percent of the 22 percent, but more like 80 percent of the 22 percent, which would have been 17.6 percent of the Palestinians' historic homeland. Moreover, Arafat had, in effect, relinquished the right of the refugees to return. According to Alain Gresh, "Arafat had already made clear to Clinton at a meeting in Washington on June 15, 2000, that … a balance had to be struck between Israel's demographic concerns and Palestinians' demands," regarding the refugees.[27]

Generous Offers and Jerusalem

Israel's "compromise" on Jerusalem, which had been brandished by segments of the U.S. media as too good of a deal to turn down, consisted of placing under Palestinian "administrative control" less than 15 percent of the forty-three square miles Israel had annexed from the West Bank after 1967. Accordingly, Palestinians were told that they would enjoy a "sense of sovereignty" in areas Israel includes in its redefinition of Jerusalem. Given that what Israel calls East Jerusalem (Jordanian Jerusalem) was only four square miles in 1967, and now has expanded to 47 square miles, giving back to the Palestinians a little of what was theirs was hardly a magnanimous act.

The twenty-eight Arab villages and neighborhoods annexed after 1967, which have no traces of Jewish heritage, include, among others, Sheikh Jarrah, Wadi al-Jouz, Shofat, Silwan, Ras al-Amoud, Beit Hanina, Kufr Aqab, al-Sawahreh. Nor is there a Jewish heritage, for that matter, in Ein Karem, Lifta, Deir Yassin, al-Maliha, al-Baqa'a, Talbiyeh, Qatamoun, among other Arab villages and urban centers annexed as West Jerusalem after 1948.

Moreover, in addition to relieving Israel of ruling over the Arab neighborhoods of what is now called East Jerusalem, the Palestinians would have had to acquiesce in yet a further enlargement of Jerusalem, comprising the settlements of Ma'ale Adumim to the east and Givaat Ze'ev to the north and northwest. Of course, all the other major blocs of illegal settlements in the Hebron-Bethlehem area and in the Jenin-Nablus area are expected to be annexed by Israel.

In addition, with regard to the holy places in Jerusalem, Israel would have retained sovereignty over the land on which the Muslim and Christian holy places are built while the Palestinian Authority would have exercised control over only the buildings. Under Camp David's "generous offer," this was certainly a recipe for a perpetual conflict rather than peace.

The Oslo process could never have culminated in an honorable compromise, but in the permanent bantustanization of the West Bank. Oslo was a mere pause along the path of Israel's conquest of the whole of mandated Palestine. It did not take the eye of a scrutinizing analyst to see in Barak's red lines disdain for international law (borders, Jerusalem, settlements, refugees); the reaffirmation of apartheid ("separation" in the Afrikaans language); and the lack of remorse for ethnic cleansing (Jerusalem, refugees). Could it be that even the hapless Arafat, with his penchant for the trapppings of power, could not bear to see his future realm as a collection of disconnected Bantustans, his people as disenfranchised refugees and maquiladora laborers, his capital as an unknown village, and himself as the first Palestinian leader to completely surrender legally established and historic rights? Could that have been the reason for his initial reluctance to accept Clinton's summons to Camp David? Arafat was obviously facing his moment of truth at Camp David. It was one thing to talk about the size of land ceded to his authority and the extent of that authority during the interim phase; it was quite another to broach the intractable issues that had been deferred since 1993—and which somehow were thought to have been deferred indefinitely, or resolved in Israel's favor.

Was the Collapse of Camp David a Failure of Oslo?

A quick glance at the Oslo Accords reveals that the failure at Camp David was largely due to certain structural defects in the DOP. There was almost no transition connecting the interim issues to the intractable final status issues, leaving unanswered questions about the rationale for two phases of negotiations and for three levels of authority in Oslo II. Oslo's interim arrangements had proven to have little relevance to the final status phase. The so-called confidence-building measures of the interim phase have proven more effective as propaganda tools than practical measures. It therefore made very little sense to divide the negotiations into two unconnected phases.

Hardly anything that was accomplished during the seven years of Oslo could have been utilized to bridge the gaps. Instead, the central feature of Clinton's methodology of conflict resolution was arm-twisting, as if a lasting peace could ever emanate from salesmanship techniques and coercion. The pursuit of a negotiated settlement, based on two states, seemed to have run its course. That project was dealt a severe blow by a colossal imbalance of power between Israel and the Palestinians, by a steady and growing Israelization (and more recently Likudization) of American Middle East policy, by a vigorous drive of settler colonization, and by Arab disarray. The Oslo process demonstrated that the so-called peace partners were not only far apart conceptually, but also were hopelessly divided over interpretations and what the end results of the process should be. Meanwhile, Palestinians saw one agreement after another—from Oslo I all the way to Sharm al-Shaykh and Taba—in which Arafat seemed to have accepted, by implication, that U.N. resolutions do not necessarily constitute the basis for a final settlement.

Israel's Strategy in the Oslo Process

It should be recalled that when Rabin diverted the negotiating venue from public talks in Washington to secret talks in Oslo in 1993, he was making an important shift away from the stalling tactics of his Likud predecessor, Yitzhak Shamir, while creating his own gridlock with the appearance of diplomatic progress. In a subtle divergence from Shamir, Rabin opted for an agreement with a built-in conflict over meaning, goals, and objectives. It is because of that gridlock and the built-in conflict that the Oslo process was born and remained in a stalemate, despite the continuous staging of diplomatic progress.

Another serious flaw in Oslo relates to the pattern of segmentation and deferral. For the Palestinians, segmenting the negotiations by issues, population categories, regions, towns and villages, and stages of negotiations remained one of the biggest obstacles to peace. Had the issue of land and settlements not been deferred during Oslo's "interim phase," the question of settlement security would not have become a barrier for redeployment. Had the issue of Hebron not been singled out and deferred, the question of "further redeployment" would not have arisen. Had the issues of Jerusalem and sovereignty not been delayed, the violence associated with the Israeli military's closure of Palestinian population centers, the 1996 tunnel crisis, settlement-building crises in Ras al-Amoud and Jabal Abu Ghoneim (Har Ha'oma), and similar "individual" crises would not have replaced its root causes on the agenda of the "honest broker." Had the deferral pattern not been set, matters relating to self-governance, further redeployment, easing the closure, releasing tax funds, and even resuming negotiations would not have been treated as probationary.

The Inherent Flaws of Oslo: A Process Doomed from the Outset

Under Oslo, terms such as "occupation" and "withdrawal" were excised from the lexicon. New terms surfaced, such as "redeployment," "external security," "sense of sovereignty," "super-sovereignty," "sub-sovereignty," "shared sovereignty," "reserves," and "custodianship." Others, such as "state," acquired a new definition, which excluded sovereignty. Even Prime Minister Sharon, the architect of Palestinian politicide in March and April 2002, and George W. Bush have declared their support for a Palestinian state, a commentary on the real meaning of the nation-state being envisioned for the Palestinians.

For the U.S. and Israel, a Camp David agreement was the natural last step in a series of capitulations and concessions extracted from Arafat, beginning with the open-ended Oslo. Clinton was banking on his penchant for creative diplomacy to produce one more agreement, even in the face of great skepticism at the time he summoned the parties to Camp David. This time, however, the "creative diplomacy," which had produced the earlier agreements by deferring the substantive issues, had been exhausted. Having resisted Clinton's usual browbeating at Camp David, Arafat spoiled the party and surprised his host by failing to sign off on a final surrender. As a consequence, he and his people would face the most severe punishments that the Palestinian people have endured since 1948. The Barak period will probably go down in history as a mere prelude to Sharon's bloody rule, comparable to no other period in its contempt for international morality and law and for its total disregard for human life and property.

Israel's Provocations and U.S. Supporting Propaganda

Anyone reading the Israeli press at the time when the Camp David talks collapsed would have noticed the number of editorials and opinion pieces predicting that Arafat's rebuff would not go unnoticed.[28] Reports about preparations for a war against the PA were rampant from May 2000 onward. Arafat, together with his people, would be given a taste of what the Middle East's superpower could deliver. In fact, Sharon's plan to destroy the civilian, social, and security infrastructure of the Palestinians in the spring of 2002 was prepared long before, in the year 2000, and updated the following year.[29] According to Israeli professor Tanya Reinhart, the plan to crush the Palestinians was prepared in October 2000 under Barak:

> "Foreign Report" (*Jane's Information*) of July 12, 2001, disclosed that the Israeli army [under Sharon's government] had updated its plans for an "all-out assault to smash the Palestinian Authority, force out leader Yasir Arafat and kill or detain its army." The blueprint entitled "The Destruction of the Palestinian Authority and Disarmament of All Armed Forces," was presented to the Israeli government by chief of staff Shaul Mofaz on July 8, 2001. The assault would be launched at the government's discretion, after a big suicide bomb attack in Israel, causing widespread deaths and injuries, citing the bloodshed as justification. It was a calculated plan long in the making.[30]

Israel had never had any difficulty finding pretexts for its military adventures—not in 1948, 1956, 1967, 1976, 1982, and not now. This time, Ariel Sharon, the master of provocation—who in a multilateral world would have been contemplating the possibility of being captured like the former Chilean dictator Augusto Pinochet and tried for war crimes—made a triumphant entry into the compound of al-Haram al-Sharif (known to Jews as the Temple Mount) on September 28, 2000, surrounded by more than a thousand soldiers and armed police officers, in a clear attempt to provoke the Palestinians.

Israel's newly trained sharpshooters, with orders to kill, went into action against Muslim worshipers the very next day, killing and injuring dozens. The Al-Aqsa Intifada had, thus, been ignited, with a multitude of young people demonstrating nonviolently at checkpoints and some throwing stones. Segments of the U.S. media began to call the uprising "Arafat's war" and even suggested that he deliberately provoked it, parroting the racist Israeli accusation that Palestinian parents send their children to the street to throw stones, get killed, and thus score a propaganda victory. Such gratuitous attitudes were based on the premise that Palestinians did not value human lives, as did Israelis and Westerners—a well-known and well-documented phenomenon in the Western discourse about third-world societies challenging colonialism. Moreover, the accusation assumed that Arafat was directing and orchestrating the uprising by remote control, despite the fact that the uprising was in part waged against his own regime.

This was not, of course, the first time that the U.S. media have distorted the essence of popular revolution among oppressed peoples. South African, Vietnamese, Central American, and African American activists in the 1960s were also portrayed as having been instigated, if not led, by "external" forces whenever they challenged the oppressive status quo. What the media failed (or refused) to understand was that all these struggles and the popular discontent throughout the Arab world are really a consequence of the efforts of the imperial powers and their regional collaborators to restructure and rearrange the political systems of the region to suit their interests, contrary to the interests of the common people.

Clinton Grasps for a Settlement:
Sharm al-Shaykh, Taba, Tenet, and Mitchell

Rescuing Washington's diplomatic turf remained a Clinton priority, despite mounting evidence that even the pretense of impartiality had been forfeited when Israeli forces put aside all restraints against unarmed Palestinian civilians after September 2000. The excessive use of force, resulting initially in a kill ratio of three to seventy in favor of Israel,[31] and the introduction of newly trained Israeli sharpshooters impelled the Security Council to convene a session on October 3, 2000, despite vigorous U.S. opposition. A scandalously watered-down resolution (1322) adopted on October 7 condemned violence without mentioning Israel, the price for U.S. abstention instead of a veto. All the other fourteen members of the Security Council, however, voted for the resolution. On December 18, the U.S. lobbied strongly against a similar resolution and succeeded in convincing six members to abstain, thus assuring defeat without even having to cast its veto.[32] With the increase in Israeli killings and stepped up repression, the Security Council convened five months later to consider a resolution sponsored by seven nonaligned countries urging the creation of an unarmed international observer force to protect civilians in the West Bank and Gaza. The United States used its veto this time to kill that resolution on March 27, 2001.[33] Only four West European countries abstained; the rest voted in the affirmative.

U.S. Damage Control

Meanwhile, to maintain the facade of a peace process and to thwart any potential international intervention, the Clinton administration introduced two new entries into the Middle East diplomatic lexicon—the Tenet Plan and the Mitchell Committee. For the next two years, various U.S. envoys would shuttle back and forth to the area with palliatives and promises to implement Tenet and Mitchell, the latest ceilings of the "peace process." Pre-empting any genuine international effort at conciliation, Clinton arranged to have President Mubarak convene a conference at Sharm al-Shaykh on October 17, 2000, in order to keep the process going, even as peace seemed hopelessly remote. It would still, however, be a "peace process," and the U.S. would still be the custodian.

As the most recent codicils of the Oslo process, the Mitchell and Tenet documents are the only remaining tangible components of a dead enterprise. They bring to mind Resolutions 242 and 338, which are repeated over and over but have yet to produce peace after thirty-five years. Now that the "peace process" is seen in a state of prolonged hybernation, the two documents are treated as signposts of a possible revival. But as Sharon's veto of a political horizon seems to resonate with George Bush, these so-called plans sound more like the last gasp of the "peace process." While neither one of them talks about peace, Tenet addresses the question of how to restore Palestinian contributions to Israel's security and that of its settlers; Mitchell attempts to lay out a fictitious political framework, whose real purpose is to obviate the need for international protection.

The Origins of Tenet and Mitchell

At Sharm al-Shaykh, in October 2000, Arafat and Barak were encouraged by representatives of the United States, Jordan, Egypt, the United Nations, and the European Union to reach decisions on a cease-fire, renewed security cooperation under the CIA auspices, and a modality for inquiry into the causes of the uprising. The seeds that were planted between Netanyahu and Arafat at the Wye Agreement had thus been nurtured, as it was agreed that CIA observers would be dispatched to the field as part of a restructured trilateral security arrangement. As for international observers, Israel remained adamantly opposed to them in the face of great international, Palestinian, and Arab pressure for some type of an international inquiry. The United Nations Commission on Human Rights (UNCHR) adopted a resolution on October 19, 2000, condemning Israel's "disproportionate and indiscriminate use of force," and the Commission accused Israel of committing war crimes and crimes against humanity. The resolution called for the establishment of an "inquiry commission" and asked Mary Robinson, the human rights commissioner, to investigate Israel's violation of human rights. After completing her fact-finding trip, Robinson accused Israel of using "excessive force" and called for an international monitoring presence.[34] During her extended visit to the Occupied Territories, her own vehicle came under Israeli fire. But as expected, the U.S. deferred to Israel—hence the Mitchell Committee, which consisted of safe and trusted individuals not likely to create waves, was Clinton's substitute for a credible commission of inquiry and international monitors. Former Senator George Mitchell's background has already been covered, highlighting his close connections with the pro-Israel PACs, which kept him among the very top recipients of their contributions during his tenure in the U.S. Senate. His former colleague and fellow Mitchell Committee member Senator Warren Rudman was equally indebted to the pro-Israel lobby. Former Turkish president Suleyman Demirel was an ardent proponent of strategic cooperation between Israel and Turkey. Norwegian foreign minister Thorbjoern Jagland's association with Oslo is well-known and finally European Union representative Javier Solana was deemed to add credibility. What the Palestinians needed more than anything at that time, and even more now, was international protection. Neither that nor a legitimate inquiry would be undertaken, as U.S. diplomats systematically lobbied U.N. delegates to oppose real monitoring.

The second product of the October 2000 meeting at Sharm al-Shaykh was the Tenet Plan, which called on the security organizations of the PA and Israel to "reaffirm their commitments to the security agreements forged at Sharm al-Shaykh, embedded in the Mitchell Report of April 2001."[35]

The Bush Administration and the Mitchell Committee Report
The Mitchell Committee made it clear from the beginning that it did not constitute a tribunal and that it would refrain from conducting any in-

vestigation on the ground. In fact, having conducted its work in Washington, it had to rely largely on reports submitted to it by the two protagonists. Despite that, Israel decided to stop cooperating with it in January 2001, pending high-level talks with the incoming Bush administration. The Palestinians, on the other hand, who were denied a true international monitoring process by this Committee, expressed their satisfaction and even pleasure. The Committee's report, released on May 20, 2001, during the administration of George W. Bush, opted for a road map back toward the discredited Oslo process, which had already caused the collapse of Camp David.[36] Palestinian writer Mouin Rabbani described the prospects in a perceptive article: "Yet, by refusing to deviate from Oslo's conceptual framework and political assumptions, and seeking to reinforce them instead, the Mitchell report has set the stage for its own failure. Future historians are likely to consider it Oslo's last gasp."[37] The recommendations of the report were a mere repetition of familiar cliches: ending the violence, resuming security cooperation, seeking a cooling-off period, rebuilding confidence, and resuming negotiations. There was nothing creative or innovative in the familiar sequence and phraseology, which has proven to be more sanctimonious than practical over many years of futile American diplomacy. But, again, the *raison d'etre* of the Mitchell Committee was the pre-emption of any incorporation of an international effort into peacemaking after the effective demise of Oslo. There was no distinction made between the violence of an occupying power and the resistance of an occupied population. In fact, Palestinian "violence" and "terrorism" were juxtaposed against Israel's quest for "security."

Trying to appear evenhanded, the report placed some of the blame on "some" Israelis who appear not to comprehend the humiliation and frustration that Palestinians must endure every day as a result of living with the continuing effects of occupation, sustained by the presence of Israeli military forces and settlements in their midst, or the determination of the Palestinians to achieve independence and genuine self-determination.

By the same token, the report places blame on "some" Palestinians who appear not to comprehend the extent to which terrorism creates fear among the Israeli people and undermines their belief in the possibility of coexistence, or the determination of the government of Israel to do whatever is necessary to protect its people.

The report summarizes the charge to the Committee as comprising three things: What happened? Why did it happen? And how can the recurrence of violence be prevented? It answers the first question by taking the easy way out: "We are not a tribunal," but proceeds with a chronology of events starting with Sharon's entry into Haram al-Sharif on September 28, 2000, again indicting both parties in a disingenuous attempt to appear evenhanded:

> However, we were provided with no persuasive evidence that the Sharon visit was anything other than an internal political act; neither were we provided with persuasive evidence that the PA planned the up-rising…. However, there is no evidence on which to conclude that the PA made a consistent effort to contain the demonstration and control the violence once it began, or that the government of Israel made a consistent effort to use nonlethal means to control demonstrations of unarmed Palestinians.

Concluding its answer to the question of what happened, the report exonerates Sharon by saying, "The Sharon visit did not cause the 'al-Aqsa Intifada.' But it was poorly timed and the provocative effect should have been foreseen."

As to the second question—why it happened—the report devotes a page for each one of the protagonists' perspectives and, except for some nuances, attempts to strike a balance, placing the committee in a seemingly neutral posture. On how to end the violence and put Oslo back "on track," the report offers nothing new, relying on worn-out cliches such as the need to improve the confidence climate and pave the way to negotiations.

To the extent that the report placed most of the emphasis on the need to end the violence, Israel found a convenient excuse to procrastinate further, a strategy it adheres to at the present time. It formally accepted the Mitchell report but stipulated that the settlement freeze called for by the report would only be discussed *after* the complete cessation of all violence and "terrorism." This precondition was extended later to the mere idea of resuming any kind of political talks. The PA, on the other hand, accepted the report, in keeping with its pathetic policy of appeasing the principal players and wanting to appear "constructive." To date, however, the Mitchell report has not been on any active agenda, perhaps because peace talks, in themselves, have become hostage to escalating conditions, most of which were impossible to meet.

Clinton and the Pro-Israel Establishment in the U.S.

In a last attempt to rescue his diplomatic investment, President Clinton gave a major foreign policy speech on January 7, 2001, at the Israel Policy Forum Gala in New York.[38] The first fifteen minutes of his speech revealed the high degree of rapport he enjoyed with numerous American Jewish leaders in the audience, making specific references to his relations with each one, which left no doubt about his devotion to their cause and his dedication to the future of Israel. He made it clear that he was using his remaining time in office to narrow down the differences between Barak and Arafat by suggesting five principles on which a final settlement would be built.

First, the principle of two separate homelands, which requires land swaps, annexations, and consolidation. There can be no genuine resolution to the conflict without "a sovereign viable Palestinian state that accommodates Israel's security requirements and the demographic realities." That suggests Palestinian sovereignty over Gaza, the vast majority of the West Bank, and the incorporation into Israel of settlement blocs, with the goal of maximizing the number of settlers in Israel while minimizing the land for Palestine.

Second, the Palestinian refugees will exercise their right of return by "returning" to the Palestinian state, or they may wish to remain where they are or move to other countries "consistent with those countries' sovereign decisions." The burden of compensation falls on the international community, with the U.S. taking the lead, but there was no mention of Israeli responsibility whatsoever.

Third, the need for "lasting security guarantees for Israel," which should not "come at the expense of Palestinian sovereignty or interfere with Palestinian territorial integrity." Such security needs, however, require a nonmilitarized Palestinian state, international monitors, and a "phased Israeli withdrawal to address Israeli security needs in the Jordan valley."

Fourth, Jerusalem will be an open city and the capital of two states. "What is Arab should be Palestinian ... what is Jewish should be Israeli ... and what is holy to both should require a special care to meet the needs of all."

Fifth, any agreement "will have to mark the decision to end the conflict"—no more interim agreements or deadlines.[39]

These were Clinton's parameters for a settlement, which seemed to have coincided with certain leaps forward achieved by the Israeli and Palestinian negotiating teams. But Clinton had less than two weeks and Barak was not interested in what his negotiators placed on his desk. Meanwhile, the Intifada was becoming more militarized under the impact of Israeli lethal force and the reign of terror imposed upon the Palestinians by the occupation regime.

Did Arafat Have a Strategy at Oslo and Camp David?

Arafat's association with Oslo placed him in a crippling conundrum. He risked losing legitimacy if he made further compromises on Palestinian rights, yet he had gone so far down the road of concessions to Israel that withdrawing from the process became untenable. Having traded his people's legitimacy for U.S. and Israeli legitimacy, Arafat had placed himself in a no-win situation—unable to deliver either to Israel and its U.S. patron or to his own constituents, who were ready to scale down their aspirations but not to surrender their fundamental rights.

Arafat's repeated denunciations of "terror" and vows to eradicate violence, under constant urging by the United States and Israel since the mid-1980s, have been seen in the Palestinian street as an ominous attack on the legitimate right to resist an illegal occupation. By expecting Arafat to agree to a cease-fire, Clinton and Barak seemed to miss a new reality—that Arafat's commitments may have been made on behalf of the Palestinian people, but without their consent. His people were asserting their legitimate right of resistance, and paying an exceedingly high price for it—with their lives and their children's lives, with their homes and property, and with their own livelihoods. Unless the Intifada produced new and better terms for the Palestinians, it was unlikely that an end to the demonstrations and various acts of resistance was near, but the Oslo equation had become *caduc*.[40] Had Arafat decided to acquiesce in U.S. and Israeli demands to suppress the Intifada, he would have risked losing his role as the acknowledged leader of the Palestinian people. Should he have led the Intifada, he would have risked a greater punishment than what had already been inflicted upon him and his PA institutions while Barak was still in charge, and before the total devastation under Sharon had taken place.

The Intifada and its leadership denounced Oslo at the early stages of the uprising, and so did Arafat's Fatah organization (Tanzim), but Arafat himself did not.[41] His PA was, after all, the creation of Oslo, which is to say the creation of Israel, the architect of Oslo. Consequently, the PA had no alternative strategy, except to utilize the unrest for the achievement of a better deal—something that would have ranged between an improved Camp David II and a notch below the Beilin–Abu-Mazin Agreement.

Knowing that the situation was like a double-edged sword, Arafat kept hoping that, eventually, a new American administration would have to summon the two parties to yet another diplomatic parley. He calculated that Israel's maximum escalation would involve an exceedingly costly re-occupation of all the territory in Area A under his rule and Area B under his partial control. Arafat was of course later proven wrong, as Sharon was able to keep Areas A and B under his effective control, but without the cost of the daily administration and without losing the Oslo benefits even as he continued to dismantle them. Moreover, the new American administration has managed to maintain a very low level of engagement as we will see in the next chapter. Arafat's strategy faltered completely, due to his inability to fulfill contradictory obligations—to his own constituents and to their nemeses in Tel Aviv and Washington.

President Clinton, who opened the Camp David summit by calling for a "principled compromise," could have been reminded that the negotiations for a stable peace and ultimate reconciliation must be guided by principles—principles not merely designed to reflect the existing balance of power, but principles that reflect the concerns of both parties and the requirements of international law. Such a principled compromise could not be brokered without the sponsorship of the international community and the force of the relevant United Nations resolutions. Just as Barak did not hesitate to publicize his four red lines, in full violation of United Nations resolutions, as he embarked on the trip to Camp David, Arafat could have affirmed these resolutions, such as 181, 194, 3236, 242, and 338, thus upholding the right to statehood, the rights of refugees, and the inadmissibility of conquest by force. He could have insisted on the inclusion of the 1949 Geneva Convention for the Protection of Civilians under Military Control in the agenda. He could have been prepared to request a Security Council meeting under its broad peacekeeping powers in the diplomatic, military, and economic spheres, despite the knowledge that the Council has effectively become an instrument of U.S. foreign policy. Such moral pressure could eventually bring world public opinion to dissuade the U.S.

from continuing to pretend that it is a peacemaker and not a party to the conflict. Arafat also could have been prepared to request a General Assembly meeting under the Uniting for Peace Resolution, in the event the U.S. was going to use its Security Council veto. Such a move or a threat to use it might have angered his American host, but diplomatic niceties do not precede the national interest. The need for protecting Palestinian civilians under the mercy of the fourth most powerful army in the world was rather urgent at the time of Camp David, and is even more urgent at the present time. Such an effort by the Palestinian president should have taken precedence over all efforts to resuscitate a dead peace process by a lame duck U.S. president and a lame duck Israeli prime minister.

In the final analysis, negotiations between the PA and Israel were marred by conceptual and methodological gaps and the absence of a strategy for negotiations on the part of the Palestinians. Conceptually, the Palestinians and Israelis differed on the very concept and meaning of negotiations. The Israelis saw the Palestinians coming to the negotiations to see how the Israelis would give them "their 22 percent of the West Bank, along with East Jerusalem and at least at the declaratory level, the right of return."[42] For Israel, which did not see itself obligated morally or legally to empathize with the Palestinians, such a position obviated the need for negotiations. Gilead Sher, an Israeli negotiator, described the Palestinian approach as being "based on emotions of justice and grievance ... and as an instrument for righting a historical wrong."[43] It is thus a clash of cultures and conceptualization: the moralistic versus the realpolitik approach. The Israelis, on the other hand, took it for granted that negotiations must end up in compromises, but failed to acknowledge that the Palestinians had already made their compromises and were not about to compromise these compromises. Israeli negotiations preferred to start with laying out a position based on their own conception of their "vital territorial needs" and Resolution 242, which they considered inadequate as a framework for dealing with territorial matters. They expected, therefore, a qualitative change in the Palestinian position, which has been well-known since the mid-1970s. The Palestinian conception of 242, which had been modified by the U.S. government in 1993, did not match that of Israel, which denies its applicability to the West Bank and Gaza, a non-occupied but rather contested, territory. Thus, the Palestinians went to these negotiations *after* they had already made their major compromises, which forgave Israel for its conquest of 78 percent of their historic homeland. Why should they be shocked when Israel began to lay claims to an additional 20 percent of the remaining 22 percent?

Perhaps, the gullibility of the Palestinian position is nowhere illustrated better than in an interview with one of their own negotiators. Answering the question, "Was there a basic strategy that you used?" Palestinian negotiator, Hasan Asfour had this to say:

> Our strategy was to use the interim solution to continue towards the final.... Towards that, we got the Israelis to agree that the territories were based on 242, meaning that historical Palestine would be divided into two states—a Palestinian state of the West Bank and Gaza, including East Jerusalem, and the Israeli state on the other part of historical Palestine.[44]

Needless to say, Resolution 242 makes no mention of Palestinian statehood, let alone Israeli adherence to such an explanation. Perhaps, the strategic mistake made by the Palestinian negotiators was that their two-state position, reaffirmed on numerous occasions during the past quarter of a century, was at the *same time* their negotiating position. Thus there was no distinction between what they asked for and what in reality they hoped to achieve.

Notes

1 See reports by B'Tselem (The Israeli Information Center for Human Rights in the Occupied Territories), http://www.btselem.org.

2 *New York Times*, October 22, 2000.

3 "Committee Against Torture Says Israel's Policy of Closures and Demolitions of Palestinian Homes May Amount to Cruel, Inhuman or Degrading Treatment," Press Release, Amnesty International, November 23, 2001, http://www.amnestyusa.org/news/2001/israel11232001.html.

4 Ramit Plushnick-Masti, "Amnesty Accuses Israel of War Crimes," Associated Press, November 4, 2002; see also Chris McGreal, "Amnesty Calls for Arrest of Israelis for War Crimes," *The Guardian* (London), November 4, 2002; Joseph Algazy, "Amnesty Accuses IDF of War Crimes in Jinen," *Ha'aretz*, November 4, 2002.

5 See Appendix.

6   See Robert Malley and Hussein Agha, "Why Barak is Wrong," *The Guardian* (London), May 27, 2002. Malley was a special adviser to President Bill Clinton on Israeli-Palestinian affairs.

7   Malley and Agha, "Why Barak is Wrong."

8   Alain Gresh, "The Broken Dream: Camp David Revisited," *Le Monde diplomatique*, July 2002.

9   Uri Avnery, "Barak: A Villa in the Jungle," July 2002, http://www.gush-shalom.org.

10   Malley and Agha, "Why Barak is Wrong"; Avnery, "Barak."

11   Malley and Agha, "Why Barak is Wrong."

12   Benny Morris, "Camp David and After: An Exchange," *New York Review of Books*, June 13, 2002. There seems to have been no attempt made on the part of Morris to correct Barak on the historical responsibility, which he himself, as one of the "new historians," demonstrated in his book *The Birth of the Palestinian Refugee Problem, 1947–1949* (New York: Cambridge University Press, 1987).

13   Gresh quoting *Ha'aretz,* May 2, 2002.

14   Avnery, "Barak."

15   "Statement on the Middle East Peace Talks at Camp David," White House, Washington, D.C., July 25, 2000; "Interview of the President by Israeli Television," White House Press Release, Washington, D.C., July 28, 2000.

16   *Yedioth Ahronoth*, July 11, 2000.

17   Malley and Agha, "Why Barak is Wrong."

18   Malley and Agha, "Why Barak Is Wrong."

19   Malley and Agha, "Why Barak Is Wrong."; see also Morris, "Camp David and After."

20   Morris, "Camp David and After."

21   Avnery, "Barak."

22   See http://www.palestinecenter.org.

23   See http://www.palestinecenter.org.

24   See http://www.btselem.org/English/Publications/Summaries/Land_Grab_Map.asp.

25   Available online at http://www.gush-shalom.org/media/barak_eng.swf.

26   Malley and Agha, "Why Barak is Wrong."

27   Gresh, "The Broken Dream," *Le Monde diplomatique*.

28   *Ha'aretz,* July 12, 2001.

29   Tanya Reinhart, "The Field of Thorns," April 2002, http://www.nthposition.com/politics_fieldofthorns.html; *Ha'aretz,* November 23, 2001.

30   Reinhart, "The Field of Thorns"; *Ha'aretz,* November 23, 2001.

31   For statistics, see note 1.

32   Security Council, 4248th Meeting, December 18, 2000.

33   Security Council, 4305th Meeting, March 27, 2001.

34   Press Conference by Human Rights High Commissioner Mary Robinson, November 28, 2000; *New York Times,* November 28, 2000.

35   For a summary of the Mitchell Report, see http://www.al-bab.com/arab/ docs/pal/mitchell1.htm; other details in two documents: http://www.jordanembassyus.org/tenet_plan.htm and the Avalon Project of Yale University Law School: http://www.yale.edu/lawweb/avalon/ mideast/mid023.htm.

36   Suleyman Demirel, Thorbjoern Jagl, Warren B. Rudman, Javier Solana, and George J. Mitchell, Chairman, "Report of the Sharm al-Sheikh Fact-Finding Committee" (The Mitchell Report), May 20, 2001, http://www.al-bab.com/arab/docs/pal/mitchell1.htm.

37   Mouin Rabbani, "The Mitchell Report: Oslo's Last Gasp," *Middle East Report: Press Information Notes* 59 (June 1, 2001).

38   Distributed by the Office of International Information Programs, U.S. Department of State, http://usinfo.state.gov.

39   Distributed by the Office of International Information Programs, U.S. Department of State, http://usinfo.state.gov.

40   *Caduc* is the French term "passe," which Arafat uttered in the 1980s when pressed on the Palestine National Covenant. He said it was caduc—tantamount to having been superseded.

41   *Tanzeem* is the Arabic word for "organization," referring to Fateh and not necessarily to a special armed clandestine unit.

42   Yossi Alpher, "An Israeli View: Both Sides Took the Wrong Side," June 17, 2002, http://bitterlemons.org.

43   Gilead Sher, "Comments on the Negotiating Strategies," June 17, 2002, http://bitterlemons.org.

44   Interview with Hasan Asfour, "Reaping Strategic Mistakes: A Palestinian View," June 17, 2002, http://bitterlemons.org.

CHAPTER 11

BUSH AND SHARON: DEFINING THE PATH

*For more than three months now, all the electricity and water infra-
structures in the camp have been in ruins and the IDF is not allowing
UNWRA (United Nations Relief and Works Agency) to bring in the
equipment necessary for taking away the rubble and repairing the dam-
ages.... "What could I do? I thought I was going mad," he related. "I
ran to the IDF position near the Jenin hospital. The soldiers did not allow me to approach. I screamed: 'The commander, where's the commander? Just one question. I have nine children in the camp and I heard
that all of them died. May I go in and find out their condition?' The soldier pulled out his rifle and yelled at me: 'Go back.' I pleaded: 'Be hu-
mane, help me, give me an answer.' The soldier got angry and fired into
the air. 'Get out of here. I'll shoot you.' I said to him: 'Kill me,' I didn't
have anything to live for any more. I didn't want to go. I was certain that
all of them had been killed, but doctors and male nurses from the hospital pulled me inside."*

*"The crowding was terrible, the water stank and was full of worms.
In fact, we were drinking sewage water," fumed Imali Awis. All of her
children fell ill and had to be hospitalized after the IDF withdrew. "After all we went through, who wouldn't lose his health? Who didn't lose
his sanity? They made crazed beasts of us."*

—*"The Living Dead," Ha'aretz, July 19, 2002.*

September 11 as a Defining Moment

The horror that befell America on September 11 sounded the alarm of future danger but at the same time afforded George W. Bush a unique opportunity to stake out a foreign policy turf. It provided a theme and a
context for his administration, which summoned the American people to
rally behind the flag. The unprecedented assault helped transform a president with meager knowledge of and scant preparation in foreign affairs to
one who would marshal resources and exact concessions—at the expense

of basic rights, at home and abroad—to restore the nation's wounded honor. At a time of such unprecedented calamity, a fearful and exasperated public would largely embrace the government-promoted nationalist/chauvinist fervor, rarely questioning why we should be the target of such hatred.[1]

The president's dictum: "Either you are with us, or you are with the terrorists," silenced any potential domestic criticism and facilitated the government's unrestrained force and intimidation abroad. For most Americans, the aggression we visited on "others" was not only acceptable, but gratifying. American state terrorism became a substitute for diplomacy and statesmanship, and a co-opted public looked for revenge despite the "collateral damage" and potential blowback. The evil must be found and the terrorists "smoked out," while sanctuaries and "safe havens" would be placed on a roster of dishonor; their turn would come during a prolonged war that could last indefinitely.

The dichotomy in the mind of George W. Bush is so absolute that there is little room for any distinction between terrorism and resistance or cause and effect. In fact, the phrase "root cause" has been stereotyped and distorted as a scarcely veiled and disingenuous justification of the terror itself. Thus, for example, the Palestinian-Israeli conflict begins for George W. Bush, effectively, with the suicide bombings of 2001. Since he is oblivious to the events of the previous decade, let alone the wars of 1967 or the conquest of 1948, Bush's Middle East policy has been shaped and reinforced by a worldview derived from the horrors of September 11, and reconstructed by the experiences of the likes of General Ariel Sharon.

The agenda of the "war on terrorism" includes, above all, the reaffirmation of the United States in the unrivaled position of global dominance, unconstrained by economic considerations, diplomatic necessities, or domestic predilections. It would also grant a virulent attorney general a free hand to trash civil liberties and constitutional protections in the name of guarding "homeland security." It would even cover the commander-in-chief's unsavory deals with Enron, as well as those of his next-in-line, Cheney, with Halliburton and the energy industry.[2]

The "War on Terror"

Within hours of the attacks in New York and Washington, President George W. Bush declared a "war on terrorism," much like Israel's colonial wars of the past half century. The enemies in both cases are Muslims, Arabs, and Palestinians. That move, without a Congressional declaration of war and without any constitutional basis, turned what might have normally been a police action to apprehend criminals into a broad strategic play to reshape the map of the Middle East and Central Asia and to expand U.S. hegemony even further. The immediate agenda included the overthrow of the Taliban regime in Afghanistan and its replacement by a more compliant regime headed by the Northern Alliance, which had demonstrated equal brutality during the 1980s. The United States scored a quick military victory with virtually no U.S. casualties. This reconquest of Afghanistan was largely viewed in the United States as a vindication of the "hawks" in the Bush administration who favored war over diplomacy and who argued against offering the Arab world any political incentive to join the so-called coalition against terror. Administration supporters of Colin Powell's line were rebuffed and marginalized as irrelevant "softies" who exaggerated the influence of Washington's Arab clients and treated them mistakenly as allies. Thus, catering to Arab demands for a political settlement in Palestine/Israel was seen by Secretary of Defense Donald Rumsfeld and his neoconservative allies in the defense establishment, such as Paul Wolfowitz and Richard Perle, as the worst form of appeasement.[3] Moreover, the "war on terrorism" would finally exempt the U.S. from catering to Saudi Arabia in order to secure oil.[4]

September 11 has served Bush's needs, and blanketed his adventures. It provided him with a pretext to declare a prolonged war intended to crush any opposition or even potential resistance to a globalized order under unquestioned American control. In this war against terrorism, the president appears to be driven by a feeling that the world in which we live today is a Hobbesian one in need of a firm hand.

Fear of "Terror" as a Context for Bush's Middle East Policy

The American public is constantly being placed in a state of fear, as bulletin after bulletin emanates from the CIA, FBI, or the Homeland Security czar forecasting terrorist attacks. The fear and scare tactics of near weekly announcements of terrorist threats (that do not materialize) seems like it is part of a deliberate psychological warfare against the American people in order to keep everyone on edge and to pass laws and take actions that would otherwise be quite controversial. A recent *USA Today* op-ed captures the essence of this fear:

> Lost in the cacophony of military music, flying the red, white and blue and the patriotic rhetoric that marked the celebration of Independence Day and surrounds the war on terrorism is democracy's most wonderful and critical aspect: the right to dissent. Since September 11, it's as if we've been terrified, not only by the terrorists, but also by an American government that demands silent acquiescence in whatever it proposes to do as part of its vague and thus far ineffective "war on terrorism."[5]

As a war on evil, this becomes an endless war, particularly as evildoers seem to multiply with the broadening of the definition of terrorism. It is in this framework that Bush sees the Palestinian resistance to the Israeli occupation. Irrespective of the ideology, orientation, or methods of struggle, all variants of the Palestinian resistance are simplified and subsumed under the category of "terrorism."

The Imperatives of Bush's Middle East Policy

The first visit of Israeli prime minister Ariel Sharon to Washington on March 21, 2001, crystallized the foreign policy of the Bush administration toward the Middle East. In a speech by Secretary of State Colin Powell, in remarks by Secretary of Defense Donald Rumsfeld, and in the reports of senior administration officials following the Bush-Sharon meetings at the White House, the outlines of U.S. policy in the Middle East became rather clear.

Although the Arab media and many diplomats hailed George W. Bush's election victory over Al Gore as portending a salutary change in American policy toward the Middle East, it soon became clear that the Bush administration's policy toward the region had sunk even below the Clinton administration's level of dishonesty and unfairness. Indeed, a carefully articulated convergence of views on the global and regional threats facing the United States and Israel was not only confirmed by the very first meeting of Ariel Sharon and Donald Rumsfeld, but also emerged in statements and reports emanating from the State Department and the White House, which also promised increased collaboration and coordination between the two countries.[6]

What is remarkable is the rhetoric of the senior Bush advisers on foreign and defense policies. In particular, Rumsfeld and Bush have been utilizing the Cold War–like rhetoric of the Reagan administration, even though the international context is currently vastly different from that of the 1980s when the Soviet Union was intact and its threat was palpable although vastly exaggerated. Reagan's comprehensive expansion, upgrading, and modernization of the American defense establishment may have contributed to the bankruptcy of the Soviet Union in its effort to meet the American challenge and is now being imitated by the Bush-Rumsfeld team in its plans for the production and deployment of an antimissile defense system. This costly antimissile missile system is designed to defend against the potential Chinese missile threat (and any rogue takeover in Russia), but it is also of importance against an increasingly touted "threat" of the missile capability and the potential for production and deployment of weapons of mass destruction by Iraq and Iran. On that perceived regional threat there was definite convergence between Israel's strategic views and those of the new administration in the United States during Sharon's first call on Washington. Just as significant is the second perceived threat to both the U.S. and Israel. This is the threat of "international terrorism," specifically "Islamic terrorism," in the region and elsewhere. Thus the current global strategic views of the Bush administration and Israel are practically identical, as are the perceived Middle Eastern regional "threats" (missiles, the proliferation of weapons of mass destruction, and terrorism), leading the highest officials of both governments to articulate similar strategic views and to declare plans for far-reaching collaboration on the occasion of Sharon's March 2001 visit to Washington.

This convergence of outlook seems to have brought together, in mutual appreciation, America's conservative Bush administration and the right-wing government of Israel's Sharon. It is also behind the administration's current policy of uncritical support of Israel's Likud, especially given the fact that both governments seem to believe that, despite the Al-Aqsa Intifada, the situation in Palestine does not threaten regional stability or the security of the Gulf monarchies. The Palestine problem is thus seen as less of a priority than the potential "threats" of Iraq and Iran. Hence we see the evident reordering of the foreign policy priorities in the region by the Bush administration. This by and large explains the original plan of Secretary Powell's first visit to the region in the spring of 2001 that was to include only the Gulf states. It was only after strong protest and much pleading that Powell consented to extend that visit to Egypt, Israel, and the Palestinian Authority.

Rather than seeing Israel's war honestly as a war against a civilian population that breaches the 1949 Geneva Convention (involving war crime in the Nuremberg sense of the term), Bush shares Sharon's view that it is simply a defensive war to dismantle "the terror infrastructure" of the Palestinians. Bush hastened to applaud Sharon's efforts against the Palestinians as reinforcing his own crusade against terrorism, once and for all, through the use of force and raw power.

In their speeches and comments, Bush and his senior advisers have pointedly repeated the standard mantra of American government policy regarding Israel. Powell, in an obligatory speech before AIPAC in March 2001, affirmed the unwavering strategic alliance between Israel and the United States, the "special relationship" that binds the two countries, and the determination of the United States to help Israel maintain a qualitative military edge over all the Arab states. What is new in those speeches, however, was the de-emphasis of the "peace process" and the Palestine question. In fact, Powell issued a directive to the officials of the State Department instructing them not to utilize the term "peace process" anymore, but to speak of peace negotiations. This was clearly a move not only to distinguish the new administration from the legacy of President Clinton, but also a means to signal a change in the priorities of the Bush administration.

Perhaps more significant in the reprioritization of American policy toward the Palestine question are statements by both Bush and Powell in March 2001, changing the description of America's role from "catalyst for peace" (under the Bush Sr.–Baker team) to "honest broker" (under Clinton) to "'facilitator' for peace negotiations" who will "assist but not insist," according to Powell.[7] That is, the United States will facilitate peace negotiations once the initiative has been taken by the two relevant parties. The initiative will not emanate from Washington, and furthermore, for such negotiations to restart, "violence" and "terrorism" must be reduced or come to an end. The burden for stopping the violence, it insisted, is solely the responsibility of the Palestinian Authority. In celebrating the successful visit of Sharon to the United States, the first of the Middle East political leaders to visit Bush, the White House spokesperson indirectly admitted upon repeated questioning that an invitation to Chairman Yasir Arafat to the White House would depend on Arafat's formal condemnation of (Palestinian) "violence" and his efforts to take steps to reduce the "violence" in the occupied territories. After repeated condemnations by Arafat throughout 2001 and 2002, even the idea of an Arafat venture beyond his besieged and all but destroyed compound in Ramallah was a fantasy.

One was pressed to find differences between the Sharon and the Bush governments in regard to the Palestinian question. A careful reading of the speeches and statements of Bush administration officials shortly after assuming power in Washington shows little if any recognition of, much less sympathy for, the plight of the Palestinian people under a brutal military occupation. The Israeli practices of collective punishment, closure and isolation, economic strangulation, starvation, massive bombardment of residential areas with American-supplied F-16s and helicopter gunships, assassinations, and deliberate maiming of demonstrators in the Palestinian Occupied Territories have elicited no serious American government condemnation or calls on Israel to cease and desist. The most that Bush and Powell said initially, but not recently, was that it is important that economic life in the Occupied Territories is restored to a normal status. There was no implication in the comments that the call for restoring normal economic life was derived from a humanitarian concern for the suffering and brutalized Palestinian people rather than from a concern over the possibility of the collapse of the PA. Initially, the Bush administration's view was that the PA was the only agency capable of engaging in "security cooperation" with Israel.[8] By the summer of 2002, Arafat and the PA were no longer of concern to George Bush, who in June called for the ouster of Arafat and a reconstruction of the PA in order to be more compliant and less unwilling to act as Israel's gendarme and subcontractor, as will be described later in this chapter.

Even if the U.S.-Israeli conditions for resuming "negotiations" had been met by the PA back in spring 2001, the Bush administration was unlikely to support the PA's demand for resuming these negotiations according to the terms that had already been reached at Camp David II, not to mention the terms discussed at Taba or in the Clinton proposals. Secretary Powell specifically ruled out any form of U.S. pressure in his 2001 speech to the AIPAC conference, stating that the U.S. will neither pressure Israel nor follow a policy of evenhandedness. He further stated that the U.S. would not support any United Nations resolution to provide international protection for the Palestinian people in the Occupied Territories. The United States, in fact, cast a veto on March 27, 2001, on a resolution that called for an ambiguous formula of "a mechanism for defense" instead of a protection force. According to Israeli journalist Amira Hass, representatives of four European countries (Ireland, Britain, Norway, and France) said that the vote "proved that Israel is a full member of the Security Council, and has the veto as well."[9]

Meanwhile, Sharon had made it quite clear, according to Israeli sources, that he was unwilling to redeploy Israel's troops from more than 42 percent of the Occupied Territories, if at all, and would never honor the obligations of Netanyahu and Barak to the Palestinians. Neither this view, which was presumed to conflict with U.S. policy, nor his announced proposal for negotiating a long-term interim agreement in place of a permanent solution with the PA, had elicited any American reaction. Should a long-term interim agreement come to pass, it would allow Sharon more time and flexibility to pursue implementation of the 1920s concept of the "Iron Wall," developed by the revisionist Zionist Ze'ev Jabotinsky, who advocated securing an "Eretz Israel" through "Jewish military might."[10] According to Jabotinsky's "Iron Wall," only through the use of overwhelming force would the Zionists build "the largest possible state with a built-in, guaranteed Jewish majority."[11] In fact, Sharon's commitment to the "Iron Wall" ideal is shared by a broad spectrum of Israeli politicians, public opinion leaders, and parties, including the center and the so-called peace movement.

It is clear that President Bush was not indebted to the Jewish vote or financial contributions in his electoral victory over Al Gore. But the conventional wisdom that suggested that his administration would therefore more likely be evenhanded on the Arab-Israeli conflict was dashed during Bush's first meeting with Sharon. Although American policy toward the region is not determined strictly by the pro-Israel lobby, but rather is a product of America's imperial imperative and its global strategy, the pro-Zionist lobby, which now more prominently includes neoconservative and Christian fundamentalist groups, is, at the least, capable of influencing the terms of such policy and at the most punishing those politicians and journalists who deviate from its parameters. George W. Bush knows very well the failure of his own father with the lobby and Israel during the 1988–1991 battle over the $10 billion loan guarantees, the Israeli settlements in the Occupied Territories, and Jerusalem. Bush II knew from the outset that he could not go out of his way to alienate either Israel or the pro-Israel lobby and its fundamentalist supporters if he hoped to run again for president in 2004. Bush is particularly aware of the power and influence wielded by the evangelical right, as well as the secular right, whose re-entrenchment in political power goes back to the Reagan era. This is the very same political coalition that is behind the antiterrorist crusade of Sharon and Bush, believing that military aid to Israel is mandated by the Bible (with Israel itself seen in terms of Biblical prophecy). According to Professor Samih Farsoun:

> Despite the clear difference in the Christian evangelical vision for Israel, in which all the Jews will be converted to Christianity from the Zionist Jewish vision of a permanent Jewish state, the alliance is solid. In the current battle over the Occupied Territories (especially because of the second Intifada) and the future of the region, the corridors of power in Washington are a critical battleground.[12]

During his seven visits to the White House, Sharon managed to meet with luminaries of that coalition and discuss with them the critical aspect of his strategy in prosecuting the war on the Palestinians, which is creating provocations to which Israel "had" to "respond defensively." The convergence of views and strategies between an American administration surrounded by evangelical Christians and secular neoconservatives and a right-wing Israeli government has allowed Israel to use whatever brutal and illegal means it wishes to suppress the Palestinian Intifada, while the U.S. media and intelligentsia continued to keep the American public in the dark.

Suicide Bombings: A Pillar of Sharon's Strategy

Described by the Israeli media and publicists as Israel's own "Twin Towers" attack (with 26 deaths and more than 100 injured), the suicide bombings of December 1, 2001, in Haifa and Jerusalem were seized upon as a rallying cry for an all-out assault on Yasir Arafat, a convenient address for the Palestinian national movement. The suicide bombings were, in fact, retaliatory acts for the Israeli assassination of Hamas's legendary leader Mahmoud Abu-Alhonoud on November 23, 2001. General Sharon, who provoked these attacks with his policy of "targeted killings," a euphemism for assassinations, declared Arafat "Israel's bin Laden" and the PA its

Taliban. Meanwhile, Bush and Powell said they were in the same trench with Israel in its own "war on terrorism."[13] Meanwhile, no connection was ever made either by Washington or the complicit U.S. media (in contrast to the far more critical Israeli media) between the gang-style assassination of Abu-Alhonoud and the retaliatory suicide bombings in Haifa and Jerusalem. Sharon's role in provoking these incidents, subsequent assassinations, and large-scale home demolitions was simply ignored.

Sharon has repeatedly used provocative acts (such as his visit to al-Haram al-Sharif at the end of October 2000) at moments when it looked as though there might be a basis for talks between Israel and the Palestinians. It was becoming obvious in late 2001 that he was using the Intifada and the assassination of Palestinian leaders from the grassroots to provoke a reaction from Hamas and Fatah's Tanzim. The cycle continued when Sharon ordered a rocket attack killing Palestinian activist Raed Karmi on January 14, 2002, which lead to a rash of suicide bombings in Israel and justified harsh Israeli reprisals that eventually culminated in the reoccupation of the West Bank. Sharon's strategy also aimed to isolate Arafat and his leadership internationally and to erode worldwide sympathy for the Palestinian cause.[14]

The Israeli terror attack on the Gaza residential quarter on July 23, 2002, which killed seventeen (including nine children and Hamas leader Salah Shehadeh) and injured 170, provoked a retaliatory attack on the Hebrew University cafeteria on July 31 that killed seven and injured a dozen. Not unexpectedly, it provided another pretext for Sharon to send the Israeli army on a destructive mission that pogromized the people of Nablus on August 3. Nablus was still under curfew as of November 2002.

This pattern has been recognized by a variety of Israeli journalists, who openly accused Sharon of deliberately undermining all possibilities for a cease-fire. For example, Akiva Eldar wrote that Israel attacked *knowing* that the final draft of a Tanzim declaration of unilateral cease-fire was approved by Hussein Al-Sheikh, the influential secretary-general of Fateh in the West Bank.[15] Hamas was expected to add its signature to that declaration, which could have ended the Intifada. Even Sheikh Ahmed Yasin, the spiritual leader of Hamas, had called for such a cease-fire and for ending all suicide bombings.

As Gideon Samet of *Ha'aretz* wrote:

[R]eports from every direction add up to a stream of proofs that show that along with the women and children, a genuine opportunity to break the cycle of terror and retaliation was buried in Gaza. If that's true, the prime minister, along with two other ministers and a small group of senior army officials, behaved repulsively.[16]

By adding fuel to a dying fire, Sharon's "great success" was having insured that another peaceful solution was averted. In the words of Professor Menachem Klein,

Prime Minister Ariel Sharon ... together with the establishment that serves him, is abetting terrorism against Israel ... what is terrorism if not a deliberate attack on a noncombatant population in order to achieve a political goal? And what, by the same token, is a rage-directed reaction—blind or calculated, but in either case systematic and repeated, against a civilian population—if not terrorism.[17]

A further illustration of Sharon's strategy of pre-empting a cease-fire and the mere possibility of political talks was provided by an unlikely Israeli source: Alex Fishman, the veteran correspondent who covers military and intelligence affairs for the mass-circulating newspaper *Yedioth Ahronoth*, considered right of center. He wrote, "An hour and half after the heads of Tanzim agreed on publishing a declaration of a unilateral cease-fire, Israel liquidated [Salah Shehadeh] in Gaza. Thus was cut off a two-month-old move aimed at achieving a cease-fire."[18]

Bush condemned Hamas's retaliation at Hebrew University one week later and expressed his "fury," while his spokesman simply chided Israel for being "heavy-handed" in Gaza.[19] Adding insult to injury, he instructed his U.N. ambassador, John Negroponte, prior to the attack on the Hebrew University, to threaten Arab representatives at the U.N. with another veto should they persist in seeking a resolution condemning the Israeli attack. The Associated Press reported, "In a major policy shift, the U.S. on Friday told the Security Council that it will only consider Middle East resolutions that explicitly condemn Palestinian terrorism and call on both sides to pursue a political settlement."[20]

By the end of 2001, Sharon had already succeeded in establishing the suicide bombings as the single most important pillar of a strategy that would not only complete the eradication of Oslo, which was begun by Ehud Barak at Camp David, but also pre-empt any future diplomatic settlement that could end the occupation. Sharon's strategy would establish the reoccupation of the West Bank and its fragmentation into eight separate and closed enclaves isolated from each other on the ground. While the Israeli army continues to be responsible for overall security, a "reformed" PA would, in effect, function as Israel's "civil administration," assuming the burden for the welfare of the population—an arrangement that has been nicknamed by Palestinians as "deluxe occupation."[21] It would repair the streets, collect garbage, and operate a sanitized educational system, in which Palestinian history is rewritten to suit the exigencies of settler colonialism.

Significantly, Sharon was able to sell this policy to George Bush as part of a deal in which Israel broadens its geostrategic role in the region within the framework of the global strategic role that Washington is trying to establish through its war on terrorism. No more will Washington even go through the motions of urging restraint on its junior partner. The Karin A Affair of December 2001, in which Israel claimed to have captured a ship loaded with Iranian weapons destined to be delivered to the PA, with Arafat's presumed approval, gave Sharon another trump card in his strategic power play. Iran, after all, is a far better candidate than Iraq as a "threat" to Israel, hence making it a suitable target for the "war on terrorism." George Bush's later inclusion of Iran in his "axis of evil," possibly with prodding from Sharon, further elevated Israel in Washington's post–September 11 strategic planning. State Department spokesman Richard Boucher said, "We're very concerned about disturbing and destructive behaviors that Iran has undertaken."[22]

In this context, Israel was able to get away with a massive escalation of its occupation of the West Bank in spring 2002. Confronted with evidence of massive atrocities committed by the Israeli army in Nablus, Jenin, and other Palestinian towns and villages, Washington gave Israel tacit support in thwarting a U.N. mission of inquiry under the auspices of the Security Council.[23] Worse yet, following a daylong debate on U.N. Secretary-General Kofi Annan's August 1 report on events in Jenin and other Palestinian cities, the U.N. General Assembly adopted a resolution on August 5, 2002, demanding an immediate end to military incursions and all acts of violence, terror, provocation, incitement, and destruction in Israel and the occupied Palestinian territories. The U.S. isolation in the international community was starkly revealed in the voting on that resolution, which passed by a vote of 114 in favor to four against, with eleven abstentions. The four voting against were Micronesia, Israel, Marshall Islands, and the United States.

Sharon's Sixth Visit

On June 10, 2002, prime minister Sharon held his sixth meeting at the White House with President Bush. During Sharon's fifth visit, Bush had declared him "a man of peace" to the chagrin of millions around the world.[24] This time, Bush described Sharon as his teacher: "I learn from this man every time he comes here."[25] Obviously George Bush, who was not speaking from a prepared text, did not weigh the implication of such descriptions for the U.S. role as mediator or self-appointed "honest broker."

Worse yet was Bush's adoption of Sharon's position that a satisfactory "reform" of the Palestinian Authority, together with the creation of administrative and security institutions, must precede political talks. In fact, Sharon came to Washington uninvited in order to veto political talks and the idea of a deadline for setting up a Palestinian state, which he knew would be urged by President Mubarak of Egypt during his uneventful visit a few days before. George Bush had already rebuffed Mubarak's suggestion the day before he met with Sharon, thus allowing Sharon to score twice—no deadline and no political talk until Arafat delivers a virtual surrender. But the professionals at the State Department and the White House knew that U.S. policy, redefined by George W. Bush, would still have to be couched in the proper terminology and would have to meet the requirements of deception, premised on the notion of the U.S. as an honest broker. Thus, clarifying matters, the White House spokesman quickly cautioned listeners not "to read too much" into the words of the president.[26]

This disclaimer was not very convincing, particularly when Bush again aligned his position with that of Sharon on Colin Powell's idea of a regional conference. He said, "The conditions [for a conference] aren't even there yet. That's because no one has confidence in the emerging Palestinian government."[27] With that, there were hardly any differences remaining between the positions of the U.S. and Israel. And yet, the conditions for holding an international conference were not as unsuitable, according to Colin Powell, described by President Bush. Powell, it seems, was allowed to give the London-based Arab daily *Al-Hayat* a more optimistic view. The regional/international conference is still on, said Powell, adding: "I will chair the conference.... We will hold the meeting, or conference, call it what you will, this summer."[28] Moreover, Powell put a different spin on Bush's dwindling vision for a Palestinian state, by saying that the president was not backtracking from his goal, but in order to achieve it, it is possible that a "temporary state" would have to be established as a transitional step, prior to the so-called final status negotiations. By the time Bush gave his own speech nearly two weeks later, everyone seemed to have closed ranks. The president walked toward the podium at the White House Rose Garden flanked by Donald Rumsfeld, Colin Powell, and Condoleezza Rice in a show of unity. Nothing more was heard about Powell's summer conference, as war against Iraq seemed to dominate the diplomatic agenda.

The Bush Speech

The long-awaited speech by George W. Bush, delivered June 24, 2002, marked a departure from the Clinton era rhetoric in that it effectively endorsed Sharon's abrogation of the Oslo process.[29] For the first time since 1993, the U.S. government turned its back on the very idea of the sides returning to the negotiations table. For thirty-five years, the negotiations held under the auspices of Washington were largely an exercise in futility. But American "shepherding" of this farce did not come without a price. The bulk of Bush's speech was devoted to commands and conditions, and warnings to abandon "terror," addressed repeatedly to the Palestinians but rarely to Israelis. In fact, the word "terror," a staple in Bush's vocabulary since September 11, appeared ten times in a speech consisting of 1867 words, but not once in connection with Israeli state terrorism. Bush's repeated threats to the Palestinians would make anyone wonder whether his speech was written by Ariel Sharon: "Today, Palestinian authorities are encouraging, not opposing terrorism.... This is unacceptable. And the United States will not support the establishment of a Palestinian state until its leaders engage in a sustained fight against the terrorists and dismantle their infrastructure."[30]

Bush's demands on Israel were uttered without conviction: restore freedom of movement, but only after "violence subsides"; withdraw to "positions held prior to September 28, 2000"; and stop "settlement activity," in accordance with the innocuous recommendations of the Mitchell Committee. Bush's remarks about the occupation were limited to friendly advice that it "threatens Israel's identity and democracy." Other than these solicitations, Bush's commands, refrains, and threats were reserved for those "who are not with us," that is, Palestinians, Iraqis, Syrians, and "terrorists." Even America's client states in the Arab world, which qualify with reservations as "being with us," were told to establish "full normalization of relations" with Israel, ignoring the Arab League's expressed willingness to do so in exchange for an end to the occupation.

Bush's speech called on the Palestinians, who were trapped in their homes for weeks and months and were still under prolonged curfews, to change their leaders, to "build a practicing democracy," to acquire "new political and economic institutions based on democracy [and a] market economy," to adopt a new constitution, which "separates the powers of government," to conduct "multiparty local elections by the end of the year," to establish a "truly independent judiciary," to streamline the security system, and of course to stop "terrorism." Only when the Palestinians met such a long list of impossible demands would they be eligible to be invited to negotiations that could optimally offer them a "provisional" state.

Even the *New York Times* remarked on June 25, 2002: "How the Palestinians can be expected to carry out elections or reform themselves while in a total lockdown by the Israeli military remains something of a mystery."[31] Jonathan Friedland of the *Guardian* aptly remarked that the speech "consisted, from beginning to end, of fantasy.... Bush is demanding that Palestine become Sweden before it can become Palestine."[32]

In return for meeting these conditions, Bush promised to "support the creation of a Palestinian state, whose borders and certain aspects of its sovereignty will be provisional until resolved as part of a final settlement in the Middle East." Emphasizing his *quid pro quo*, Bush commanded: "embrace democracy, confront corruption, and firmly reject terror." Revealing his own disconnect from Middle East reality, he pledged to enlist the help of the Europeans and the Arab states in the task of building a democratic system, as if the Arab leaders, who normally rule for life, are paragons of constitutional government. After all these conditions were met, the provisional state might still take three years, thus prolonging the Oslo charade, and only then would the two parties address the core issues that divide them, if they so wish.

The Bush speech was devoid of any timetables, stages, guarantees, or safeguards; in fact, it hints that ultimately the settlement will be bilateral with no international supervision. If Oslo's seven years permitted Israel to double its settlements and settlers, a foreclosure on peace, the post-Oslo, post-Palestinian "reformation" period might leave nothing to negotiate about, as Sharon has been given a free hand to formalize the apartheid-like arrangements in 42 percent of the West Bank. With justification, many Palestinians fear these actions are only a prelude to their "transfer."[33]

A provisional state is a concept that lacks a proper definition and has no meaning in either politics or international law. Moreover, Bush's intent to address "aspects of sovereignty" is just a polite way to describe the permanent fragmentation of the West Bank to permit extraterritoriality for Israeli settlers and soldiers, permanent checkpoints in the name of security, and consolidation of illegal settlement blocs. A provisional state is likely to be the state that Sharon supports—a collection of eight disconnected Bantustans in the West Bank, separated from Israel by a long electronic fence, and separated from each other by Israeli checkpoints and bypass roads for Jews only.

The fact that three million Palestinians were subject to prolonged curfews in cities that have been reoccupied, totally isolated, and besieged by trigger-happy soldiers did not seem to merit any notice in the Bush "peace plan," casting a serious doubt that there is light at the end of the tunnel for the besieged Palestinians.[34] The resumption of normal life in the reoccupied territories was, after all, a necessary step for meeting Bush's impossible demands. It should be noted that Bush's demand for Palestinian "democracy"—so long as the Palestinians did not elect Arafat as their leader, which Bush implied would be unacceptable—is antithetical to the security-laden regime established by Oslo.[35] In fact, it was the inability and unwillingness of Arafat to utilize that security apparatus to the extent required by Israel and the United States that made him a pariah (in Sharon's words, "irrelevant"). Bush's criticism of Arafat's regime, however valid, was not the reason for denying the Palestinians their internationally recognized rights. Characters like Arafat and Saddam Hussein provide a ready excuse for Washington and Tel Aviv to pursue their colonial ambitions.

Reaction's to Bush's Speech

Surely, Bush did not offer a peace plan. In fact, even some of Sharon's cabinet colleagues were dismayed by the speech and its anticipated disastrous consequences. Shimon Shiffer of the largest Israeli evening newspaper, *Yedioth Ahronoth*, had a chance to watch Foreign Minister Shimon Peres watching the Bush speech on television, and he gave the following description:

> Shimon Peres' face became more and more weary and angry the longer Bush went on with his speech. "He is making a fatal mistake," remarked Peres. "Making the creation of a Palestinian state dependent upon a change in the Palestinian leadership is a fatal mistake," he repeated again and again. "The abyss into which the region will plunge will be as deep as the expectations from this speech were high. There will be a bloodbath."[36]

Another cabinet colleague, Ruby Rivlin, communications minister from the Likud Party, commented: "It looks like it was written by a senior Likud official. We are talking about a pro-Israel speech and a victory for the course taken by Prime Minister Sharon."[37]

In an article that appeared in the London *Times* by Ross Dunn, titled "Sharon Could Have Written Speech," a number of Israeli journalists are quoted repeating this theme:

> Nahum Bernea, a columnist for the Hebrew daily *Yedioth Ahronoth* said: "Sharon could demand copyright on the speech—He couldn't have dreamt of a more pleasant address." Hemi Shalev, in the newspaper *Ma'ariv*, wrote: "One can only imagine Sharon watching the speech on TV, and the smile on his face spreading wider until he cries with joy when he hears Bush demand Arafat's political head on a platter."[38]

Writing in the same vein, Robert Fisk, the veteran British journalist, commented rhetorically in the *Independent*:

> Why, I wonder, doesn't Mr. Bush let Ariel Sharon run the White House press bureau? Not only would it be more honest—we would at least be hearing the voice of Israel at first hand—but it would spare the American president the ignominy of parroting everything he is told by the Israelis.[39]

There was a consensus in the mainstream Israeli press that the Bush speech was bound to encourage Sharon to step up his military offensive, and that the lack of any timetable would not bring about any political talks anytime soon. The *Washington Post* and *New York Times* expressed similar misgivings, while the European press was almost unanimous in its cool reception to the speech. George Bush was unable to sell his speech to his allies, who were attending the G-8 meeting in Canada on the very next day. Almost every one of those leaders felt a need to distance himself from Bush's position by commenting on the right of the Palestinians to name their own leaders. Moreover, the Danish government, which held the rotating presidency of the EU at the time, expressed worries that the "United States has effectively abandoned the Mideast peace process" after Bush's speech.[40]

Why then did Egypt, Saudi Arabia, and Jordan, which offered Israel peace and normalization only three months earlier, embrace the charade? Why would they out-Israelize Sharon? Worse yet, why did the PA, which was asked to self-negate, welcome the speech and the opportunity to cooperate with a government that despises its leaders and provides the weapons, funds, and diplomatic means to kill its people, destroy their property, and marginalize their cause?[41]

Bush's "Road Map": A Short-Cut To Baghdad?

As the trumpets of war against Iraq intensified in September and October 2002, the Bush administration began to view the diplomatic paralysis on the Palestinian-Israeli front as a potential hindrance to its war effort. Russia, the European Union, and the United Nations, which constitute three quarters of the "Quartet," had to be placated, particularly as the U.S. needed to gain their acquiescence in a Security Council resolution that would rubber stamp America's plans to invade Iraq. That concern, together with an attempt to convey concern to the ineffectual Arab states, led to what was billed as a new American initiative bearing the title, "Road Map."

The plan was handed to Sharon—who "made a point to advisers that he had not bothered to read it"—during his seventh U.S. visit in October.[42] The six-page document promises to resuscitate the "peace process" over three stages: First, Israel would ease living conditions in the Occupied Territories by lifting the curfews, dismantling the so-called illegal settlement outposts built during Sharon's rule, and ceasing land confiscation and house demolitions. In return, the Palestinians would end the Intifada, issue an explicit statement recognizing Israel's right to exist, adopt a new constitution, and appoint an "empowered" prime minister. This would be accomplished during November and December 2002. The second phase, which is intended to last throughout 2003, would see Israel make a gradual withdrawal to the pre-Intifada lines of September 28, 2002, while it observes a freeze on settlement building. Meanwhile, the Palestinians would implement political and economic reforms, hold elections, and establish a provisional state by the end of 2003. The third phase is reserved for final status negotiations, ending sometime between 2005 and 2006.

Of course, this would not be the first time that the U.S. proposes a "peace plan" that is not exactly meant for implementation. It seems like an extension of Bush's June 2002 speech, having no real timeline and neither monitoring nor enforcement mechanisms. Israeli journalist Aluf Benn described the "Road Map" as an "empty shell," adding: "It is pretty certain the map wouldn't be implemented and will join the shelved Clinton, Mitchell, Tenet, and Zini plans."[43] Its vagueness will certainly enable the contemptuous Sharon to invoke all the terror-laden clauses in Bush's speech to avoid any kind of political talks, let alone a political settlement. His spokespeople reacted swiftly by saying that the Palestinians must establish a democracy and replace Arafat with leaders "not compromised by terror" before negotiations would resume.[44] Had Bush been really serious about his latest "peace plan," he might have tempered his lavish praise of Sharon and refrained from granting him a green light in dealing with Iraq: "If Iraq attacks Israel tomorrow, I would assume the prime minister would respond. He's got a desire to defend himself."[45] Sharon, who was called a "close friend" by Bush during his seventh visit on October 15, 2002, praised the president's "determined stance against international terrorism," saying that Israel has never had a better friend in the White House than Bush. "As far as I remember, as we look back toward many years now, I think that we never had such relations with any president of the United States as we have with you, and we never had such cooperation in everything as we have with the current administration."[46]

The Death of the Peace Process: Is "Transfer" the Answer?

The Bush presidency might well become synonymous with the effective death of the so-called peace process. Slowly, but steadily, George Bush patronized Sharon's strategy, which had evolved from demanding a cease-fire to expecting Arafat to "stop the violence" to "uproot terror" and to reform the PA, while utilizing suicide bombings as a pretext for avoiding a cease-fire.

Sharon's strategy, at present, represents a continuation of his strategy over the past quarter of a century: the effective redefinition of Israel's borders to include all of pre-1948 Palestine, from the Mediterranean Sea to the Jordan River. Sharon is systematically disestablishing the economic, geographic, and demographic basis of Palestinian statehood while reinstating military rule on all residents of the West Bank, irrespective of Oslo's geographic and functional classifications. Sharon has been an outspoken advocate of the specious notion that the Palestinians already have their sovereign state—in Jordan. As prime minister, he has been vigorously trying to cow the Palestinians into submission, ending their uprising against the occupation once and for all. The effective choice he is offering the Palestinians is: accept a fragmented collection of Bantustans or leave the country. Expulsion, which is euphemistically known as "transfer" in Zionist literature, is now supported by nearly half of Israel's population.

During Sharon's sixth visit to the United States, on June 10, 2002, he met with the Senate Foreign Relations Committee behind closed doors, a rare privilege for any leader, foreign or domestic. At that meeting, he made it clear to the senators that the ancient boundaries of the "Land of Israel" are guaranteed to the Jewish people by Holy Scriptures, and that he does not foresee any peace during his lifetime.[47] Alluding to the most opportune circumstances for expulsion of the Palestinians from the West Bank, he told the senators that "U.S. military action against Iraq, instead of exacerbating the Palestinian problem, would end it."[48]

Prior to the onslaught of the spring and summer 2002, Sharon had tightened the economic siege, blocked communication between towns, villages, and cities, and made the curfews a permanent feature of life for some 700,000 city-dwellers, making life unbearable for the ordinary Palestinian, with the purpose of persuading as many of them as possible to leave. The idea of "transfer" has been seriously discussed in Zionist councils and in Israel. Professor Nur Masalha has demonstrated in his book *Imperial Israel and the Palestinians* that the notion of "transfer" is adhered to by the four principal components of the Israeli body politic (Labor, Mifdal—the religious bloc, the secular right-wing, and Likud), including Sharon's Likud bloc.[49] Sharon himself made it clear that his mission is to finish the job that was not completed in 1948. In an interview with Ari Shavit published in *Ha'aretz* he said:

> The War of Independence has not ended. No. Nineteen forty-eight was
> just one chapter. If you ask me whether the state of Israel is capable of
> defending itself today, I say yes, absolutely. And if you ask me whether
> the state of Israel is facing the danger of war, I say no. But are we living

here securely? No. And, therefore, it is impossible to say that we have completed the work and that now we can rest on our laurels.[50]

Given that expulsion of the Palestinians from the remaining portion of their land has become the real policy of the Sharon government, one wonders whether the United States is willing at the start of the twentieth century to countenance ethnic cleansing? And if this is an acceptable price, which Bush is willing to pay for his own geostrategic designs and domestic political goals, how much violence and instability will the international community tolerate before it begins to ask how to restrain such grandiose schemes? In the end, will Bush's embrace of Sharon's primitive ideology and endorsement of his colonial adventures undermine U.S. interests and create chaos in the region?

Notes

1   Marc Cooper, "An Interview with Gore Vidal, The Last Defender of the American Republic," *LA Weekly*, July 5–11, 2002.

2   See Alexander Cockburn, "The Crooks in the White House," *CounterPunch*, July 6, 2002.

3   See Nicholas Lemann, "The Next World Order," *New Yorker*, April 1, 2002; for a perceptive analysis of Paul Wolfowitz's world view, see Bill Keller, "The Sunshine Warrior," *New York Times Sunday Magazine*, September 22, 2002.

4   Richard Perle revealed his contempt for the "coalition" in October 2001: "I have serious doubts about the extent to which we need a coalition ... I don't know what this coalition is, who's in it, who's out of it, where you get your membership card. Can you be expelled if you're not doing certain minimum things? Are the Saudis in it? Are they out of it? The Syrians support terror—are they in, are they out? It's a very vague concept, and an insubstantial one." See Charmaine Seitz, "Hanging in the Balance: How Might a U.S. Strike in Iraq Affect Palestinians?" http://www.palestinereport.org; on the relationship between Palestine and Iraq, see *CounterPunch*, October 28, 2002; see also Reuters, August 13, 2002.

5   *USA Today*, July 4, 2002.

6   *Ha'aretz*, March 21, 2001.

7   See also Bush's statement to the press on March 29, 2001, in which he said: "I have said all along that this nation will not try to force a peace settlement in the Middle East, that we will facilitate a peace settlement. It requires two willing parties to come to the table to enact a peace treaty that will last. And this administration won't try to force peace on the parties." Excerpted from U.S. Department of State, Washington, D.C., http://usinfo.state.gov.

8   In his March 2001 speech to AIPAC, Colin Powell said Americans want to hear from "all leaders" in the region, implying it will not freeze out Arafat. *Ha'aretz* March 21, 2001.

9   See Amira Hass, "Four U.S. Rejections Scuttled Security Council Resolution," *Ha'aretz*, April 13, 2001. She added: "The Americans did not want any mention of the settlements, the Geneva Convention and international law; they opposed mention of the word 'siege'; and they objected to any mention of the principle of land for peace."

10   See Simha Flapan, *Zionism and the Palestinians* (New York: Barnes and Noble, 1979), p. 117; see also an unpublished speech by Professor Jeff Halper, "Sharon's National Unity Government: Shoring up the 'Iron Wall,'" March 13, 2001, in which he made the following relevant remark: "In a famous article entitled 'The Iron Wall,' published in 1923, Ze'ev Jabotinsky articulated a cardinal principle of the Zionist enterprise: Zionism should endeavor to bring about a Jewish state in the whole land of Israel, regardless of the Arab response ... 'Every indigenous people,' Jabotinsky wrote, 'will resist alien settlers as long as they see any hope of ridding themselves of the danger of foreign settlement. This is how the Arabs will behave and go on behaving so long as they possess a gleam of hope that they can prevent "Palestine" from becoming the land of Israel.' Jabotinsky also wrote the following in the 'Iron Wall': 'All colonization must continue in defiance of the will of the native population. Therefore, it can continue and develop only under the shield of force which comprises an Iron Wall through which the local population can never break through. To the hackneyed reproach that this point of view is unethical, I answer, "absolutely untrue." This is our ethic. There is no other ethic.'" Ze'ev Jabotinsky, "The Iron Wall," 1923.

11   Elmer Berger, *Peace For Palestine: First Lost Opportunity* (Gainesville: University of Florida Press, 1993), p. 141.

12   Samih Farsoun, "The Anti-Terrorism Crusade of the United States," paper presented at a Conference on Terrorism, the United States, and the Arab World, University of Exeter, United Kingdom, July 14–15, 2002; for more on Christian fundamentalists, see *The Guardian* (London), October 28, 2002.

13   Professor Menachem Klein of Bar Ilan University, who also served on the Israeli negotiating team during the Camp David summit, put it this way: "Osama bin Laden did not confront the U.S. with a peace offer, whereas the

Palestinian national movement put forward a peace proposal more than a decade ago, at the end of the 1980s. Today, this has become a pan-Arab initiative." *Ha'aretz*, July 25, 2002.

14 See an article on this subject by Toufic Haddad, "Resisting Sharon," *Between the Lines*, February 2002, http://www.between-lines.org/archives/2002/feb/Toufic_Haddad.htm.

15 *Ha'aretz*, July 25, 2002; *Ha'aretz*, July 26, 2002.

16 *Ha'aretz*, July 26, 2002.

17 *Ha'aretz*, July 25, 2002; see also a subsequent article by Akiva Eldar on this subject: "If there's smoke, there is no cease-fire," *Ha'aretz*, July 30, 2002. He wrote, "Israel's propaganda machine worked overtime this week and proved its efficacy. The prime minister, the foreign minister, intelligence officers, officials, and spokesmen changed overnight from a fight for a cease-fire to a fight against a cease-fire initiative." Eldar quotes Yossi Beilin: "Yossi Beilin, back this week from talks in Washington, says that the cease-fire attempt and the Gaza bombing were the talk of the town wherever he went—the National Security Council, the State Department and Congress. He says that he was asked if it was an accident that for a third time, Sharon ordered such an operation just as the chances for a cease-fire begin to take shape."

18 *Yedioth Ahronoth*, July 24, 2002.

19 According to the Associated Press, August 1, 2002, Bush said, "I just, I cannot speak strongly enough about how we must collectively get after those who kill in the name of some kind of false religion."

20 Associated Press, July 26, 2002.

21 *Ha'aretz*, June 11, 2002.

22 Richard Boucher, State Department Briefing, Federal News Service, July 23, 2002.

23 The U.N. secretary-general felt that he was forced to disband the fact-finding mission organized in response to Security Council Resolution 1405 dated April 19, 2002. On August 1, 2002, the secretary-general released a report prepared pursuant to General Assembly Resolution ES-10/10. Summing it up, the *Guardian* wrote: "In Jenin and elsewhere last spring, as in Gaza last week, Israel exceeded the limits of its legal right to self-defense. It placed itself in *prima facie* breach of the fourth Geneva Convention and the International Covenant on Civil and Political Rights. Specifically, after an ambush on April 9 in Jenin that killed 13 soldiers, it resorted to random, vengeful acts of terror involving civilians. As we said last April, the destruction wrought in Jenin looked and smelled like a crime. On the basis of the U.N.'s findings, it still does," *Guardian* (London), August 2, 2002.

24   "Bush Reiterates Support for Palestinian State to Sharon," U.S. Embassy, Israel, June 10, 2002, http://www.usembassy-israel.org.il/publish/peace/archives/2002/june/061103.html.

25   "Bush Reiterates Support for Palestinian State to Sharon."

26   *Ha'aretz*, June 12, 2002.

27   *New York Times*, June 11, 2002; *Ha'aretz*, June 11, 2002.

28   Daniel Sobelman, "Powell: Bush Mulling 'Temporary' Palestine Before Final Talks," *Ha'aretz* June 12, 2002.

29   *New York Times*, June 25, 2002.

30   See http://www.usembassy-israel.org.il/.

31   *New York Times*, June 25, 2002.

32   *Guardian* (London), June 26, 2002.

33   On the issue of "transfer" or expulsion, see *Ha'aretz*, October 7, 2002; *Ha'aretz*, October 18, 2002; *Ha'aretz*, October 10, 2002.

34   For a thorough description of Israel's siege policy, see Amira Hass, "Long Term Sieges," *Ha'aretz*, June 12, 2002.

35   "Powell Explains President's Middle East Policy," U.S. Embassy, Israel, June 26, 2002, http://www.usembassy-israel.org.il/publish/peace/archives/2002/june/062716.html.

36   Gush Shalom (The Peace Bloc), June 25, 2002. Online at http://www.gush-shalom.org.

37   *The Times* (London), June 27, 2002.

38   *The Times* (London), June 27, 2002.

39   *The Independent* (London), June 26, 2002.

40   *Ha'aretz*, June 28, 2002.

41   For the PA's reaction, see Nabil Shaath, "Bush's Tune is Promising but the Words Need Work," *Los Angeles Times*, June 27, 2002.

42   *New York Times*, October 25, 2002.

43   *Ha'aretz*, October 24, 2001.

44   *New York Times*, October 25, 2002. On the "Road Map" plan, see Graham Usher, "Road to Nowhere," *Al-Ahram Weekly*, http//:www.Ahram.org.eg/weekly/2002/609/fr1.htm; see also Jonathan Cook, "Selling Snakeoil," *Al-Ahram Weekly*, http//:www.Ahram.org.eg/weekly/2002/609/re2.htm.

45   *Ha'aretz*, October 17, 2002.

46   *Ha'aretz*, October 17, 2002.

47   Robert Novak, "Sharon and the Senators," June 17, 2002, http://www.townhall.com.

48   Novak, "Sharon and the Senators."

49   Nur Masalha, *Imperial Israel and the Palestinians* (London: Pluto Press, 2000).

50   *Ha'aretz*, April 12, 2001.

CHAPTER 12

REDRESS, THE SINGLE STATE, AND INTERNATIONAL SOLIDARITY

A new reality has been unwittingly produced by the Oslo Accords—a reality which had conceivably escaped the minds of many who watched the "historic" signing around the globe on September 13, 1993. The requirements for a just and durable peace are far different today from what they once were. The Oslo Accords have dealt a crippling blow to the foundations of the global consensus on the solution to the question of Palestine, which was predicated on the right of the Palestinian people to establish their own independent state alongside Israel. The two-state solution has run its course, having been dealt a severe blow by a colossal imbalance of power between Israel and the Palestinians, by a steady and growing Israelization of American Middle East policy, by an unrestrained drive of settler colonization, and by Arab ineptitude, disarray, and political failure to respond to the Zionist challenge.[1]

In 1999 and 2000, we witnessed how the lone superpower had to employ vigorous diplomatic resources to persuade Prime Minister Benjamin Netanyahu, and later Prime Minister Ehud Barak, to meet simple obligations under the Oslo agreements. After the Palestinians embarked on the path of negotiations, they realized that they were still at the stage of determining whether they have rights, instead of trying to claim rights that they were internationally guaranteed. They proceeded as if Israel's continuing military occupation did not even exist, and therefore Israel's claim to the now "disputed" (rather than "occupied") territories was at least as good as theirs. They proceeded as if Jerusalem were virtually an Israeli city and as if the Palestinian struggle for emancipation—from the status of refugees and of occupied people—would be dependent on Israeli goodwill. The letter of Oslo rendered the goal of Palestinian statehood impractical and obsolete. Yet the Palestinian Oslo dream continued to hang on nothing more than a thin thread of hope devoid of any substance.

Paradoxically, the Oslo process led to an inevitable conclusion that its own architects had neither contemplated nor pursued: the future of the Palestinian struggle is toward integration, not separation; toward a pluralistic existence, not exclusion; and toward parity, mutuality, common humanity, and a common destiny. This remains the new and important reality that the Oslo process generated. Ironically, this reality might lay the foundations for a joint Palestinian-Israeli struggle, emanating from a realization that the lives of Palestinians and Israelis are inextricably intertwined. There was and remains a common interest in the economy, employment, water distribution, ecology, human rights, and foreign relations. But after the Israeli onslaught of the spring and summer of 2002, readiness to translate that commonality into a structural framework that would enable both people to derive equal benefits remained out of reach. Today, even the idea of living together seems unfathomable to Palestinians and Israelis alike.

Even if the Oslo process miraculously led to some kind of a breakthrough, the maximum gain for the Palestinians that seems possible at this point is a fractured collection of Bantustans, noncontiguous enclaves, on about 40 to 50 percent of the West Bank and 65 percent of Gaza. Under optimal conditions, something called the state of Palestine would likely emerge, but would be only nominally independent. Genuine independence was ruled out by the agreement between Labor and Likud in January 1997. Entitled "National Agreement Regarding the Negotiations on the Permanent Settlement with the Palestinians," it rejected Palestinian sovereignty, the removal of the Israeli settlements, negotiating the status of Jerusalem, repatriating the refugees, and dismantling the occupation. The only difference between Likud and Labor is that the latter is better able to disguise the structural flaws and asymmetrical nature of the enterprise.

As to the argument that Labor's classical Zionist doctrine, which presumably espouses separation, would grant the Palestinians their separate political existence, it must be kept in mind that the doctrine of separation had already been adapted to Likud's notion of "population mixture." The mixture idea, first enunciated by Begin and Shamir and inherent in the autonomy scheme, was reborn as Labor's cantonization plan. Rabin's peace, which Arafat often described as the "peace of the brave," converged with Netanyahu's approach of the bantustanization of the land of about one-third of the Palestinian people, leaving the other two-thirds living in permanent exile or as second-class citizens in Israel itself.

Likud supporter and *New York Times* columnist William Safire has suggested that this brand of apartheid was inevitable: "The map of a workable final deal stares us all in the face: A Palestinian flag in a majority of the West Bank land and 98 percent of its people, with road tunnels and overpasses making the new state's large enclaves contiguous and independent of Israel."[2] The key words in Safire's statement were, of course, enclaves, tunnels, and overpasses—which together negate contiguity and preclude meaningful Palestinian independence. After the signing of Oslo II (1995), the Palestinians in the West Bank and Gaza began to realize that they were residents of enclaves separated from each other and from Israel, but functionally indeed part of a "Greater Israel." They were separated from the settlements, from Jerusalem, and from each other (from other Palestinian cities and even villages, as well as from the Palestinian diaspora). This fragmentation is now social, economic, physical, and of course, regional, despite Oslo's call for a contiguous Palestinian entity.

In view of all that, Labor's conception of the "state of Palestine" is one that will be physically fragmented, economically strangled by Israel, dominated by the United States and the global financial institutions the U.S. dominates (the World Bank, International Monetary Fund, and World Trade Organization), and constrained by regional interests and global requirements. It will continue to be intolerant and repressive toward dissent, now conveniently classified as "terrorism." It will likely be pressed to seek a confederative relationship with Jordan and some kind of association with Israel, in which a Middle East version of the North American Free Trade Agreement (NAFTA), with maquiladora-style tax-free and low-wage industry, would substitute for development. Moreover, the price of the facade could include a renewed, even permanent, deferral of the final status issues. And yet, Labor is as far as it can be from holding power at the present time.

However, with Israel having already declared the final status issues, in effect, nonnegotiable, the absence of any significant change in the status quo could, in the long run, result in a renewed struggle by Palestinians and Israelis for equality in a joint democratic and binational society.

The Single State Solution

The Palestinian people did not struggle and sacrifice for most of the past century for a truncated, divided Palestinian state. The current struggle for an independent state within the Oslo framework is hardly likely to succeed. But, outside of the Oslo strictures, a new discourse is developing about a broader social-economic struggle for equal rights, equal citizenship, and equal legitimacy within a single Israeli-Palestinian polity. Different versions, either a democratic secular state or a binational state, are today viewed by a growing number of people on both sides as viable alternatives to perpetual conflict.

Palestinians in Support of a Single State

On the Palestinian side, Columbia University professor Edward W. Said emerged as one of the key champions of a one-state solution, advancing it in various writings and interviews, one of which appeared in the *Christian Science Monitor*:

> The whole idea of trying to produce two states is at an end. The Oslo peace process is really in tatters.... The lives of Israelis and Palestinians are hopelessly intertwined. There is no way to separate them. You can have fantasy and denial, or put people in ghettos. But in reality there is a common history. So we have to find a way to live together. It may take 50 years. But ... the Israeli experience will gradually turn back towards the world they really live in, the Islamic Arab world. And that can only come through Palestinians.[3]

In an interview with radio journalist David Barsamian, Said again endorsed secular binationalism, not only as a desirable oucome, but also as a necessary reality:

> Of course, on the West Bank, the settlers and Palestinians interact, through antipathy and hostility, but physically they're in the same place. This is something that can't be changed by pulling people back to separate boundaries or separate states.... Then there is the demographic reality: By the year 2010, there will be demographic parity between the two, Palestinians and Israelis. The South Africans, in a country twenty times bigger than Israel, couldn't for long maintain apartheid. And it is unlikely that a place like Israel—which is surrounded on all sides by Arab states—is going to be able to maintain what, in effect, is a system of apartheid for Palestinians. So, although a binational state now seems like a totally long shot and completely utopian, not to say to many peo-

ple a crazy idea, it is the one idea that will allow people to live with—and not exterminate—each other.[4]

Other Palestinian intellectuals in the Occupied Territories, inside Israel and in exile, including Nadim Rouhana, As'ad Ghanem, Azmi Bishara, and Adel Samara, among others, joined the call for a single state. Samara, for example, wrote, "[T]he only just and feasible form of binational state ... will have to be a state which will dissolve the Zionist regime ... cancel the Law of Return, stop importing new settlers, [and] guarantee the Palestinian right of return, equality of land and resources."[5] Azmi Bishara, an outspoken member of the Israeli Parliament (Knesset), considers Israel as a de facto binational state, albeit without equality for one of the two nationalities—the Arab one. He is presently leading a struggle for equal rights and citizenship inside Israel, and is consequently being tried for treason for having exercised free speech and for having arranged for elderly Palestinians in Israel to meet with their relatives who are refugees in Syria, considered an enemy state. Interviewed by *Middle East Report,* he said:

> We cannot sustain our national identity unless we demand equality in Israel. Otherwise, our national identity becomes merely a product of negating forces, that is to say, a negative national identity, or a product of Israel's refusal to accept us. So, if your national identity is created through inequality only, it becomes shaky and negative. We must build our national identity on the positive forces inherent in it. We do not exist only because Israel rejects us.[6]

For Bishara, the struggle for equality and group rights is inextricably linked to the struggle for democratic binationalism: "Individual equality in Israel cannot be achieved without having group rights. It is impossible for the Arabs in Israel to fuse with Jewish Israelis into a single nation as happened in France and the U.S., because this invalidates the essence of Israel's structure."[7]

Other Palestinian intellectuals, like Nadim Rouhana, perceived the connection between Oslo's failure and the eventuality of a single binational state in all of historic Palestine:

> The failure of the Oslo process to yield a viable Palestinian state could lead to the convergence of interests of all segments of the Palestinian people in calling for a unitary state in Palestine. Indeed the most likely response to the fading hopes for a Palestinian state will be not the acceptance of a Bantustan system of government in the West Bank, but the

development of a mainstream political program that redefines the Israeli-Palestinian conflict from one over territory and sovereignty to a
conflict over power sharing and equality of Palestinian and Jew in historic Palestine in the form of a binational or secular state—the same issue that the Palestinians in Israel are struggling for.[8]

Dr. Ghada Karmi, a Palestinian intellectual based in London, wrote a
seminal article analyzing the Oslo foreclosure on the two-state solution
and advocating the single state as the only possible solution remaining.
The following sums up her cogent argument:

> The Palestinian sense of injustice, which fundamentally derives from
> the loss of their homeland and the denial of their right to return to it, will
> not be redressed by an unequal arrangement of two states. And if the in-
> justice is left unresolved, it will remain a source of instability and a
> cause of "terrorism" in the region. No one denies that there will be mas-
> sive obstacles in the way of implementing a one-state solution in Is-
> rael/Palestine. Nor can the past be reversed, but a solution even at this
> late stage, which permits the equitable sharing of the whole land be-
> tween the two peoples and repatriates the refugees will help lay the
> foundations for a stable future. Given the present structure of Israel and
> the Occupied Territories, which is binational in all but name, a formal
> policy of binationalism is not unthinkable. It may even ultimately pave
> the way to the secular democratic state in historic Palestine. This might
> seem utopian now, but is it any more so than the Zionist enterprise of
> contructing a Jewish state in someone else's country?[9]

Israelis in Support of a Single State

On the Israeli side, endorsement of binationalism comes from an un-
usually diverse group, including liberal politicians, secular leftists, and,
strangely enough, from right-wing rabbis. From the Zionist left, for example, Meron Benvinisti, a former deputy mayor of Jerusalem, described how:

> The reality in Eretz Israel ["greater Israel"] is a binational one. The real-
> ity inside the green line is also binational ... The model which is closest
> to my heart is that of Belgium. Two people, the Flemings and the Wal-
> loons; two regional governments, and one central government.... The
> direction I would prefer is cantonization, the division of Eretz Israel
> West of the Jordan River into Jewish and Arab cantons; I want it to be
> clear that I include the Galilee and the Triangle [translation of the
> Arabic al-Muthalath referring to an area in today's Israel inhabited by
> Palestinian Arabs] in this proposal.[10]

Haim Baram, a secular Israeli leftist known to Western audiences through his regular columns in the London-based *Middle East International*, also endorsed the concept of binationalism as a way to avert the creation of an apartheid regime.

On the religious right, a March 1997 *News From Within* article by Yair Sheleg noted that Israeli Rabbi Menachem Fruman supported the idea of binationalism on the grounds that it would guarantee the "wholeness of the land of Israel," as well as the continuation of the settlements in the West Bank: "I prefer loyalty to the land over loyalty to the state. I see the whole Israel movement as a post-Zionist movement which represents an advance for Zionism over what it is today."[11] Fruman, however, expressed no apologies for advocating two separate legal standards in the single state—one for Jews and one for Arabs. His single state had no problem accommodating apartheid, the roots of which, he said, had prevailed in the hierarchy of classes during the Middle Ages: "If you want, you can write down that I want to take us back to the 'darkness' of the Middle Ages."[12]

Obviously, it is difficult to propose a blueprint for either binationalism or a democratic secular state, in view of the fact that a variety of models may exist depending on the degree of exclusiveness and/or the extent of cultural autonomy each community might be willing to give up or preserve. The important thing is that the lives and fate of the two peoples have been interconnected, and, consequently, a just solution will require that Israelis and Palestinians explore the basis for a common existence, the redress of grievances, and paths to a common vision of a mutually democratic, shared future.

Stephen P. Cohen, a Middle East expert with the Israel Policy Forum, a left-leaning think tank, expressed the view that the status quo in the Occupied Territories could only lead to the institution of apartheid; hence the single state vision becomes the only alternative to perpetual conflict: "There is a growing realization in Israel and among Palestinians that the situation on the ground is becoming defined by the erasure of the Green Line as previously understood.... You now have a Jewish state on both sides of the Green Line, one where there is a Jewish majority and one where there is a Jewish minority ruling an Arab majority. So you have the feeling we are back to the notion of Palestinians getting civil rights in a single state."[13]

Palestinian Strategies

For the Palestinians, the post-Oslo path of the single state was not a new form of political development. Indeed, the first program of Palestinian liberation after the 1967 occupation included the call for a democratic secular state. That program, however, which was linked to armed struggle, was summarily dismissed in order to accommodate the Arab states' agenda of diplomatic struggle, and even the latter was often rhetorical until it became totally ineffectual by the early 1990s. According to the unwritten agreement between the PLO and the Arab states, the renunciation of the unitary state idea came as a *quid pro quo*: the PLO would scale down its national ambitions and accept a two-state approach while the Arab states would provide diplomatic and material help for an independent Palestinian mini-state alongside Israel. On the surface, diplomacy was declared a great success, particularly as Israel was isolated in much of the world, while numerous international forums endorsed the idea of Palestinian self-determination. In reality, however, it was a Pyrrhic victory, as the widely-endorsed Palestinian state was never actually established and had little or no hope of being established given the methods being used to achieve this goal.

By contrast, the South Africans, who had also declared armed struggle, continued to cling to the goal of a unitary state and to reject pressure to renounce armed struggle. A separate independent existence was not high on their diplomatic agenda. In the case of Palestine, the United Nations focused on the human rights of the people under military occupation and only formally on their right to a separate existence. But, in spite of international recognition of their right to independence, they were never able to experience true emancipation. Palestinians continued to endure the status of refugees, of occupied people, and of an ethnic minority in a country in which they had constituted a majority of the population during the lifetime of many who remained.

When the Palestinian struggle finally shifted toward the political dimension during the 1987–1992 Intifada, the goal of a separate independent existence remained intact. It was, however, a struggle suited more to empowerment and social and economic progress than toward coexistence in a single state. Its principal goal was to end the occupation.

Alternative Strategies

When the pursuit of independence was impeded by the structural limitations inherent in Oslo, the Palestinians were challenged more than ever to resurrect the political struggle of the first Intifada: building mass organizations and alternative institutions that would enable them to address the social, economic, and political needs of the populace. Israel's ever-increasing land grab would not be halted by diplomatic action, but would be slowed (if not halted altogether) only by popular mobilization and mass action. Undoubtedly, the task was daunting, for it challenged not only Israel's continuing occupation regime, but the Palestinian Authority, as well. For the PA, any form of extra-Oslo struggle, even that designed to implement principles of international law, was subject to repression under the guise of fighting terrorism, guarding Israel's security, and meeting the requirements of what Israel and the U.S. called "reciprocity."

The privations and hardships associated with the status of refugees, of occupied population, and of second-class citizens, continued to thwart Palestinian political development, despite all the trappings of statehood. The PA created a president without executive power, a council without legislative powers, courts with insignificant jurisdiction, an overblown civilian bureaucracy prone to corruption, and a pervasive military apparatus focused on suppressing dissent. Oslo was calculated to put the onus on Arafat to prove his ability as an effective gendarme for Israel. The minute normal oppositional politics turned into resistance, Israel declared an all-out war and blamed the victim for its own atrocities. Arafat could not deliver what Israel wanted without becoming Israel's puppet and quisling.

There can be no shortcuts to genuine emancipation. Any realistic alternative to Oslo must address the concrete situation of Palestinians living in the Palestinian territories of the West Bank, Gaza, and East Jerusalem; those inside Israel; and those in the far-flung diaspora. No degree of independence or liberation will be meaningful without removing the legal, social, and economic inequalities and divisions facing these groups of Palestinians. That will require a determined, systematic, and protracted struggle, combining the three segments of the Palestinian people jointly with Israeli Jews who wish to be neither master of another people, nor privileged in an apartheid system, nor colonial settlers denying the existence of the indigenous natives of the land, nor ethnic cleansers organizing a "transfer."

The goal of the struggle must be equal protection under the law in a unified state—much like that required in the Fourteenth Amendment to the U.S. Constitution: the illegality of any disparity or classification in protection by the law, the end of group segregation, and its removal from the social, economic, and legal fabric of society. Equality for every single human being in Palestine/Israel should be the motto of the new struggle.

This vision, of course, is bound to collide with the interests of the major players, whether in Washington, Tel Aviv, or Ramallah. It would signal that U.S. domination of Middle East diplomacy had failed. It would serve as an indictment of Zionism—the classical Labor version of Rabin, Peres, and Barak, as well as the revisionist brand of Jabotinsky, Begin, and Sharon. It would serve as an indictment of the narrow brand of Palestinian nationalism that seemed either unwilling or incapable of reexamining the past, with all its errors, pitfalls, and misconceptions.

This kind of struggle may sound unrealistic, and the goal idealistic or utopian, but it certainly has more prospects for success than the open-ended Oslo formula, whose fate was settled in advance by a grotesque disparity in power. The Palestinians have been given no choice but to struggle for equal rights and equal dignity, despite Oslo's constraints. Not only has Oslo foreclosed their option of a sovereign separate existence, it also denied them the right to struggle for that existence. Even the PA has finally realized that Israel's land grab has forfeited the two-state option. In a surprising move, the PA has communicated to the Bush administration that the expansion of settlements in the West Bank may have already pre-empted the two-state solution, which has ostensibly been the basis for two decades of negotiations. Two top Palestinian officials submitted written documents to the State Department and to the White House expressing apprehension that the two-state solution is still possible. The veiled threat was embodied in a ten-page memo and five detailed maps of settlement activity on October 7, 2002, delivered by Finance Minister Salam Fayad to Secretary of State Colin Powell and his senior aide David Satterfield. A similar message was delivered to the White House one week later by Ahmed Qureia, the speaker of the Palestinian Legislative Council.[14]

A Reconsideration of Zionist Ideology?

The fundamental nature of the Israeli state precludes genuine coexistence with the Palestinian people on any equal basis. As long as the Zionist ideology of acquiring Palestinian land and resources while excluding the Palestinian people prevails, a negotiated settlement based on the right of the two people to dignity and self-determination is not possible. Any serious forward movement beyond the intolerable present situation requires a profound debate about the nature of Zionist ideology and history, in which the difficult questions, suppressed since the establishment of Israel, must be raised. The dominant Zionist narrative and its negative portrayal of Arabs and distortion of history must be at the heart of this debate.

A post-Zionist debate that had been taking place inside Israel during the 1990s has come to a grinding halt under the impact of Sharon's strategy of provocations, which continues to generate Palestinian suicide bombings, turning the Israeli population against all Palestinians. The Israeli political scientist Ilan Pappe, who studied the post-Zionist phenomenon, delineated some of its salient manifestations in the various Israeli cultural products, including films, music, novels, and short stories. He touched only slightly on the extent to which this critique has become available to the general public and the degree to which it affects public attitudes toward Arabs and Palestinians.[15] Pappe revealed, however, how intertwined have the lives of ordinary Palestinians and Israelis have become. There is an implication in his work that Israel cannot prosper as an isolated Western outpost in the region:

> There is a need to dissolve the sharp contradictions between a Zionist and Jewish state and human rights and democracy. A democratic pluralist Israel as a part of the Mediterranean is also Israel with many historical narratives. Such an Israel has a chance at a common future.[16]

The question of whether Zionism is a movement of national plundering or a movement of a persecuted people, acting according to a human ethic, seeking compromise, and peace, is being increasingly raised by some Israeli intellectuals. The Israeli historian Benny Morris, for example, framed the question in terms of the accuracy of the "Zionist ethos claims that we came to this land not to exploit the natives and expel them, and not to occupy them by force."[17] Today, in the aftermath of the second Intifada, Morris himself characterizes the ongoing struggle as an existential one for Israel, a sad commentary on the decline of the post-Zionist debate. In a recent article, Morris argued that the Middle East might now be at peace if Israel had driven out *all* the Palestinians in 1948.[18] And yet, only when this kind of critique is broadened to include the mainstream and penetrate the consciousness of the average Jewish Israeli will the so-called peace process begin to assume truly peaceful dimensions. Only when the Palestinians decide to rediscover and reconstruct their democratic secular state framework, and transform it from a propagandistic slogan to a viable program that can be adapted to the present realities, will hopes for real peace be rekindled.

No matter by what name we refer to this phenomenon—a binational state, a federal system, a cantonal arrangement on the Swiss model—the common denominators would still be equal rights, equal citizenship, plurality, and coexistence. It would manifest a common humanity in which the very identity of the citizens would have to be reexamined, taking into consideration psychological and ideological factors, and not only ethnic, religious, and nationalistic factors. The very concept of citizenship and identity would be transformed, as has been suggested, for example, by Edward Said, who described a Palestinian as anyone who identifies with the sufferings of the Palestinians, who resists the limits of what the Oslo final status negotiations have to offer, who participated in the liberation struggles throughout the 1970s and 1980s—and not only who was born in Palestine and is willing to live in whatever ghetto has been chosen for her or him by the architects of Oslo. He wrote:

> We stand firm on the matter of identity as something more significant and politically democratic than mere residence and subservience to what Israel offers us. What we ask for as Palestinians is the right to be citizens and not just numbers in the ultimately losing game being played by the Oslo participants. It is worth pointing out, moreover, that Israelis will also be the losers if they accept the narrow-minded and ungenerous definition of the Palestinians as a subject people confined to a "homeland" being manipulated by their government. In a decade, there will be demographic parity between Jews and Arabs in historical Palestine. Better that we accommodate to each other sooner rather than later as full members of a binational secular state than to go on fighting what has been demeaningly called a shepherd's war between feuding tribes. To choose that identity is to make history. Not to choose is to disappear.[19]

Seeking Redress Through International Civil Society

For the Palestinians, redress and restitution have been impeded by having had to confront a powerful enemy fortified by a strategic alliance with the world's only superpower. Moreover, an inept leadership and complicit

Arab "allies" have proven disastrous to the cause, while the Palestine question itself remains deliberately surrounded by disinformation. Any efforts, therefore, toward compensation and reparations have to be creative, innovative, and directed toward building an international solidarity movement whose goal is to force the hand of states and international institutions of justice.

The Palestinians have experienced the historical process of conquest, dispossession, and domination, and have never, contrary to other colonized people, experienced the process of decolonization. A commission of truth and reconciliation, South African–style, is not in the offing, and official "sorry days" and "sorry books," such as exist in Australia, are very far away. Neither Prime Minister Ariel Sharon nor Shimon Peres is likely to entertain the thought of making apologies similar to those Queen Elizabeth and President Bill Clinton made to India and Guatemala, respectively, however empty those words may have been. They wouldn't even countenance the questioning of Israeli members of the armed forces for their roles in the spring massacres of Jenin, Nablus, and Ramallah—let alone their own roles in the crimes of Sabra, Shatila, and Qana. What Menachem Begin said years ago ("Nobody should preach to us ethics, nobody!") is a dictum that remains alive and well in the most intransigent government in the entire history of Israel.

In the current context, the Palestinians have to look for restitution far from established governments and conventional means, aiming instead toward building an international grassroots movement. The structure of inequality is global, and thus reparations and restitution have emerged as central issues separating the affluent North from the poor South, with the United States leading the anti-reparations camp. The World Conference Against Racism, Racial Discrimination, Xenophobia, and Related Intolerances, which was held in Durban, South Africa, in September, 2001, was portrayed in the United States as an anti-Israel parley worthy of a U.S. boycott. The issue that loomed high on the real U.S. agenda was the question of financial reparations for the transatlantic slave trade. Essentially, however, the conference represented a historic event that aimed to eradicate the legacy of slavery, colonialism, and racism.

Beneath the issues of Zionism and slavery lay the economic underpinnings of the conference on racism, which are quite worrisome to the world's rich and powerful. The United States and some of its allies have unsuccessfully attempted to distort the real meaning of the Durban conference and diminish its significance as a pivotal event in the ongoing confrontation between the forces of colonialism and racism, on the one hand, and those of liberation and equality, on the other. The Durban gathering constituted a critical juncture on the road toward democratization, economic and social emancipation, and indeed a more egalitarian world.

The Durban conference unmistakably revealed the futility of seeking justice from governments with agendas that clash with the needs of colonized people and their aspirations for justice and redress. The resolutions on Palestine and Zionism presented by the nongovernmental organizations (NGOs) at that conference stood in sharp contrast to the determined attempts by the U.S. government, supported by Western European governments and Mary Robinson, the U.N. commissioner for human rights, to undermine the very concept of reparations.

The NGO resolutions supported the Palestinian cause strongly and universally, expressing the sentiments of international civil society. By contrast, government representatives led by the United States simply echoed George W. Bush's crude formulation that the conference should not be allowed to "pick on Israel." It was tantamount to a rapist claiming he was being picked on by his victim because he was being prosecuted for his crime.

By elevating the question of Zionism and Israel to the status of a principal issue at the Durban Conference, Washington was hoping to defend the global status quo, with all its socioeconomic ills and its autocratic nature. It was also hoping to maintain its own hegemony, as well as the prevailing taboo against any form of reparation payments as compensation for past injustices. What was interesting is that such strategic goals had been advanced in the name of protecting Israel and the Jewish people, who have suffered immensely from bigotry, slander, and discrimination.

In the NGO gathering, the issue of Zionism created a vigorous discussion. Western advocates of "compromise" and "practicality," led by Reverend Jesse Jackson, posited that the conference was far too important to become a victim of ideological collisions. While that logic had predictably gained the endorsement of the official Palestinian leaders—specifically Nabil Shaath, Palestinian Authority minister of planning and international cooperation—it was, effectively, repudiated by a forthright speech to the conference by Hanan Ashrawi, a leading Palestinian NGO spokesperson unaffiliated with the Palestinian Authority.

Nabil Shaath argued: "We are not interested in raising an ideological issue against Israel. Therefore, we will not support statements against Zionism, nor are we going to support statements equating Zionism with racism." By contrast, Hanan Ashrawi, voicing the opinion of a vastly broader sector of Palestinian public, told the conference:

> I appeal to you ... not to adopt the stance of "cowardly neutrality," for in the struggle against oppression, injustice, racism, intolerance, colonialism, and exclusion, there can be NO neutrality.... Here, there is no U.S. veto to deprive us of protection and our rights, nor is there censorship or blackmail to intimidate governments ruled by self-interest.[20]

Indeed, there was no formal U.S. veto in Durban, but there was a great deal of intimidation and manipulation, as the more official, though unrepresentative, voice of the PA clearly indicated. The token U.S. delegation was using corridor diplomacy to "repair" the language in the hope that a watered-down version of the "practical" school of thought would finally emerge. The aim was to produce a final resolution that would, as always, condemn slavery, condemn the unjust legacy of colonialism and racism, but only after insuring that Zionism was not included in these definitions. When that effort failed, the U.S. and Israel withdrew, branding the event as a "farce."

The American decision, which was widely criticized, even by the Reverend Jesse Jackson and the obliging U.N. Secretary-General Kofi Anan, made it all the more urgent that Palestinian and Arab NGOs cling tenaciously to their position of naming Zionism exactly as it should be, as a racist-colonialist ideology. Concurrently, the Americans staunchly opposed any substitution of a mere condemnation of slavery for actual payment of reparations. Only by adhering to that twin strategy were they able to guard against being placed in a no-win situation. Only then could they claim to have been acting as active participants in the dialectical struggle between colonialism and racism, on the one hand, and liberation, justice, and equality on the other.

When the issues at hand fall within the arena of crimes against humanity, redress must be legal and must also be guarded against pragmatic solutions. As such, slavery and racism should not be dealt with only in terms of what is "practical," but in terms of what is just. Descendants of slave traders may apologize and even atone, but they must also compensate. Similarly, descendants of racist Zionists and contemporary Zionists must also apologize, atone, and compensate. Watered-down resolutions will only serve to embolden them and give them comfort that the atrocities they commit are beyond the reach of law.

After the invalidation of the U.N. resolution equating Zionism and racism, Israel was able to claim the removal of the conflict from its colonial context, rendering it one between a state fighting for its survival and "terrorists" bent on its destruction. As long as the paradigm of the "peace process" remains intact, with the term "occupation" excised from the diplomatic lexicon, Israel will continue to argue that the Palestinian liberation struggle is not what it claims to be and that Israel's own apartheid is not what it is.

In short, the issues at Durban were linked and inseparable. Colonialism, racism, and slavery are responsible for the present social and economic evils that keep Africa's black laborers in a state of terrible exploitation and permanent poverty, and their effects are reinforced by the current process of globalization. Similarly, Israel's colonial and racist practices must be halted before the Palestinians end their Intifada (in contrast to Bush's demand that Palestinians end their Intifada before the United States will reactivate its insipid diplomatic role). Today, that role is nonexistent.

In fact, America is part of the problem, and, as such, it cannot be part of the solution. Resuming the "peace process" is going back to the very conditions that had produced the chaos leading to the entrenchment of apartheid, land alienation, and consolidation of the occupation. For the Palestinians, it has been a process of suffering and denial. Durban was a milestone event, especially for international civil society, which has effectively launched a process of adjudication and tried to foster future reconciliation that can put an end to the last colonial wars.

International Solidarity: Beyond Durban

The beginning of the twenty-first century witnessed the emergence of a new international solidarity movement with varied groups supporting the struggle of the Palestinian people. The Madrid and Oslo processes created a major transformation in the Palestinian movement. Unlike the 1970s and 1980s, when an international solidarity movement was harmoniously behind the Palestinian people and their leadership, the 1990s Oslo ar-

rangements created a schism between leadership and grassroots, leaving
the solidarity movement in a quandary. No one wanted to preach to the
Palestinians what their interests were. Nevertheless, Arafat's decision to
become Israel's enforcer and America's client began to alienate broad
segments of Palestinian society everywhere, leading eventually to Palestinian self-reliance at the grassroots, as reliance on the goodwill of the
U.S. government proved disastrous. The outcome of that interaction with
the international NGO movement produced a new form of international
solidarity focusing on protection, return, and the use of economic pressure
to gain redress. It was a public response to the ongoing U.S. pressure on
Arafat to relinquish the right of return and denounce resistance as a form
of terror, even as the U.S. continued to veto U.N. resolutions calling for
protection of Palestinian civilians under occupation.

In 2000, the Palestine Right to Return Coalition (Al-Awda) was established in the U.S. with a branch in the UK.[21] It has been mobilizing
support for the right of the Palestinian refugees to return to their homes
and to gain restitution. During the following year, a divestment campaign
modeled on the 1980s antiapartheid struggle was launched on U.S. campuses. Petitions calling for universities to get rid of their investments in Israel have been circulating at Harvard, MIT, Princeton, Cornell, the
University of California campuses, and many others, and more are being
planned. A battle is currently raging on U.S. campuses for and against investment in Israel, with thousands of faculty signatures being collected.[22]
Other components of the solidarity movement include the "internation-
als," who act as witnesses to Israeli atrocities and perform the duties of a
volunteer international protective force. They are vulnerable to deportation orders, but many of them have managed to stay.

The Palestine Solidarity Campaign and the Boycott Israeli Goods
Campaign also derive their inspiration from the struggle against South
African apartheid. They call for boycotting Israeli goods, sporting events,
and even academic conferences.[23] In early July 2002, the boycott campaign in the UK was able to secure a ban on settlement-produced products
illegally labeled "made in Israel." A cultural boycott is also emerging in
addition to the economic boycott. For example, two professors, Hilary
Rose and Stephen Rose, drafted the "Israel Academic Moratorium Call,"
again justifying it in terms of the anti-apartheid struggle:

The international academic, cultural and sporting communities had played a major part in isolating South Africa, and we have increasingly learned of individuals who thought that cooperating with Israeli institutions was like collaborating with the apartheid regime. A writer refused to have her play acted in Israel, a musician turns down an invitation to perform, or an academic to attend a conference. It was these individual ethical refusals which led us to make the restricted call for a moratorium on European research and academic collaboration with Israeli institutions until the Israeli government opened serious peace negotiations.[24]

Moreover, a new U.S. Campaign to End the Israeli Occupation was established in the United States in 2002 to work through organized constituencies already working against settlements, land confiscation, house demolitions, and other violations of international law, with a common platform to challenge U.S. policies supporting the Israeli occupation of Palestine.[25] Other initiatives emanate from a variety of existing and new organizations, such as the International Socialist Organization (ISO), Adalah: The Legal Center for Arab Minority Rights in Israel, the Alternative Information Center, Gush Shalom, Badil: Resource Center for Palestinian Residency and Refugee Rights, the American Friends Service Committee, and Sabeel: Ecumenical Liberation Theology Center. These and others have become part of a worldwide solidarity movement operating on the assumption that governments have failed to bring about an equitable settlement, while the U.N. has become an instrument for U.S. foreign policy. An honorable outcome of the Palestinian-Israeli conflict can only emerge from successful organizing by the international solidarity movement, which could counteract the ongoing obstruction of peace by the United States under the conditions of global autocracy.

Justice can never be delivered by the lone superpower, which supplies the very tools and political protection that enable Israel to commit war crimes. It can only be obtained through international alliances of individual activists amd organizations, which, in turn, pressure and transform governments and the international institutions of civil society. Justice in the final analysis will not be achieved by appeasing and accommodating one's oppressors, but rather through solidarity with the struggles of others who demonstrate their support for Palestinian rights. The battle in Durban was one and the same for the Palestinians, Africans, African Americans, native people elsewhere, and other victims of exploitation, colonialism, intolerance, racism, and xenophobia. They are the natural allies of the Palestinian people.

Notes

1   For an analysis of the decline of the viability of the two-state solution, see *CounterPunch*, November 4, 2002.
2   *New York Times*, September 10, 1997.
3   *Christian Science Monitor*, May 27, 1997.
4   David Barsamian, "An Interview With Edward W. Said," *The Progressive,* April 1999, p. 35; see also As'ad Ghonem, "Zionism, Post-Zionism and Anti-Zionism in Israel: Jews and Arabs in the conflict over the nature of the state," in *The Post-Zionist Debate in Israel*, ed. E. Nemni (London: Zed Books, 2002).
5   *News From Within*, April 1997.
6   "Equal Rights for Arabs in Jewish State: A Goal Unrealizable: An Interview with Azmi Bishara, Knesset Member," *MERIP Press Information Note* 12 (December 14, 1999).
7   "Equal Rights for Arabs in Jewish State."
8   Nadim Rouhana, "The Test of Equal Citizenship," *Harvard International Review* 20 (1998), p. 78.
9   Ghada Karmi, "A Secular Democratic State in Historic Palestine: An Idea Whose Time Has Come?" July 2002. First published in al-Adad, Beirut, Lebanon, http://www.caabu.org/press/articles/secular-state.html.
10 *News From Within*, April 1997.
11 *News From Within*, March 1997.
12 *News From Within*, March 1997.
13 *The Forward*, October 25, 2002.
14 *The Forward*, October 25, 2002.
15 See Pappe's series of three articles on the subject: Ilan Pappe, "Post-Zionist Critique on Israel and the Palestinians," parts 1–3, *Journal of Palestine Studies* 26: 2 (Winter 1997): 29–41; 26: 3 (Spring 1997): 37–43; and 26: 4 (Summer 1997): 60–69; see also Ilan Pappe, "Review Essay, Israeli Television's Fiftieth Anniversary 'Tekumma' Series: A Post-Zionist View?" *Journal of Palestine Studies* 27: 4 (Summer 1998): 99–105.
16 *Ha'aretz* (Weekend Supplement), June 10, 1994.
17 *Ha'aretz*, June 24, 1994.
18 *Guardian* (London), October 3, 2002.

19   Edward W. Said, "By Birth or By Choice?" *Al-Ahram Weekly,* October
         28–November 3, 1999.

20   Hanan Ashrawi, Address to The World Conference Against Racism,
         Racial Discrimination, Xenophobia, and Related Intolerances, Durban,
         South Africa, August 28, 2001.

21   See http://al-awda.org.

22   *Ha'aretz,* July 17, 2002; see also the Michigan Divestment Conference at
         http://www.divestmentconference.com; SAFE, University of Michigan at
         http://www.studentsallied.com; U-M President's Statement on the
         Divestment Conference at http://www.umich.edu/pres/coleman/PSC.html;
         Harvard and MIT divestment petition at http://www.harvardmitdivest.org;
         University of California's faculty petition at http://www.ucdivest.org; and
         Palestine Solidarity Committee of South Africa at http://mandla.co.za/psc/
         Default.htm.

23   See http://www.palestinecampaign.org, http://www.boycottisraeligoods.org.

24   *Guardian* (London), May 27, 2002; *Guardian* (London), July 15, 2002.

25   See http://endtheoccupation.org.

A PEACE PROCESS OR A NEGOTIATING STRATEGY?

The Madrid and Oslo processes yielded to Israel important benefits—full peace with Jordan, de facto normalization with many Arab states, and full relations with most of the Islamic and third-world states that had previously boycotted Israel. The separate tracks approach, devised by Israel and sold to the Arabs by James Baker III, enabled Israel and the international Zionist movement to accomplish a broad strategic goal: a separate peace with the Arab states not contingent on the necessity of meeting Israeli obligations to the Palestinian people as spelled out in various U.N. resolutions. Thus, the withdrawal clause of Security Council Resolution 242 was an issue between Israel and Jordan regarding a little-known patch of desert in southern Jordan, and possibly an issue in suspension between Israel and Syria regarding the Golan Heights, but not in the West Bank and Gaza, and certainly not in Jerusalem, which Israel does not consider occupied.

The second diplomatic instrument of Madrid—negotiations in stages, reinforced by Oslo, enabled Israel to accomplish another strategic goal: deferral of the Palestine question in its entirety, while normalizing relations with the Arab world and reorganizing its occupation of Palestinian lands, with Yasir Arafat's implicit complicity and "legal" commitment. These diplomatic devices also produced the Palestinian Authority, which helped effect that reorganization, simultaneously pre-empting and marginalizing the PLO as the voice of the Palestinians and anchor of their national rights. Further conquest of land and resources under presumed peaceful conditions was the ultimate dividend of Oslo. Israel consolidated the 1967 occupation while mortally fragmenting all that remained of Palestine—the site of the future Palestinian state.

Rarely were nations able to achieve so much in negotiations while making so few cosmetic concessions in return. Until the 2000 Intifada, Israeli diplomats and businessmen shuttled freely between Arab capitals, all the way from Qatar in the east to Casablanca in the west. The Arab boycott of Israel was effectively ended, until it was resumed by broad sectors of Arab civil society and a vibrant solidarity movement abroad. The concept of Arab defense was rendered illegitimate by Oslo and became increasingly identified as "terrorism," now punishable under post–September 11 military doctrines of the right to launch "pre-emptive strikes" and eliminate "terrorist bases." As a result, the Arab states have emerged as subcontractors for the dishonest broker, the United States, whose major assignment is to impress on Arafat to contain and criminalize Palestinian resistance, now redefined as "terrorist" activity. By opting for the separate Oslo route, after the closure of Madrid, Arafat gave Arab leaders an easy way out. They did not wish to be more Palestinian than the Palestinians. Hence their recruitment by the dishonest broker as willing messengers and advice givers. The latest mission assumed by Jordan and Egypt in August 2002 involved a failed attempt to participate in the training of a new Palestinian security force to contain the resistance to Israel's occupation and to help insure Israeli security.

Clearly, de facto normalization between the Arab world and Israel has sidelined the Palestine question, which served as a prominent symbol of just liberation struggles against colonialism. Arafat's apologists blame the Gulf War and the end of the Cold War for the Palestinian travail, but rarely, if at all, do they accept responsibility for their fatal mistakes or acknowledge having been fooled into a no-win strategy. Nor was any admission ever made by Arafat himself or by his top echelons that their corruption has diminished a just cause. Worse yet was their inability and unwillingness to utilize the democratically elected institutions and the immense talents and skills of their own people when Israel's diplomatic resources and legal expertise were fully mobilized against their haphazard efforts and extemporaneous methods. Global and regional considerations aside, Arafat cannot escape responsibility for having exchanged the Madrid framework, in which autonomy was deemed the beginning of a transitional phase, for the Oslo framework, which effectively made limited autonomy the end of the road.

Having opted for the Oslo path, Arafat was able to negotiate without a proxy. But while he temporarily ceased to be a pariah himself, together with his organization, he managed to place the Palestinian people and their entire cause under probation. And together with the bureaucrats of his organization, he was tempted by the prospects of international donations and a place he could call home, even if it was Gaza. He assumed Israel's burden, while Israel gave up nothing, and his people paid the heavy price.

The diplomatic instruments of Madrid have been utilized by Israel to lure the Palestinians into a blind alley, while at the same time using them as the green light for entry into Amman and beyond. The penetration of the Arab world is being achieved with virtually no cost to Israel, as Arafat tried to qualify as an enforcer for the occupation but would eventually flunk out and be demonized like Saddam Hussein and Osama bin Laden, consigned to irrevocable condemnation.

Israel's nonrecognition of the Palestinians as a sovereign people is the singlemost important obstacle to a genuine peace. Having overlooked the importance of that negation, Arafat has effectively enabled Israel to give the derivatives of the Arab-Israeli conflict—the Arab factor—precedence over the essence—Palestine—of that conflict. It is in this context that Israel's negotiating strategy becomes crystal clear: the Gaza-Jericho First formula (1994) was simply the bait. Ironically, for Israel, it opened the gateway to the Arab world, but left the doors to the West Bank tightly closed in the face of the Palestinians. Instead of saving Arafat's career, it served as his trap. Unlike Egypt's Anwar Sadat, who concluded a single agreement with Israel to be implemented in stages, Arafat had merely concluded an agreement to reach agreement, which would be negotiated in endless stages but never allowed to reach closure. His path to the West Bank has, therefore, been arduous, while the road to Jerusalem was shut tight.

Now, seven years after "Gaza-Jericho," there is a new "Gaza-Bethlehem First" agreement, reached on August 18, 2002 between Israeli defense minister Benyamin Ben-Eliezer and the PA minister of interior, Abdul Razzaq Al-Yahya, which was supposed to lead to a gradual Israeli army withdrawal from Palestinian cities located in Area A in the West Bank and a relaxation of the draconian measures imposed on more than three million Palestinians under occupation and semi-permanent curfews. According to Palestinian journalist Khalid Amayreh, "as soon as Israeli occupation troops left the streets of Bethlehem, Israeli political and military leaders started issuing statements emphasizing the insignificance of the agreement and stressing that it wouldn't change anything on the ground."[1] In fact, the Israeli government was directing two contradictory messages during the autumn of

2002, one by Sharon to Israeli hardline constituents and another by the author of Gaza-Bethlehem First, Defense Minister Ben-Eliezer, directed to
Western public opinion. Sharon, responding to charges by his far-rightist
coalition partners that the deal amounted to a return to the Oslo path, assured critics that he "only removed two or three jeeps from the streets of
Bethlehem, that is all we've done, and our forces are clamping a siege on
the city, preventing anyone from getting in or out."[2] Ben-Eliezer, who is
in full agreement with Sharon on the overall strategy for the West Bank,
authored an op-ed article in the *Wall Street Journal* expressing the message that the plan is genuine and creative:

> The Gaza-Bethlehem plan has already yielded some positive results. Is-
> raeli troops have evacuated Bethlehem, allowing Palestinians to take
> security control of the city.... Unlike other plans, this is an initiative that
> has come from within—from people living in the region.[3]

Any expectation that "Bethlehem-Gaza First" will prove more successful than its predecessor, "Gaza-Jericho First," is indeed a false hope.
The state-in-waiting implied in the term "first" will probably wait much
longer—so as long as the Sharon government, which looks more like a
military junta than a cabinet, remains in office. Ben-Eliezer's boasting
about his plan underscores its lack of substance, open-ended character
and absence of timetables:

> Rather than setting its sights on broader, long term objectives, the plan fo-
> cuses solely on the pressing need to calm tensions first.... This is a pro-
> cess with a different rhythm. We will proceed according to the pace of
> events on the ground. There is no pressure to meet deadlines, and we are
> not asking that the process be rushed. We do, however, ask to see results.[4]

In fact, the present conversion of the state-in-waiting to what Israeli
journalist Nahum Bernea called Israel's "penal colony" was the logical
result of Israel's strategy and Arafat's ad hoc strategy (if he can even be
said to have a strategy). Dreaming about final status talks while paying no
attention to the interim phase has taken a heavy toll on Arafat's people.
Gaza became their purgatory, while life in the West Bank has become
hell. And for the diaspora Palestinians, there is only permanent exile.

Redeployment Reconsidered

By determining the framework and the scope of the "peace process," Israel was able to keep the course of diplomacy consonant with its national

goals and acceptable to its various constituencies across the entire political spectrum, including the expansionist settler movement. Thus, while the Gaza-Jericho agreement had initially enjoyed a broad consensus in the Israeli body politic, a replication of it in the heavily colonized West Bank was out of the question. Seven years ago, Knesset member Hisham Mahameed was quoted as saying that settlement activity has come to "enjoy a consensus within Israel, even among the Israeli left."[5] This is even more true today than it was in the past.

Rabin's government was deeply aware in 1993 and 1994 of the fact that the redeployment of the Israeli army to the fifteen Gaza Strip settlements was much more feasible, in political and security terms, than a redeployment in the West Bank. And yet, according to a May 1994 report of the Gaza Center for Rights and Law, an estimated 4,000–4,500 Israeli soldiers were assigned to fifty-four settlements, camps, and checkpoints. The demographic and geographic character of the numerous Jewish settlements in the West Bank would make it nearly impossible for any Israeli government to find a satisfactory arrangement accommodating settler colonialism and Palestinian independence. A negotiated settlement based on the right of the two peoples to dignity and self-determination, therefore, continued to be elusive. The Gaza-Jericho agreement, itself, was part of Israel's negotiating strategy, calculated to release Israel from the pressure to find a solution to its continuing occupation of the West Bank and Jerusalem. And as long as Hamas and Islamic Jihad persisted in responding to Israel's calculated provocations, Arafat's obligation to Israeli security under Oslo continued to dominate the diplomatic agenda.

Palestinian obligations for Israeli security under the various Oslo agreements came to include the security of the settlements. Thus, as early as December 1994, Rabin's government made it clear to the Palestinian negotiators that the redeployment clause in the Cairo agreement was contingent on "settlements security." Not unexpectedly, the dishonest broker defended that policy. Former U.S. Secretary of State Warren Christopher announced: "No one expects Israel to redeploy outside the territories during the second stage of the interim agreement unless the PLO assures security in the area under its control." That onus, placed on the Palestinians by Washington, has continued to be a linchpin of U.S. policy to the present day. Israel and the United States succeeded in changing not only the global consensus on the Palestine question, but also the rules of Madrid, which supposedly linked Israeli security and Palestinian rights. How then could the Palestinians ever argue in future final negotiations that these settlements exist illegally on occupied land and must, therefore, be dismantled? Having accepted the paramountcy of settlement security in the "interim" stage, how could they reasonably expect their destruction later? The settlements and the military forces that protect them are the foundation upon which the Israeli occupation is built and maintained, and the excuse to pre-empt an independent Palestinian state. In the words of the late Yehoshofat Harkabi, the former Israeli military chief of intelligence, settlements have become "an instrument to prevent the establishment of a sovereign Palestinian authority west of the Jordan River."[6]

As the so-called negotiations continued between 1994 and 2000, acceleration of demands and conditions on Arafat became all too familiar as an integral part of the Israeli negotiating strategy, irrespective of who was in power. Thus Rabin's successor, Benjamin Netanyahu, was also awarded time to develop a "peace" plan (that is, for procrastination and developing additional impediments). The pattern was continued under Netanyahu's successor, Ehud Barak, in May 1999. Barak was given time by Mubarak, Nabil Sha'ath, and of course Bill Clinton, only to discover in the end that his peace plan was nothing but a gimmick to escape responsibility for further redeployment and instead proceed directly to final status talks (a policy that issued the death certificate of Oslo). By the time Sharon came to power in February 2001, Israel's obligations for further redeployment and for reaching a final settlement were totally abandoned on the pretext that Arafat, the subcontractor turned into terrorist who can no longer stop the violence, must self-negate altogether. Thus Oslo has come full circle, having enabled Israel to realize strategic goals by ensuring that the area between the Jordan River and the Mediterranean can only accommodate a single sovereignty, hence Sharon's "deluxe" reoccupation and South African strategy. [7]

Sharon's South African strategy was recently analyzed by Avi Primor, a former Israeli diplomat and currently vice president of Tel Aviv University:

> There are two elements that characterize Sharon's policies toward the Palestinians: the siege of the Palestinian cities and the subversion of the central Palestinian authority—with or without Arafat. Clearly, such a situation requires local authorities in the besieged towns, if only to pro-

vide elementary services to the population. Those local authorities cannot be subordinate to the gradually disappearing Palestinian Authority, nor can they operate without being subordinate to the Israeli authorities. Why hasn't this plan reached full fruition yet? It's possible that if not for American pressure, the PA would be only a historical memory by now. But even so, when U.S. Defense Secretary Donald Rumsfeld refers to the "so-called" Occupied Territories, it's clear the U.S. is only slowing down, not stopping the Sharon strategy. Without anyone taking notice, a process is underway establishing a "Palestinian state" limited to the Palestinian cities, a "state" comprised of a number of separate, sovereign-less enclaves, with no resources for self-sustenance. The territories of the West Bank and Gaza remain in Israeli hands, and its Palestinian residents are being turned into "citizens" of that "foreign country."[8]

A "No-Win" Situation for Arafat

The Israeli and U.S. framework of the "peace process" placed Arafat in a no-win situation. His deal with Israel was predicated on an impossible equation. No serious discussion of Israeli redeployment or extension of limited self-rule to the West Bank was to be undertaken until Arafat decided to utilize the "strong police force" on behalf of Israel's settlers. Yet, while Arafat might appear to Israel as more qualified when pursuing that course, he would be condemned by his fellow Palestinians as a puppet and a quisling. That became starkly clear when his police force committed its first major act as Israel's surrogate by firing on demonstrators after Friday prayers in Gaza, killing thirteen and injuring 200 on November 18, 1994.[9] Ten days before the incident, in words that can be seen as prophetic, Arafat's chief negotiator, Nabil Shaath, expressed the Palestinian dilemma when he told the Israeli newspaper *Yedioth Ahronoth*, "I would suggest not making Arafat look like an Israeli agent, like an 'Uncle Tom' serving his masters."[10]

But the agreement was collapsing almost from the beginning and was impossible to implement. Beyond all the specific reasons Oslo failed that I have explained in *Dishonest Broker,* the very nature of the Israeli state precludes genuine coexistence with the Palestinian people on an equal basis. Any forward movement on a "peace process," now discredited by the sponsor and its strategic ally, would require a genuine debate about the history of Zionism in which the difficult questions, submerged since 1948, would need to be raised. Otherwise, "peace" will simply be the continuation of war through other means. Indeed, Israeli strategists speak rather candidly about the "peace process" as "part of a military strategy." The *Boston Globe* reporter Ethan Bronner quoted an Israeli general as saying, "That is how Israel will turn Clausewitz on his head." Through the peace process, he said, "we're making diplomacy into war by other means."[11] The process is designed to enable Israeli strategists to focus on the high-tech war for the twenty-first century, building long-range missiles and antimissile missiles, developing enormous fire power, laser-guided projectiles, and night vision equipment, while leaving the day-to-day police repression role to Yasir Arafat. It was a cost-effective strategy based on the notion of the "small smart army." But the Intifada in 2000 changed the equation. In the words of former Likudist Defense Minister Moshe Arens, Israel concluded that the Palestinians would have to be defeated before Israel could make peace with them.

President Bush again reinforced Israeli intransigence in his speech of June 24, 2002. Bush asserted that Palestinians must give up their basic right of resistance in order to sit at the negotiating table with the party that now denies them a sovereign existence. These stipulations made by the lone superpower are being made to supercede the rights conferred upon the Palestinians by international law and the dictates of the Universal Declaration of Human Rights.

The prospects for a serious breakthrough toward a settlement will have to await a return to diplomacy, and the whole process will be dependent on an unlikely, but much needed, Israeli debate of Zionist history and the nature of the Israeli state. If the Zionist claim is correct about coming to Palestine "to build and be built," rather than to conquer and plunder, then Israel will have to make hard choices: between peace and the settlements, between peace and a permanent exile for the Palestinian refugees, between peace and Jerusalem as the eternal capital, between peace and Israel as a Western imperial project.

The latest chapter of the "peace process," ongoing without real success for more than three decades, is less about peace and more about bureaucratic procedures designed to reconfirm the existing situation while creating the pretense of negotiation toward a diplomatic breakthrough. The illusion of peace produced by the agreements is far more dangerous than the untenable status quo. The driving forces behind that illusion have distorted the essence of the conflict and paralyzed the efforts to achieve a real solution. Consequently, they have prolonged the occupation and obstructed the opportunity for a peace with justice—the only peace that can promise an enduring coexistence between Arabs and Jews, and the only peace capable of transforming the political landscape of the Middle East from a perpetual battleground to a terrain of dignity, reciprocity, mutuality, freedom, and self-determination.

Notes

1   Khalid Amayreh, "Gaza-Bethlehem First … and Last!" IAP News, August 27, 2002.
2   Amayreh, "Gaza-Bethlehem First … and Last!"
3   *Wall Street Journal*, September 16, 2002.
4   *Wall Street Journal*, September 16, 2002.
5   *Palestine Report* (Jerusalem Media and Communication Center) 8: 2 (February 13, 1995): 9.
6   *Ha'aretz*, September 1, 1994.
7   *Ha'aretz*, June 11, 2002.
8   *Ha'aretz*, September 19, 2002.
9   *New York Times*, November 19, 1994; *New York Times*, November 20, 1994.
10   *New York Times*, November 9, 1994.
11   *Boston Globe*, August 30, 1994.

SETTLEMENTS AND SETTLERS IN THE WEST BANK: 1967–2001*

Year	Number of Settlements**	Population (in thousands)
1967	1	Unknown
1968	3	Unknown
1969	8	Unknown
1970	10	Unknown
1971	12	Unknown
1972	14	Unknown
1973	14	Unknown
1974	14	Unknown
1975	19	Unknown
1976	20	3.2
1977	31	4.4
1978	39	7.4
1979	43	10
1980	53	12.5
1981	68	16.2
1982	73	21
1983	76	22.8
1984	102	35.3
1985	105	44.2
1986	110	51.1
1987	110	57.9
1988	110	63.6

Year	Number of Settlements**	Population (in thousands)
1989	115	69.8
1990	118	78.6
1991	119	90.3
1992	120	100.5
1993	120	110.9
1994	120	122.7
1995	120	127.9
1996	121	141.5
1997	122	154.4
1998	123	166.1
1999	123	177.5
2000	123	191.6
2001***	123	198

* Not including East Jerusalem
** These figures relate to the number of settlements recognized by the Ministry of the Interior.
*** As of September 31, 2001 (provisional data).
Source: Yehezkel Lein, in collaboration with Eyal Weizman, "Land Grab: Israel's Settlement Policy in the West Bank," May 2002.

INDEX

Arad, Moshe, 132
Arafat, Yasir: Camp David II and,
xii, 169–71, 175–79, 186–89;
concessions by, 93, 118, 123;
demonization of, xii–xiii, 70–71,
142, 201–2; as enforcer, 233,
238–39, 241, 243–44; failure of,
5, 84, 187, 237–40; Hamas and,
108; Hebron and, 112–13; Intifa-
das and, 84, 180–81, 186–87; Jerusalem and, 138, 172;
marginalization of, 89–90, 105,
111, 171, 242–43; Oslo and,
81–82, 84, 162, 186–87, 225,
237–39; reciprocity and, 114;
refugees and, 157–58, 175, 233;
removal of, xii, xviii, 208–9,
211; security and, 105; statehood
and, 53, 95, 122; terrorism renounced by, 65, 72, 122–23, 186,
199
Aran, Oded, 132
Arens, Moshe, 27, 244
Arms Export Control Act, 27, 42,
168
Aronson, Geoffrey, 139
Asfour, Hasan, 189
Ashrawi, Hanan, 84, 231
Asia, Central, xviii, 46, 195
Al-Assad, Hafez, 75, 90
Associated Press, 42
Ataturk, Kemal, 16
Atlanta bombing, 109
autonomy: Camp David I and, 9,
62, 64–65, 98, 115; interim, 8,
76–78, 82; Israeli policy and, 74,
109, 115–16; Jerusalem and,
114, 142, 170, 175, 178; limited,
42–43, 78, 89, 115–16; in the

Occupied Territories, 64, 69,
185; self-rule, 42–43, 78, 90–92,
95, 98, 150–51. *See also* sover-
eignty; statehood
Avnery, Uri, 169–70, 170–71, 173
AWACS sales, 35, 40–41
Al-Awda, 233
Awis, Imali, 193
"Axis of Evil," 45, 204

B

B'nai B'rith, 135
B'Tselem, 85
Badil: Resource Center for Palestin-
ian Residency and Refugee
Rights, 234
Baghdad Pact, 16
Baker, James, III: Arabs and, 237;
Jerusalem and, 132; Madrid and,
7–8; peace plans and, 51, 66–69,
71–75; reassessment by, 5, 45;
on settlements, 128–29
Balawi, Hakam, 91
Balfour Declaration, 1
Ball, George, 23–24
bantustanization: Intifada and, 11;
of Occupied Territories, 105,
111, 116, 174–76, 208, 212, 243;
Oslo and, xiv, 10–11, 218–19,
237; statehood and, 221
Barak, Ehud: Al-Assad and, 170;
Camp David II and, xii, 167,
169–72, 174–75, 187; cease-fire
and, 181; Clinton and, xi–xii,
185–86, 242; Intifada and, 186;
Palestinian rule and, 156; procrastination by, 169, 217, 242;
racism of, 172–73; redeployment
and, 200

Interim Agreement on the West Bank and Gaza. *See* Oslo II
International Commission for Palestinian Refugees (ICPR), 160
International Convention on the Elimination of All Forms of Racial discrimination, 159
International Covenant on Civil and Political Rights, 159, 215n23
International Socialist Organization (ISO), 234
Intifada (1988), 43, 65–67, 69–70, 73, 84, 224
Intifada, Al-Aqsa: effects of, 66, 197, 237–38, 244; ending of, 227, 232; media on, 168, 179–80, 203; observers and, 180–83; Oslo and, 167–68, 186–87; peace efforts during, 180–84; start of, 11, 179; suppression of, xvii, 180, 182, 193, 201–2
Iran: Iraq and, 6, 16, 31; Karin A Affair, 204; revolution in, 23–24, 39; Shah of, 23, 39, 41; terrorism and, 109, 197; U.S. and, xiv, 23, 124, 204
Iraq: coup in, 18; democracy and, xviii; Europe and, 210; Gulf War, 8–9, 24, 28–32, 69–73, 81–82; Hussein and, 7–9, 28, 30–32, 70, 208, 239; Iran and, 6, 16, 31; Israel and, 26–27, 31–32; nuclear raid on, 26–27, 35; Palestinians and, 69–70, 152; U.S. and, xviii, 6–9, 197, 210–12, 213n4; war on terrorism and, xiv, xvii, 31–32, 197
"Iron Wall" (Jabotinsky), 200

Islam, as menace, xvi–xv, 23, 46, 197
Islamic Jihad, 241
Israel: 1948 war, 1; 1967 war, 2; "Comprehensive Plan," xiii; diplomatic recognition of, 27, 53, 104, 237–40; economy of, 96, 104; history of, 1, 151; invasions by, 19, 35; Iraq nuclear raid by, 26–27, 35; isolation of, 224; obstruction by, 7–8, 27–28, 42–43, 56, 65, 68–69; October 1973 war, 51; philanthropy towards, 36; polls on, 45; restitution and, 11–12, 98–99; right-wing rule in, 77. *See also* Israeli lobby; strategic politics
Israel: U.S. Foreign Assistance (Congressional Research Service Report), 37
Israeli lobby in U.S.: Camp David I and, 64; comprehensive settlement and, 55; Geneva and, 56; influence of, 182, 200–201; on Jerusalem, 129, 132, 140; Occupied Territories and, 63; policy making and, 35; Zionism and, 44
Israeli-Palestinian Interim Agreement on the West Bank and Gaza. *See* Oslo II
Israeli Peace Now, xiv
Israeli-U.S. Mutual Defense Assistance Agreement, 42
Israel Policy Forum, 185, 223

J

Jabotinsky, Ze'ev (Vladimir), xviii, 200, 214n10
Jackson, Jesse, 230–31

South Africa: apartheid of, 233–34;
demography of, 220; media on,
180; reconciliation by, 229;
Sharon and, 242–43; statehood
of, 224; U.S. and, 23
sovereignty: Camp David I and, 62;
delay of, 178; as final status issue, 89, 141–42; marginalization
of, 95–97; preclusion of, 4, 10,
22, 111, 115–16; two-state solution, 185; U.S. and, 4. *See also*
autonomy; statehood
Soviet Union: decline of, 7, 21, 36,
45, 71; Egypt and, 16; Gulf War
and, 31; peace process and,
51–52, 54–57, 63, 74–75, 81–82;
refugees and, 152; Russia, 210;
strategic politics and, 6–7,
15–17, 21–22, 24–29, 41, 63; as
threat, 26, 41, 197
statehood: Arafat and, 53, 95, 122;
Gulf War and, 70; Israeli avoid-
ance of, 8; Labor and, 116,
218–19; leadership change and,
208–9; Likud and, 68, 218; Madrid and, 8–9; marginalization
of, 9, 91, 205, 218, 239, 244;
meaning of, 178; Oslo and,
90–92, 217–22, 226, 228; PLO
and, 64, 150–51, 224; provisional, 207–8; refugees and, 151;
settlements and, 116, 221, 242;
Sharon and, 178; single state solution, 220–26, 228; two-state
solution, xii, 3–4, 72, 185, 189,
217–18; U.S. and, 7–8, 185. *See
also* autonomy; sovereignty
Stauffer, Thomas, 37
"Stockholm Document," 53

Strategic Defense Initiative, 43
Strategic Petroleum Reserve, 37
strategic politics, United States/Is-
rael: communism and, 17–18;
containment and, 15, 25, 29; crisis in, 17–18; growth of, 3–5,
19–23, 35–37, 39–41;
Israelization of, 177, 217; Jerusalem and, 130, 132; oil and, xviii,
25–26; peace plans and, 8; proxy
role and, 19–21, 23; Soviet Union and, 6–7, 15–16, 21–22,
24–28, 41, 63; Wye River and,
123–24. *See also* Cold War
Sudan, xiv, 46
Suez, 17–19, 54
suicide bombings: Israeli response
to, xiii, 105, 112, 115, 179,
203–4, 211; media on, xvi–xvii,
202; polarization and, 227; redeployment and, 100; as retaliation,
202; settlements and, 204
Syria: Golan Heights, 8, 26, 42, 62,
106; Israel and, 6, 17, 20, 27,
237; Lebanon and, 6; peace process and, 51, 55, 57, 71, 75; Resolution 242 and, 105; as threat,
xiv, 109; U.S. and, 22, 31
Szep (cartoonist), 70

T

Taba (talks), 170, 177, 180, 199
Taliban, 195
Tanzim, 186, 202–3
Temporary International Presence
in Hebron (TIPH), 94–95
Tenet Plan, 182
terrorism: Arafat and, 65, 72,
122–23, 186, 199; Intifada

ABOUT THE AUTHOR

Naseer H. Aruri is Chancellor Professor (Emeritus) of Political Science at the University of Massachusetts, Dartmouth. His many publications include *Occupation: Israel Over Palestine* (1983), *The Obstruction of Peace: The U.S., Israel, and the Palestinians* (1995), and *Palestinian Refugees: The Right of Return* (Pluto, 2001). He is a contributor to *The Struggle for Palestine* (Haymarket Books), president of the Trans-Arab Research Institute (TARI), a member of the executive committee of the Center for Policy Analysis on Palestine (Washington, D.C.), a member of the Independent Palestinian Commission for the Protection of Citizens Rights (Ramallah) since its inception in January 1994, a founding member of the Arab Organization for Human Rights, Cairo and Geneva in 1982, a member of the editorial board of *Third World Quarterly* (London), and a former president of the Arab-American University Graduates. He was also a member of the Board of Directors of Human Rights Watch/Middle East, 1990-1992, and a three-term member of the Board of Directors of Amnesty International, USA, 1984-1990. He has appeared on the Lehrer News Hour, CNN Crossfire, ABC News, and he is a commentator on Pacifica Radio, the BBC, Radio Monte Carlo, and the Voice of America. He has been a contributor to *Middle East International* (London), *Al-Hayat*, *Al-Mustaqbal*, and other Arab dailies and weeklies.

ABOUT SOUTH END PRESS

South End Press is a nonprofit, collectively run book publisher with more than 200 titles in print. Since our founding in 1977, we have tried to meet the needs of readers who are exploring, or are already committed to, the politics of radical social change. Our goal is to publish books that encourage critical thinking and constructive action on the key political, cultural, social, economic, and ecological issues shaping life in the United States and in the world. In this way, we hope to give expression to a wide diversity of democratic social movements and to provide an alternative to the products of corporate publishing.

Through the Institute for Social and Cultural Change, South End Press works with other political media projects—Alternative Radio; Speakout, a speakers' bureau; and *Z Magazine*—to expand access to information and critical analysis.

To order books, please send a check or money order to: South End Press, 7 Brookline Street, #1, Cambridge, MA 02139-4146. To order by credit card, call 1-800-533-8478. Please include $3.50 for postage and handling for the first book and 50 cents for each additional book.

Write or e-mail southend@southendpress.org for a free catalog, or visit our website at www.southendpress.org.